Building to Save Energy: Legal and Regulatory Approaches

Building to Save Energy: Legal and Regulatory Approaches

Grant P. Thompson

Environmental Law Institute State and Local Energy
Conservation Project

*This work was supported in part by a grant from
the National Science Foundation.*

Ballinger Publishing Company • Cambridge, Massachusetts
A Subsidiary of Harper & Row, Publishers, Inc.

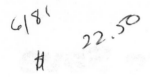

This book was prepared with the support of NSF Grant APR 7504814. However, any opinions, findings, conclusions, or recommendations herein are those of the authors and do not necessarily reflect the views of NSF.

International Standard Book Number: 0-88410-059-6

Library of Congress Catalog Card Number: 79-11754

Printed in the United States of America

Library of Congress Cataloging in Publication Data

Thompson, Grant P
   Building to save energy.

   Bibliography: p.
   Includes index.
   1. Building laws—United States. 2. Buildings—United States—Energy conservation. I. Environmental Law Institute. Energy Conservation Project. II. Title.
KF5701.T5   343'.73'078   79-11754
ISBN 0-88410-059-6

Dedication

**To Sharon, Ben, and Carrie
with love and gratitude**

Contents

List of Tables

Preface

American buildings have a justifiable reputation for architectural vigor and liveliness. But they also have an unhappy record of energy consumption. Sitting unprotected in the blazing sun, depending on supplies of energy thought to be without limit, they consumed one-third of the nation's energy at a time when energy was cheap. Those days are now past. It is worth our time thinking about the cost of energy and the steps we can take individually and collectively to make energy-saving changes and investments.

This book is about buildings, how energy is used in them, and the building and operating practices that state and local law can affect. It is designed in part as a teaching book. A reader who knows nothing about building energy use will not find any technical mysteries here; one purpose of the book is to increase understanding about where big opportunities exist for improving energy performance and what can be done to capture those opportunities. In part, this book is a history of where we are in energy regulation, how we got there, and where we are heading. It contains texts of novel regulations and statutes and guides for finding more. Moreover, it tries to suggest new ways that states and localities might wish to explore in improving energy regulation. Finally, it contains a call for more systemic improvements in the way we control building design, the way we price energy, and the way we think about the resources we consume. The viewpoint is proconservation, proenvironment, and proconsumer (although the consumer in this book includes future generations as well as those living now).

This book is one volume of the Environmental Law Institute's State and Local Energy Conservation Project, a series of books that examines legal and administrative strategies that states and localities can use to promote energy conservation. Funded by a grant from the National Science Foundation, the series offers a range of legal and regulatory approaches to eliminate uneconomic energy waste in various sectors of the economy. Other books in the series deal with land use planning for more energy-efficient cities, government procurement and operations for energy efficiency, industrial energy use, energy use in agriculture, and government fiscal policies. The recommendations are based on a study of existing laws and regulations and experience with conservation programs that have already been adopted. The books have been shaped to fit the energy information needs of state and local government officials who are charged with preparing and implementing effective energy conservation programs. But the books are also written to be accessible to citizens and legislators concerned with enhancing energy conservation efforts.

The opportunities for energy conservation in buildings are around us, ranging in drama from caulking leaky window frames to rediscovering the subtle use of shade and sunlight once known to the Pueblo Indians. The challenge will be to discover how to organize our complex society, with its conflicting interest groups and goals, to seize the opportunities. Yet it is exactly this kind of challenge that Americans are best at meeting through ingenuity and inventiveness.

Grant P. Thompson
Principal Investigator
Energy Conservation Project

Acknowledgments

It is self-evident that for a lawyer to write a book about energy conservation in buildings, he must have had a lot of help from colleagues and friends. This book is no exception. When they see the result, no doubt some will be re-affirmed in their belief that I was not a star pupil!

I will never forget my colleagues on the Energy Conservation Project at the Environmental Law Institute. The working atmosphere, combining professional critiques with moral support when needed, will be hard to duplicate.

I have been assisted in my study of regulation of American buildings by conversations over the years with Bernard Adams, Pamela L. Baldwin, Max Berking, Duncan Bremer, Clark Bullard, Claudia Burton, Sheldon H. Cady, James Cegla, William Downs, Melvin H. Chiogioji, Charles J. Cicchetti, Jeffrey C. Cohen, Paul P. Craig, Richard Crenshaw, Joel Darmstadter, Hershel D. Davidson, Gene DeLaTorre, Joseph Derringer, Ronald Doctor, Fred S. Dubin, John Eberhardt, Eugene P. Eccli, Stephen L. Feldman, Charles G. Field, Frances E. Francis, John H. Gibbons, Herbert T. Gilkey, Paul C. Greiner, Joan B. Habib, Ernst R. Habicht, Jr., C. Alexander Hewes, Jr., Richard M. Kalt, Henry C. Kelly, Ralph Knowles, L. Lee Lane, Jonathan Lash, Susannah Lawrence, Kai N. Lee, Gerald Mara, Philip J. Mause, John M. McGinty, Frank O. Meeker III, Alan S. Miller, Laurence I. Moss, Sandy Motley, Harold Olin, Michael J. Power, Richard E. Rowberg, Andy Sansom, Roger Sant, Maxine Savitz, Lee Schipper, Joan Shorey, Richard G. Stein, Erik Svenson, Hines Trechsel, Jack E. Tumilty, Seth Tuttle, Gordon Vickery, Henry S. Wakabayashi, Isabelle Weber, and Ellen Winchester.

My research assistants, who worked on sections of this book over the years, contributed much of its meat; explaining, arguing, discussing, and convincing (or being convinced) helped me more than they might have suspected at the time. Thanks to Richard A. Reeve, Bruce Ishimatsu, Barrett Stambler, and Ted McConnell.

Barbara L. Shaw and Patricia Sagurton Machir, who worked on the project as part of the *ECP Report* program, provided statutes, cases, and administrative support without fail or complaint.

Anyone who has written a book knows the debt he owes to his editors—and is grateful that no reader ever suspects. Juliet Pierson, Kathleen Courrier, Sharon R. Thompson, and Gail Boyer Hayes were careful editors. Often unsung is the copyeditor. In this case, I was grateful for the assistance given to me by Arks Smith; I hope she excuses the many lapses from grace that still remain.

David Engel and Nancy Naismith each read through the entire manuscript. They are good and valuable friends; their criticisms helped me clarify my thoughts. Eric Hirst, Robert Socolow, Stephen Anderson, and Denis Hayes each read shorter portions, giving me the benefit of their expertise and insights.

No principal investigator could ever count on having a program officer as wise and as supportive as Arthur F. Konopka of the National Science Foundation. The entire staff was continually struck by his solid, thoughtful support throughout this project.

Carol Franco of Ballinger Publishing Company has been an informative, flexible, and patient editor; I am relieved for her patience and thankful to her for her other qualities.

Friends who know my work style will recognize that I owe special thanks to my miraculous Xerox 850 electronic text editing typewriter that made composing at the typewriter a perfect man-machine relationship, allowing swift and relatively painless revisions, re-revisions, and re-re-revisions.

Finally, although they are mentioned in the dedication of this book, I want to repeat my thanks to my wife and children. Families of people writing books should unionize: no government agency would permit an employer to ignore a factory worker as writers ignore their families. Their quiet, unfailing support makes it all worthwhile.

With all the help I have received, I persist in making mistakes and committing lapses of judgment. I can only hope that readers will be as generous as those acknowledged here have been.

Building to Save Energy:
Legal and Regulatory
Approaches

Chapter 1

American Buildings and Energy Use

But for the very earth itself, no feature of the landscape has the durability of man's buildings. Willa Cather, speaking of the southwestern cliff dwellings, evokes this timelessness as she writes of a "city of some extinct civilization, hidden away . . . for centuries, preserved . . . like a fly in amber."[1] Even in our newer cities, there are many sections of commercial and residential buildings that are thirty, fifty, even a hundred or more years old. In the throwaway society that many consider America to have become, it is comforting to contemplate how relatively permanent our built environment is. Less comforting is the extent to which our buildings, both old and new, were and continue to be constructed for an earlier era of cheap energy. Poorly insulated, unshaded against the blazing summer sun, heated and cooled by machines that toss away half or more of the energy supplied—American buildings stand as monuments to a defunct, profligate time.

The longevity of existing buildings and the relative inefficiency of past and present American structures are two facts that, taken together, provide the framework within which energy analysts must plan: first, the country is saddled with most of its existing buildings for a long time, and second, if we don't start improving building efficiency quickly, the country will pay the energy price for buildings we are now constructing for many years into the future. Recent projections show that between now and the year 2000, we will build about 45 percent of the homes that will then exist and double the commercial floor space.[2]

Depending on one's views of the ability of modern Americans to learn and change, perhaps there is one fact to be cheerful about when we consider energy efficiency in buildings. Buildings, and thus the energy efficiency designed into them, are totally human artifacts. This means that it is within human power to change fundamentally the way buildings are built, equipped, and operated. It is even possible to build structures that depend only on the sun for their heating and hot water and on the wind for cooling and minimal stored electrical needs.[3] But the cost of completely untying from the central grid, the convenience of being part of an energy system whose operations are largely attended to by others, the reliability that being tied to a system provides, and the sheer weight of habit now prevent all but the most wealthy or the most daring from taking this step. Most of us are content to depend on what the market offers. Our homes, our offices, our fast food shops, and our factories are designed from standard plans, following the custom of years past (often frozen into law or regulation) to create our habitat.

Now a new factor has appeared to jolt us from this easy custom. Energy prices are rising, and a major source of energy for this country is controlled by others, whose intentions seem unclear at times. How are we to respond? Unfortunately for the recent past, we have responded in two equally unproductive ways. On the one hand we have ignored the problem, while on the other we have tried to find some devil to blame for the shortages. Citizens have blamed the utilities and the oil companies, business has blamed government regulation, and government administrators have faulted the public for underestimating the seriousness of the situation. The call has been for a national policy. The first national policy offered—that we should be independent of foreign energy sources by 1985—was so patently unconnected to reality that it served only to trivialize the debate. The second call for a national policy was grander in its scope, calling as it did for a wartime mentality on the energy issue, but presidential urgings did little to move Congress to act swiftly. Now, six years after the embargo of 1973, the outlines of a national policy for energy are only just beginning to emerge from scattered pieces of legislation that attack the energy problem bit by bit.

The impacts of sharply higher energy prices and the economic and social discomforts that followed from the cold winters of 1976-1977 and 1977-1978 provide an opportunity for change. Changes will have to come from many of the actors in the cast of builders, financiers, owners, landlords, unions, architects, manufacturers, and others. For example, the manner in which energy is priced, our habits of using energy, expectations of customers, invention of new materials and techniques for construction, and willingness of labor to use those new techniques are a few of the changes that must come. Although not every change needed is within the power of government to carry out, government can influence many of the factors that will in turn cause energy usage to move downward. Over half of the energy used by ultimate consumers in this country is regulated by some form of public body.[4] Research and development can be influenced by government funding. Government testing and certification of new materials can hasten their introduction. Even the most intractable problem of making changes in a pluralistic society—the problem of changing the way people carry on their daily lives—can be strongly affected by governmental encouragement and example.

This book looks at some of the tools that government can employ to help citizens use less energy in the construction and operation of their buildings. The reader versed in energy research literature will find no surprises here in the form of new technologies or new methods for using old technologies. This book is not about technology. Instead, it is about people and institutions and how government can organize those institutions and itself to motivate actions ultimately in everyone's best interests. Because this book is designed to meet a very specialized need, persons interested in building an energy-conserving house will find that there are much better books available.[5]

This book is not intended to be read by an expert in buildings or in building energy use. It draws upon the work of such professionals in order to provide information to them about possibilities for energy savings. Instead, this book is for the political actor, whether he or she be a state legislator, a local official, or a citizen. Energy and its use cannot avoid being ultimately a political question; public officials can help make energy conservation happen, or they can prevent it from occurring.

This book, and the series of which it is a part,[6] looks at the role of state and local government in encouraging or requiring energy conservation. Since it looks to the role of state governments, a number of important issues are left out because they refer to national markets or to items of national interest where the federal government can better act. Because it looks to the role of government, a large number of voluntary actions are not covered.

The purpose of this book is to consider the vast array of energy conservation actions that might be taken and to select from that array those actions that fit two criteria: First, they must be worth doing in terms of the amount of energy saved. It is simply not worth cranking up the entire mechanism of government in order to save a few BTUs per year. Second, actions considered should be ones in which laws or regulations have the potential for being effective and efficient. Although it is a book about law and about technical options for improving efficiency, it is written with the nonlawyer and the nontechnically trained person in mind. Energy policy is too important to leave to the lawyers or to the technocrats! Changes in energy use might have substantial effects on the way we live and the items on which we spend our money. Larger initial capital expenditures will be necessary; paying for cheap buildings with cheap energy may no longer be an option. In a democracy, decisions of this nature deserve to be made at the local or state level and must be made by those affected. Technically trained people should present options and methods to citizens, but the final decisions will be more informed and more enforceable if they come from choices made by those who are affected by the changes. It is for this reason that this series exists.

This book deals with buildings. This first chapter presents some of the statistics that are known about buildings and the energy they use in this country. The second chapter deals with the institutions (both public and private) that regulate building design and construction. The next several chapters look at the components of the building, examining the development of legal controls for insulation, air seepage, and ventilation; equipment used to heat and cool the building; and lighting. Finally, the broader question of legal controls to change the way buildings are designed and look are considered. The careful reader will notice that there is no "conclusions and recommendations" chapter. This series is not intended to answer the question, What set of strategies shall our city or state follow? Instead, it is designed to inform policymakers and citizens about what other jurisdictions have done, to suggest improvements or modifications of those actions, and to set out alternative models. The choice of which energy menu to follow properly lies not with the author of this book, but with the political process of the locality or state.

ENERGY USE IN BUILDINGS:
FACTS AND FIGURES

In 1972, about 23 percent of America's power was consumed in the residential and commercial market.[7] But this figure understates the true amount of natural resources that were devoted to the building sector. Because so much of the energy use in buildings is electricity, to get a true percentage of energy used we must look at the amount of primary energy (that is, coal, oil, natural gas, and fissile material) that it takes to produce that electricity used in buildings. Those figures are larger because it is impossible to take 100 units of energy in the form of coal, oil, uranium, or natural gas and turn it into 100 units of electrical energy. (Unfortunately, for residences at least, the fastest growth rate for energy use is in the use of electricity, which represents about 45 percent of energy used in homes.) The "conversion losses" arise from the inherent inefficiencies of changing one form of energy into another form. Added to these conversion losses are the losses that occur in sending electricity over long distances; these are "transmission losses." Taken together, conversion and transmission losses add about half again as much to the total amount of energy used. Thus, a better estimate is that buildings use about one-third of the nation's energy.

How much energy could be saved by building energy-efficient buildings? The amount varies according to the type of building, as we will see in later chapters, but the aggregate amounts are impressive. The American Institute of Architects has stated that "[i]f we adopted a high-priority national program emphasizing energy efficient buildings, we could by 1990 be saving the equivalent of more than 12.5 million barrels of petroleum per day."[8] Denis Hayes suggests that

> Thirty to 50 percent of the operating energy in most existing buildings can be conserved, and 50 to 80 percent can be saved in new buildings. The lower figures assume optimal insulation and employment of efficient furnaces and air conditioners. The higher figures assume the use of more sophisticated technologies, including solar devices, heat pumps, and total energy systems.[9]

A study done for the Federal Energy Administration found that using the relative modest goals of ASHRAE 90-75 (an energy standard for new buildings), new office buildings could reduce their total energy consumption almost 60 percent over designs current in 1973.[10] A house in Denmark, "Zero Energy House," relies on solar energy and on heat from lighting, appliances, and its occupants. The 1,290 square foot house uses only 2,300 kilowatt hours of electricity per year, one-ninth that of a typical home in Denmark. No fuel is used for winter heating![11]

These figures suggest the enormous potential for producing more energy by saving it in buildings. A kilowatt hour saved because it is not leaked through a dripping faucet or a crack in the insulation can be used to provide useful work in a factory or comfort in someone else's home. Later chapters in this book suggest more detailed savings possible from various technical, design, and operating strategies; nonetheless, the overall picture is clear. As a nation, we have a long way to go in constructing buildings that match our technical ingenuity.

THE ROLE OF THE STATE GOVERNMENT

The federal government gets most of the headlines in newspapers; nonetheless, state and local governments carry the enormous burden of day-to-day governance in this country. Ordinary citizens have almost no contact with the federal government, save through the Post Office and the Internal Revenue Service. On the other hand, zoning commissions, police, roads, building codes, health regulations, garbage collection, schools, and liquor commissions are only a few of the hundreds of ways that local and state governments directly influence American life. Even many programs that are federal in origin are administered and enforced by state and local officials. Welfare programs for needy children, air and water pollution control, and mass transit systems are only a few of the programs that exhibit this federal-state relationship. This tendency to make the states (and, through the states, the localities) the primary implementors of federal policy has been particularly pronounced in the energy field. There have been three major pieces of federal legislation designed to affect energy consumption since 1974; all of them have placed a major share of the burden for carrying out energy conservation programs on the states; in many cases, states have been charged with designing the very programs mandated by federal law.

This federal-state relationship makes American energy conservation policy a combination of large decisions and small decisions. Standards for automobile efficiency would be difficult for a state to enforce alone, and would probably be constitutionally suspect as well. But an enormous number of decisions—and particularly decisions that affect energy use in buildings—are purely local. In this country, as we shall see, although building codes are developed nationally, they are adopted either state by state or city by city. Enforcement and inspection are local almost everywhere. Zoning decisions that affect the siting and orientation of buildings are local with minor exceptions. Building practices vary regionally. For this reason, local and state control of building design, operation, and construction are particularly appropriate because the machinery for carrying out the regulation is already in place on the local level.

There is another reason for placing energy conservation initiatives at the state and local level. Energy conservation, with all of its possible social effects, is a new concept for America. Our experience has been solely with increasing energy supply, and members of the public have been minimally involved in the process, preferring instead to leave supply questions to the regulators and the utilities. When no very clear national policy is apparent, the variety that is offered by different state approaches is a strength. Often new programs are difficult to design, and it is even more difficult to guess in advance what all the ramifications of a particular program will be. Therefore, the "laboratory of the states" allows a variety of different approaches to be tried simultaneously. It may be that no one plan will emerge as clearly superior. More likely, several different mixes of energy-conserving strategies will be suitable to different parts of the country that have different climate, tastes, industrial bases, power sources, and commuting patterns.

Thus, the policy of permitting latitude to the states to experiment and innovate is a wise one. But that policy demands that sufficient guidance, information, and resources be provided. This book is one small contribution to helping those who have been asked to implement national energy conservation policies to understand the present regulatory framework within which they must work and the opportunities for new directions.

A theme of this book is that the participation of an informed public will help improve the final results of government's actions. This is not a universally accepted notion. Many technically trained people would prefer that hard questions of engineering, architecture, land use planning, or power supply were left to those who are professionally trained in the area. Yet increasingly in American life we are seeing laws and customs made after consultation with those who will be affected. No rule is promulgated without public hearings; no complex area of the law is administered without having organizations such as the League of Women Voters, The Conservation Foundation, or the American Institute of Architects active in training their constituency on the issues.

Public participation is a fact. But it is also an improvement when the public has an opportunity to participate early, fully, and openly in setting the agenda of relevant issues, the menu of options, and the range of acceptable solutions. A technical expert, no matter how well trained in the discipline, will tend to forget the human dimensions of decisions he or she makes. The internal consistency may tend to obscure the difficulties that laypersons will see with the solution.

A key to success for public participation is that the public be well informed about the issues. This book is an aid to citizens interested in the issues of legal controls on building energy consumption. The other actors in the field are introduced in Chapter 2. The public should and will take an active part in these battles in coming years.

NOTES

1. *The Professor's House* by Willa Cather. Copyright 1925 by Willa Cather. Used with permission of the current copyright holder, Alfred A. Knopf, Inc.

2. U.S. Department of Energy, "Status Report on Solar Energy Domestic Policy Review (Public Review Copy)," August 25, 1978, p. V-7.

3. *Insulation Reporter*, December 1976–January 1977, p. 1.

4. I am indebted to Richard Sclove of Resources for the Future in Washington, D.C. for providing me with the calculations that support this assertion. Sclove calculates that approximately 39 Quads of energy (or 51.44 percent of consumption) are regulated as to price.

5. Among the many excellent books for the general reader interested in energy conservation in homes are Eugene Eccli, ed., *Low-Cost, Energy-Efficient Shelter for the Owner and Builder* (Emmaus, Pennsylvania: Rodale Press, 1976); Jim Leckie et al., *Other Homes and Garbage: Designs for Self-Sufficient Living* (San Francisco: Sierra Club Books, 1975); National Bureau of Standards, *Making the Most of Your Energy Dollars in Home Heating & Cooling* (Washington, D.C.: Superintendent of Documents, U.S. Government Printing Office, n.d.); and Department of Housing and Urban Development, *In the Bank . . . or Up the Chimney? A Dollars and Cents Guide to Energy-Saving Home Improvements* (Washington, D.C.: Superintendent of Documents, U.S. Government Printing Office [Stock Number 023-000-00297-3] September 1975).

6. Environmental Law Institute State and Local Energy Conservation Project Series, published by Ballinger Publisher Company, 17 Dunster Street, Harvard Square, Cambridge, Massachusetts 02138. Among the titles in this series are: Corbin Crews Harwood, *Using Land to Save Energy*; Ivan J. Tether, *Government Procurement and Operations*; Robert A. Friedrich, *Energy Conservation for American Agriculture*; Norman L. Dean, *Energy Efficiency in Industry—A Guide to Legal Barriers and Opportunities*; and Joe W. Russell, Jr., *Economic Disincentives for Energy Conservation*.

7. This figure is drawn from the National Petroleum Council's study, *Potential for Energy Conservation in the United States: 1974-1978: Residential/Commercial* (Washington, D.C., 1974).

8. American Institute of Architects, *A Nation of Energy Efficient Buildings By 1990* (Washington, D.C., 1975).

9. Denis Hayes, *Energy: The Case for Conservation*, Worldwatch Paper 4 (Washington, D.C.: World Watch Institute 1976), p. 34.

10. Federal Energy Administration, "Energy Conservation in New Building Design: An Impact Assessment of ASHRAE Standard 90-75," *Conservation Paper Number 43B*, p. 5.

11. *Insulation Reporter, supra* note 3.

Chapter 2

Pressures Affecting Energy Use in American Buildings

A striking feature of the modern American architectural environment is the similarity of cities throughout the country. New housing developments, downtown office districts, and shopping malls—each could as easily be in Des Moines as in Durango. And yet, in a contradiction born of time, the French Quarter of New Orleans is as distinct from the marble step districts of Baltimore as the New England town square is from the broad plazas of southern California.

The move from the distinctive, regional styles to the new, more uniform American style has been influenced by many factors: a mobile population, national markets for building materials, nationwide advertising that sows the same desires everywhere, and the resort to architectural uniformity to cut construction costs are only a few of the pressures that could be listed. Factors that affect the amount of energy used in American buildings are the subject of this chapter. Many indirect, though important, pressures are ignored. Depreciation provisions, the capital gains laws, and federal programs for housing are important influences that lie beyond state control and thus the scope of this book.

This chapter is designed with two purposes in mind. First, it provides readers with a guide to some of the pressures and pressure groups that influence building design and construction and, thus, energy use. Knowledge of activities of these groups and the pressures they bring to bear is fundamental to understanding both the energy situation in which we now find ourselves and the actions that we must take to extricate ourselves from it. A second function of this chapter is to serve as a warning to those who believe that a simple change in one area can be accomplished without taking the entire web of groups and interests into account. In fact, as we will see, the complexity of the regulatory process for affecting the shape of American buildings is an accurate reflection of the variety of different groups who feel that they have a financial stake in the completed building. Labor unions, home material manufacturers, architects, builders, real estate groups, and local, state, and national governmental officials—all want to have a say in the total process, because each believes it represents a unique, important interest.

Five classes of influences will be explored in this chapter. First is the force that nature exerts on buildings and, consequently, on building design. Second is the constraint that initial cost places on energy conservation features in a building. Discussion of this constraint includes the potential role of lending institutions in financing energy conservation programs, using as an example the role that savings and loan institutions play in the residential market. The third category of influence includes both the general search for improved materials and government-sponsored research. Discussion of this subject calls for a brief consideration of the potentials for training construction workers and building firms in new techniques. The fourth influence is regulatory. Building controls and building codes in particular, model code groups, and zoning controls (considered in more detail in Chapter 7) are all part of this influence. The last shaping force of building design consists of the major interest groups that help form rules (written and informal) and trade practices.

A reader with special knowledge of any one or more of these topics will find that the summary treatment given here does not begin to exhaust the complexities of any one subject. But the beginning student of design or energy conservation may find a foothold here.

NATURAL FACTORS INFLUENCING BUILDING ENERGY USE

When designing or constructing a building, no architect or builder can ignore nature. However, the history of both residential and commercial American architecture shows a movement away from design that harmonizes with nature. This movement, made possible in part by the abundance of inexpensive energy, has been characterized by increasing disregard for important natural influences on building energy use. Two such influences, climate and site characteristics, are particularly worthy of attention.

Climate

Man builds for a host of reasons, but protection from climate is surely one of the most important. In common parlance, we even refer to buildings as shelter, as though humans were escaping some fearsome creature named Weather. But in fact, human beings can tolerate temperature and humidity variations much wider than those expressed on the typical American thermostat, which labels 72° to 76° F as the "comfort range." People from other countries, countries that are commonly believed to be otherwise civilized, find American buildings intolerably hot or cold. Although the extremes of winter or summer climates actually do require shelter from the weather, virtually all of the United States lies in temperate zones in which natural forces can keep most people comfortable most of the time—if buildings were designed to side with weather instead of to fight it.

Climate once determined the overall style, orientation with regard to the sun, and the window placement of most buildings. The steep-roofed New England saltbox house, shedding snow so that the wooden framing would not crack under the crushing weight, was an inventive design solution to a climatic problem. Similarly, the thick-walled, inner-directed adobe houses of Santa Fe, absorbing heat during the day and warming the house during the cool desert night, reflect a responsiveness to climate that contemporary housing design seems to have lost.

In like fashion, many cities themselves were apparently once designed to take account of the influences of the climate. The important compromises and innovations found around the world to deal with solar and wind patterns are traced by Victor Olgyay in his landmark study, *Design With Climate.* Speaking of the American Southwest, Olgyay says:

> [L]ong experience and practical knowledge must have guided the builders of the Pueblo Indian towns such as Acoma, which is oriented slightly east of south, with long streets of massed dwelling units running east-west. In these row houses the radiation-vulnerable east and west sides are practically eliminated by being joined together, and leave only the north and south elevations to receive solar impacts.[1]

This same concern for the impact of solar heating and cooling is what makes the southern veranda so pleasant. The veranda provides both shade for the house and a pleasant place to enjoy the evening breeze.

Climatic patterns have been intensively studied and documented in the United States, first by private citizens and, from 1870 on, by the Weather Bureau (known at first as the Division of Telegrams and Reports for the Benefit of Commerce, Signal Corps, U.S. Army, now officially known by the blander title of the National Weather Service of the National Oceanic and Atmospheric Administration (NOAA), Department of Commerce). Temperature and rainfall records as far back as 1758 are available for some cities, and the Environmental Data Service of NOAA now records on computer tapes hourly temperature, humidity, and rain conditions for many major cities. Additionally, NOAA keeps wind records that show not only the strength and direction of the wind, but also for some areas its constancy. Readings of solar intensity and duration are being improved as interest in solar energy heating, cooling, and electrical generation grows.[2]

The effects of the weather on the heating and cooling loads of buildings is also well understood. Standard texts and handbooks— of which the *1977 Handbook of Fundamentals*,[3] published by the American Society of Heating, Refrigerating, and Air-conditioning Engineers, Inc. (ASHRAE), is the best known and most widely used—are consulted routinely by building designers. Unfortunately, such handbooks are customarily used to calculate the size of the mechanical equipment that will be necessary to combat the heating of the sun and the cooling of the wind through large expanses of glass, rather than for calculating the supporting role that the sun and the wind could play in heating and cooling buildings.

In spite of this constantly improving understanding of the behavior of the climate and of how it affects energy use in a building, climate now plays a relatively small part in building orientation, design, or construction. To be sure, porches appear more frequently in Florida than in Alaska, and storm windows are sold in Minnesota but not in Texas. But post-World War II construction and design has tended more and more to reflect a self-defeating argument against climate, rather than a compromise with it. Mechanical space-conditioning equipment (particularly air conditioning), high-speed elevators, and plumbing innovations that divorce water and sewage service from considerations of building height have all contributed to our ability to shut climate out.

The costs of this American solution to the climate "problem" have rarely been noted. Only in times of stress has the fragility of our solutions emerged. The November 1965 electricity blackout in the northeastern states left people trapped in elevators and unable to manage the seventy flight trudge down seldom-used stairwells in total darkness. Had the blackout occurred on a summer day or lasted long enough for water storage tanks on the top of buildings to run dry, the consequences would have been extremely serious.

Now it appears that another, longer term, stress is emerging, one that will not be solved by fixing a few defective pieces of equipment in our electrical system. And the new stress, the rapid escalation in energy prices, cannot be simply waited out. Although the oil embargo dramatized the price rises, the underlying trends of more expensive supply and of imbalance between supply and demand because of artificially low prices had long been apparent to experts. Rising energy prices alone may not be sufficient to eliminate all of the economic and other advantages of tall, sealed glass buildings in the central city; but price rises will slowly begin to assert themselves, so that designs that take advantage of placement, shading, and natural ventilation will become increasingly attractive.

Site Selection

A second characteristic of nature, one that is less frequently considered in the context of energy use than climate, is site selection. Even a book as sensitive to nature as the Sierra Club's *Other Homes and Garbage*, devotes little more than two pages to "Site Determinants in House Design."[4]

Just as climate once determined building design, the land itself used to shape our cities. Hills served as windbreaks, while rivers defined the course and orientation of streets and thus of the buildings built along them. Skill and technology appeared to help man prevail over nature, but the collapse of dams betrayed the foolishness of building on floodplains, and the loss of houses to mudslides underscored the proverbial wisdom of building on firm foundations. These and other examples illustrate the importance of taking site selection characteristics into account. Much less dramatic are the effects of local microclimates—sites warmed by sunshine reflected off a body of water, moistened by protecting hillocks, or chilled by a wind gulley. Unfortunately, little evidence suggests that state, local, or federal regulations have given any attention to these subtle influences, though the more dramatic phenomena, floods and slides, are attention getters.[5] While it may be too much to expect that present centers of population will change drastically, we may hope that natural windbreaks, water, wind gulleys, forests, and other natural phenomena will be considered in the selection of sites for buildings.

THE EFFECT OF FIRST COST PRESSURES ON BUILDINGS

Neither human beings nor human laws can alter climate or geography. We must simply accept both as given and do whatever is necessary within the limits of our budgets and skills to design structures that are compatible with them. The role of law is limited to drawing the attention of the designer and the builder to such factors and to encouraging them both to cooperate with, rather than to fight, nature. This subject is dealt with more fully in the final chapter of this book and in a companion book in this series, *Using Land to Save Energy* by Corbin Crews Harwood.[6] This in mind, we can now turn to factors affecting building energy use that man and law can influence. The most intractable of these factors is that of the "first cost" of a building, a problem that is not very susceptible to government intervention over long periods of time without serious and usually undesirable consequences but that must nevertheless be faced explictly if energy conservation is to become a part of the American building habit.

Stated simply, persons paying for the construction of a building, whether for their own use or for eventual resale to others, have strong incentives to minimize the initial cost of construction. This desire increasingly conflicts with the economic pressures on the eventual owner, who would benefit if the building were more soundly built, so that maintenance and operating expenses would be lower.

As this pressure of first cost minimization applies to energy conservation, there is a widespread fear (generally unsupported by the studies that do exist on this question[7]) that energy conservation investments in the construction of a building will further drive the market down. Therefore, there is a cry either for less regulation that would require energy conservation investments or for government subsidies to builders.

Adding to the political pressure for keeping first costs of housing low is the fact that a variety of non-energy-related factors have made the price of homes skyrocket. Recent studies have shown that in the ten years between 1965 and 1975, the average price of a new house went from $22,900 to $42,600. Since 1975, that trend has accelerated dramatically, with inflation and pressures on the housing market contributing to the rise. Mortgage interest rates have gone from below 6 percent to more than 9 percent; indeed, some cities report 11 percent rates or more. According to one lenders' trade journal, "somewhere between one-half to two-thirds of American families could not swing the financing on last year's (1975) average new home"[8] The single family home continues to be the American dream, a dream only partially subsidized by the federal government's loan guarantee programs and by the tax deductability of mortgage interest payments. Clearly, other ways must be discovered to meet the two apparently conflicting social goals—decent housing for us all and decent energy futures for our children.

First cost pressures can be reduced by a variety of means. The government has a powerful set of tools for making mortgage money less expensive to individuals and businesses. Some energy conservation purchases could be paid for directly by the government or indirectly through tax credits. Lower interest, longer term loans, with the difference between what the market requires and the government wishes to promote being made up from the public treasury is a time-honored American tradition. However, government subsidies of this type are increasingly disfavored. They are hard to manage and audit; they distort the market in ways that are hard to predict in advance; and they cost money in a time of financial limits. Subsidies also must come from some source, and frequently such subsidies are drawn from the payments of all taxpayers, home-owners and apartment dwellers; thus, it is open to the charge that it unfairly takes from those least able to afford a home and gives support to those who already own one. The private market can also provide mechanisms for easing the burden of higher first costs. There is considerable movement in that direction already. From time to time, a combination of government assistance and private initiative proves to be the most powerful stimulus of all. The following sections concentrate on the role of lending institutions in making money available for energy conservation investments. In particular, residential loans from savings and loan institutions provide a telling case study of the routes open to all lending institutions to encourage energy conservation investments. Such strategies balance increased first costs against reduced life cycle costs.

Cost

The first costs of both design and structural features constrain every purchaser of a building more than any other consideration. Though funds are intrinsically limited, human desires seem to know no end, and so the potential buyer must rank and choose among various combinations of space, location, and equipment. A builder, in turn, must worry about whether his own choice of a mix of features will appeal to buyers. Unfortunately, many of the energy-conserving mechanical, electrical, architectural, or design features that can easily be put into a building at the construction phase are not immediately attractive to the potential purchaser. Thus, with an eye to salability, a builder puts in a high quality kitchen floor rather than spending the same amount on ceiling and wall insulation. Yet kitchen floors can be changed fairly inexpensively at any time, while insulation is often difficult or impossible, and always expensive, to add once construction is completed.

The mistake that builders and purchasers alike make is ignoring the total cost of owning a building over its entire life. The initial cost may be only a small portion of the real costs of ownership. Commercial buyers tend to be somewhat more sophisticated in calculating operating expenses, but even such sophisticated buyers frequently fall into the trap of small homebuyers in considering only the real estate taxes, the mortgage, and the insurance when calculating the cost of operation. Few buyers understand that spending more on design or construction features or on the equipment used to heat or cool a building can lower future operating expenses. As a leading federal official later responsible for much of the work on federal energy conservation standards noted in 1976, many designers continued to ignore energy conservation guidelines even three years after the oil embargo because they were not convinced that the costs for energy conscious design could be recovered.[9]

Shortsightedness does not constitute the only reason that builders concentrate too little on energy conservation. The effect of the real estate tax structure also tends to discourage energy conservation. Money spent on improving the thermal integrity of a building may increase first costs and real estate taxes alike. As we will discuss in more detail later in this volume, this tax penalty should be eliminated.

Even in the extreme case—where builder and tenant are the same—the power of calculations that ignore energy costs is obvious. This is dramatically the case with government buildings, where real estate taxes are not the issue. Governments, which typically occupy the same buildings for very long periods of time, have followed the commercial trend of concentrating on the first cost rather than the life cycle cost of their own buildings. In an extreme example of forgetting that expensive buildings need to be heated and cooled for a long time, the financial officer of one major city reported that a number of departments had to be dissuaded from using federal revenue-sharing payments for building large, inefficient buildings; although revenue sharing provided construction funds, there would have been insufficient normal tax revenue for later heating and cooling! Governments thus apparently also make the mistake common in the private sector of separating capital budgets from operating budgets. (Of course the reasons for this fallacious separation differ. In the case of the private market, the builder may not have to pay utility bills in the future or understands that he will sell the buiding quickly. In the case of the government, future costs of building operation are politically easier to deal with when compared with a higher one time expenditure.) If governments, whose time horizons should stretch beyond those of private individuals, fall into this trap, it is not surprising that homebuyers and commercial operators do as well.

Finally, energy policymakers should not be blind to the impact that regulation and market forces have on the poor—those least able to pay for decent housing. There are roughly twenty-five million people living below the federal poverty level. According to an article in *The Wall Street Journal*, it is common for many of those to pay 20 to 30 percent of their monthly income for heating and other utility services. That same article cites a study in Milwaukee conducted in the winter of 1978-1979 showing that among 800 poverty families, 45 percent of their winter income went for heat; including rent or mortgage costs, a full 93 percent of their income was spent on shelter.[10]

Yet the solution to this problem is not to force energy-inefficient housing on all of us for the sake of protecting those less able to pay. The amount that citizens as a whole would pay in wasted energy costs would far exceed the cost of making special arrangements for the poor. Moreover, it is a cruel trick with consequences far into the future to let the poor live in poorly designed, drafty homes and apartments. Such a strategy simply consigns them forever to living in homes that are more expensive to operate, thus insuring their continued poverty and dependence. A more humane social policy would be to spend the capital necessary to inprove their housing stock and energy-using equipment, thus freeing the poor from inefficiency. The poor do not deserve to be treated as second-class citizens; solutions that are good for the country as a whole, for the middle class, and for the well to do are also suitable for the poor.

Role of Financial Institutions

Thus far, the institutions that should have the strongest direct interest in making the distinction between initial and life cycle costs—the lending institutions—have done relatively little to develop a set of formulae that will take this distinction into account, and where they have, the response of the consuming public has been less than expected for the rewards offered. Although evidence suggests that energy-efficient buildings can be built at no more cost than ordinary inefficient buildings, many lending institutions have shown little interest in undertaking innovative energy conservation lending programs.

Virtually no buildings are purchased for cash. Homeowners cannot afford cash payments, and businessmen wish to leverage their equity both to make it go as far as possible and to take advantage of tax deductions granted on interest payments. On the other hand, lending institutions will almost never lend money without some kind of security, such as a mortgage on the building purchased by the loan money. This security interest protects the lender's money and lowers his risk.

What factors has a lending institution in mind when it makes a loan? First, the lender does not wish to lend so much money that the borrower will be unable to repay the loan. Lenders do not want defaults; they want repayments according to schedule. Consequently, the buyer feels a pressure either to put up more of his own (limited) money or to hold down the first cost of the building he purchases. In principle, if not in practice, lending institutions should be willing to finance those energy conservation additions to a building that repay their first cost within the time period of the mortgage note. Installation of energy conservation items that save the owner of the building $50 per month in energy costs should free that money to be applied to paying off the mortgage. At 9.25 percent interest, a monthly payment of $50.38 on a twenty-year mortgage note would support an initial expenditure of $5,500 for increased energy conservation features.

Exact calculations made by a New York savings bank illustrate this point more clearly. The bank built a demonstration house called "Centenergy 76" that incorporated fourteen features designed to conserve energy. Among those features were orientation, earth berms, adequate insulation, an electric heat pump, a solar hot water heater, and an energy-efficient fireplace. The bank's description of the costs and benefits tell the story:

> In total, the cost of these innovations and components would add only $4,000 to the cost of building the home. This will cost out in 4 to 5 years by saving up to one half the cost of heating and cooling the home as measured against a standard built tract home of the same size. In actual dollars, this comes to about $800 per year, which on a $40,000 mortgage would reduce your interest rate by 2 percent.[11]

The second pressure on lending institutions is to finance buildings that are fairly conventional in design and execution so that, in case of a default, they can be resold easily. Conventional designs also give the lending institution's appraisers some measure of security; they can assume with relative certainty that the building's valuation is correct and that the building design will not create any unusual problems such as inadequate heating or improper ventilation. Of course, many of the most important energy conservation changes are hardly innovative. Better insulation makes almost no change in the design or functioning of the building. But as fuel prices rise, greater thicknesses of insulation may demand different roof designs for example. Lending institutions depend on dependability. The proven design is sure to work; the innovation provides an additional measure of risk that is difficult to evaluate. Since loan safety is an important driving force in loan decisions, cutting the risks associated with innovation has economic value to the lender.

Large commercial buildings are often financed by life insurance companies, and a few commercial structures are financed by the internal earnings of the companies that own them. But in general, savings institutions such as banks, savings and loan associations, mutual savings banks, and pension and trust funds are the chief providers of construction funds. For renovation and remodeling, commercial banks and savings and loan associations provide most of the funding. Because of the great variety of lending institutions, each type of which raises different legal and regulatory issues, no attempt will be made in this survey chapter to deal with even a sampling of them. But the single example of the savings and loan associations, commonly called S&Ls, illustrates the variety of financial incentives that could be applied to lower or spread the sometimes higher first cost of energy conservation features in buildings.

Savings and Loan Associations:
An Illustrative Case

In 1975, savings and loan institutions provided approximately 88 percent of the residential one to four family home mortgage credit of all depository institutions. S&Ls loaned about $55 billion in 1975, financing about one million existing single family houses and about one-quarter million apartment units. In that same year, S&Ls financed the purchase of about 230,000 single family new construction homes and 100,000 new apartment units.[12] Thus, S&Ls are a dominant force in providing the residential market with home-building and buying money. The majority of S&Ls are state chartered; out of 5,102 institutions in existence on December 31, 1974, 3,042 (or 59.6 percent) were state chartered. However, the

40 percent of federally chartered S&Ls accounted for about 60 percent of the assets of the industry. In spite of the large number of state chartered S&Ls, the influence of both federal and state controls is substantial. Almost all state and federally chartered S&Ls are subject to the regulations of the Federal Home Loan Bank Board; 4,141 of the institutions, which hold 97.5 percent of the total assets of S&Ls, are insured by the Federal Savings and Loan Insurance Corporation (FSLIC). FSLIC regulations cover such subjects as the dollar limits of any individual loan, the ratio of the amount of the loan to the total value of the building, and the amount of time over which repayment may be spread. But even with this strong federal regulation, federally chartered S&Ls are also subject to some state controls. State laws often control prepayment penalties and future advance clauses, features that if adopted with an energy conservation purpose in mind could make such investments more attractive.

Both state and federal regulations and self-initiated programs provide opportunities for innovations in energy conservation. A small selection of the devices that could be used by an S&L interested in promoting energy conservation are as follows:

- *Graduated payment mortgage.* This plan permits the buyer to make relatively small payments early in the mortgage period, in exchange for the pledge to make somewhat higher payments later during the mortgage. Federal regulations permit this practice, which is frequently discussed as a way to permit young people to purchase homes and to pay for them when their incomes would most likely be higher.[13] This method of payment also enables persons who can afford a home of a given size to add more energy conservation features to the home and to pay for them with the savings.

- *Loan to value ratio.* In general, a savings institution is limited as to the percentage of the value of a home it may lend. Under some circumstances, federal regulations permit an S&L to lend 95 percent of the value of the property, providing those loans do not exceed 15 percent of the association's assets.[14] The part of the loan in excess of the ordinary loan-to-value ratio must typically be either insured or guaranteed, and the loan is subject to a maximum repayment period of thirty years (unless the entire loan is insured or guaranteed).[15] With changes in federal regulations, higher loan-to-value ratios might be permitted for energy conservation investments. Similarly, longer payback periods might be allowed. Finally, state or federal guarantees of the amounts of the loan above the ordinary loan-to-value ratio could be offered. All of these devices would either lower the monthly cost of the loan or lower the down payment required.

- *Prepayment penalty clauses.* State laws often require S&Ls to permit prepayment of a loan, although they usually permit a penalty if the loan is prepaid in full before the loan's term is expired. The premium penalty is often limited: a penalty of 2 percent limit of the amount prepaid is common.[16] A penalty-free prepayment clause might induce homeowners to convert energy operating savings immediately into capital.

- *Lower interest rates for energy conservation features.* The lower operating costs of an energy-efficient home should, in principle, enhance the security of the lending institution in two ways. First, lower utility costs would free an additional amount of the borrower's income for payment of the debt. Second, should the loan be foreclosed, the lower operating costs for the home should enhance its value to possible purchasers; thus, the energy-efficient home offers better security than other homes because it could be liquidated more easily. Both of these features tend to lessen the risk of the loan. Since part of the interest charged on any loan is used to compensate the lender for the risk of his money, a lower risk should translate into a lower interest rate.

A lending institution in Seattle pioneered in this field by offering "energy conservation loans" to prospective purchasers of homes and other energy-consuming goods; other lending institutions have now followed suit in many areas. The Seattle plan is typical. Automobiles and boats are rated on their efficiency, with higher efficiency vehicles receiving lower interest rates; sail boats, for example, qualify for lower rates than do motor boats. Homes can be remodeled under the energy conservation loan program too. The Seattle lender has stated that his institution is "thinking about what homes without adequate insulation and efficient heating systems are going to be worth in two or three years."[17]

In evaluating homes for conservation loans, the Seattle lender uses a list of twenty-one features, grouped in three categories—house shell insulation, heating systems, and appliances with energy conserving features. Each item within a group is awarded points according to its potential for reducing energy use. Solar energy systems receive five points; a ceiling insulated with R-19 insulation earns five points; and window and door weatherstripping earns two points. Homes worth $75,000 or more are required to score at least twenty-five points to qualify for lower interest rates; homes worth less than $75,000 must score at least fifteen points.

The rewards for meeting the goals established in the Seattle program can be substantial. Using figures from 1976, homes meeting these standards were eligible for loans at 8.5 percent interest instead of the 9 percent rate usual at that time. On a twenty-five year mortgage for $45,000, this interest rate differential can mean a monthly payment reduction of $15.29 and a savings of $4,585.85 in interest over the life of the loan. An even greater interest rate differential is permitted for home improvement loans when those improvements raise the home's total conservation points to at least fifteen. Again using 1976 figures, qualifying loans—at least 30 percent of which must be used for energy conservation purposes—were offered at 8.75 percent instead of 9.5 percent. The loan program has generated interest among prospective borrowers, the press, and members of Congress. Thus, it has brought the lender immediate benefits, in addition to the economic advantages of receiving improved security in better homes.

The Seattle lending institution was not required to seek permission from any regulatory authority before beginning its program.

In the case of small loans for putting in comparatively inexpensive energy conservation improvements in existing homes, a Georgia bank offered a substantial discount from its home improvement rates. In early 1977, the bank routinely charged 18.84 percent for such loans; however, if the money were used for insulation, weather stripping, caulking, storm windows and doors, the bank agreed to loan money at 10 percent. Over the course of a year, this saved $50 in interest to the consumer.[18]

As we will see later in this volume, a number of institutions in addition to the traditional lenders have undertaken on their own initiative more or less extensive loan programs for energy conservation in existing buildings. Brooklyn Union Gas, for example, has been helping to install home insulation for decades. At one time, the company was required to insulate before furnishing natural gas in a building; although that requirement is no longer in effect, the gas company continues to inform its customers about its program and urges them to participate. It also encourages participants with a loan program for gas customers. Following the lead of Brooklyn Union Gas, in 1976 Consolidated Edison Company of New York received regulatory permission to make loans for insulation.[19] (The role of the public utility companies in insulation has been recently restricted, however, by the 1978 National Energy Act.)

One advantage of having utilities lend money for insulation and other energy conservation measures is obvious: utilities are already in regular communication with energy users. Existing billing procedures can, with minor modifications, be adapted to a loan program, thus assuring administrative ease in handling the programs. Finally, since utilities are controlled by public bodies, the state governments have the power to force utilities to participate in programs designed to maximize the public interest through energy conservation. All of these matters, as well as a more detailed description of two state-authorized insulation retrofit programs, are treated in greater detail in Chapter 3. That chapter also details how this type of program has been severely limited by recent congressional action.

Conclusion

Although subsidies, special tax preferences, and favorable loan provisions give the appearance of lowering the first cost of energy conservation programs, it is important to remember that frequently the first costs will actually be higher. Thus, choices will have to be made by consumers and by governments. Even though economically worthwhile energy conservation will pay for itself, the benefits will come over time, sometimes quite quickly. But to the consumer, the higher price may be the most visible result. Regulatory actions that have the effect of raising prices are difficult and politically unpopular. Therefore, such programs must be accompanied by a program of strong educational efforts to convince citizens that the trade between short term benefits and long term savings is worth making. Some may actually welcome uniform regulation. For example, it is difficult for a small builder to be innovative in energy conservation, lest he lose money. To the extent that small builders worry that taking such action by themselves might serve only to price themselves out of the market, concerted action (forced by governmental regulation) might even be welcomed.

MATERIALS, LABOR SKILLS, AND BUYERS' EXPECTATIONS

So far, we have dealt with the forces of nature (including climate and siting) that affect building energy performance and the pressures that a desire to keep the first cost low puts on increased capital expenditures. Next, let us consider three miscellaneous factors, difficult to weight and judge, which have a potentially strong effect on the rate at which energy conservation goals are incorporated into building design and construction. These are factors that legal and regulatory means can affect only in a limited way, yet they must be understood as a prerequisite to changing any design and construction practices.

Materials Available

To a large extent, the way buildings are built has been influenced by the development of new materials. Structures above a certain height can be constructed only with steel. Curtain walls depend, among other things, on tempered glass. New materials can also influence the way energy is used. For example, the use of metal window frames without thermal breaks, instead of wooden ones or metal ones with adequate thermal breaks, increases heat loss by about 22 percent. On the other hand, not all construction innovations precipitate energy waste: reflective windows can keep out summer heat, and improved insulation materials can retard the transmission of heat in either direction.

The secondary effects of the choice of construction materials are also important, although such effects fall outside the scope of this volume. To smelt a pound of aluminum requires around 8.2 kilowatt hours of electricity,[20] while wood grows naturally and requires relatively little energy to mill and transport. This indirect cost of energy contributes significantly to the energy intensiveness of American buildings. However, it is difficult to decide what action to take to change materials selected for buildings or whether to act at all. Data on the total energy intensiveness of particular materials in use are hard to get and their soundness is hotly disputed. For example, some economists argue that the price of a good includes all of the information a purchaser needs to know about the cost to society of producing that good and that adding an "energy price" for goods would add confusion to the marketplace. Without clear information or agreement on policy, it is certainly unwise to take legislative action.

The federal government could dispel much of the confusion surrounding the question of the indirect energy costs of materials by supporting further research to discover what materials are energy-efficient both in production and in use. It could also assist development of new materials through funding research. Testing and standard setting for safety, performance, and use characteristics might take place under official auspices. Thus, highly promising new energy-saving products may be given a boost by means of large government purchases, which assure a steady market for a new product. The government can also help introduce new products by financing studies to remove barriers to consumer acceptance, a technique explored in a companion volume in this series, *Government Procurement and Operations* by Ivan J. Tether.[21]

Skills of Existing Workforce

Brand new construction techniques often call for brand new skills. They often require workers who can handle new materials or adopt new methods of handling old materials. Unfortunately, the building trades tend to be conservative in this respect. This hangback attitude prevails at least in part because using known construction techniques simplifies bidding on jobs; if a work force is to be introduced to a new construction technique, the builder will be hard pressed to set completion dates and to identify potential pitfalls and delays. In the case of buildings constructed in part or in whole with federal government funds, the provisions of the Davis-Bacon Act apply, requiring in effect that union labor be used. Unions, because one of their functions is job protection for their members, may also be extremely conservative about the introduction of new materials because they fear that it will reopen jurisdictional questions with other unions that would mean loss of jobs for their members.

Retraining workers and using government buildings as showcases for new construction methods smooth the transition from old materials and techniques to new ones. But governmental demonstrations and purchasing cannot render the process completely painless. Major institutional obstacles to better buildings will still exist when new methods are perceived to violate the important social goal of a job for all who are willing to work.

Expectations of Building Purchasers

Tradition and custom, along with their progeny, consumer tastes, play an important role in the design of buildings. Radically innovative designs are unlikely to sell quickly in the housing market. Even in the commerical field, with the exception of prestige buildings (such as the Seagram Building in New York City or the John Hancock Building in Chicago), almost every building will be built to maximize the amount of rentable space in the most conventional fashion, serving most people's tastes.

Conventional buildings, constructed with the experience gained in designing and building similar structures in mind, are also easier than experimental structures to design and build because the imponderables of innovation do not weigh upon those in charge. Thus, in the residential market, where about one-fifth of all new homes are mobile homes and where only between 4 and 10 percent of the rest are architect-designed, it is not surprising that most homes satisfy most prospective buyers. The forces of tradition that appeal to the buyer also appeal to the builder and do not inspire efforts to conserve energy.

Fortunately, many energy-conserving features do not require any radical change in the conventional design of American buildings.

Although its panes may be double- or triple-glazed instead of single, an energy-conserving window will still look like a conventional window. Walls with thicker insulation look no different from the inside than walls with no insulation at all. Attic fans and improved furnaces and air-conditioning equipment are hidden out of sight, so what they look like matters little. On the other hand, smaller windows, overhangs, and extensive flourescent lighting will all have to find acceptance, perhaps against the tides of taste. Initial costs of housing and the costs of operating a building will provide powerful incentives to accept new designs.

THE REGULATORY FRAMEWORK FOR BUILDING ENERGY USE

Although we customarily think of regulation as a function of government, the building field is notable because of the strong and open relationships that exist between the government and the private, voluntary groups that develop standards, test materials, and draft regulations for possible adoption by government. The technical job of regulating buildings is enormous, and government alone, with its present resources at least, could not begin to cope with the variety of functions that voluntary groups perform. For example, techniques for calculating the heating and cooling loads on buildings are developed and published by a technical organization composed of heating and cooling engineers, the American Society of Heating, Refrigerating, and Air-conditioning Engineers, Inc. Although there are some biases inherent in the methods ASHRAE chooses to evaluate and the assumptions concerning comfortable heating and coolings ranges, these biases are firmly based on current American practice. Furthermore, no one challenges the usefulness, accuracy, and fairness of the methods developed by ASHRAE for calculating the loads within their stated assumptions. In a rather different field, the American National Standards Institute (ANSI) approves standards for product designs that range from the exact size and shape of electrical plugs to the design of typewriter keyboards. The American Society for the Testing of Materials (ASTM) develops standard testing procedures so that competitive materials may be subjected to identical tests for rating purposes.

Most of these groups reach agreement on standards or tests by following what is known as the "consensus" approach. This means that those who develop the standards and tests are drawn from a variety of interest groups within the industry and that their work is widely reviewed in draft form before it is finally accepted. Testing and standard setting are highly technical and take place in a forum that most people do not even know exists. For this reason, there is relatively little public input into the consensus process. This exclusion is not deliberate—most members of the public simply have not known the process existed. Participation by the public requires participants informed enough about the technical issues so that the professionals cannot claim that a cherished tradition has to be the way it has always been for technical reasons. Because participation is voluntary, members of the public with no direct economic interest in a particular standard have almost no way to finance their participation in the endless meetings (frequently held in different locations each time) that go into agreeing on a standard. In this area, as in so many other areas where public participation is desirable, the continuing problem of finding able, technically trained people outside the currently existing system is almost overwhelming.

One example of public participation in standard development, detailed more thoroughly in a later chapter, is the role of the federal government in expediting the development of ASHRAE Standard 90-75, which deals with energy conservation in new buildings. Because of the interest that the federal government and Congress have shown in energy conservation in buildings, it is certain that Washington will monitor, participate in, or even control the development of subsequent energy conservation standards. State governments and citizens should be aware that they can also demand to participate in this standard-setting process; indeed, they should be encouraged to do so. Public participation could be improved by requiring that no building code or other regulatory device be adopted unless members of the public took part in its development through full, paid participation in the standard-setting process.

Outside the area of building practices developed by private groups in association with the government, direct regulation of land use and building construction is the most easily recognizable form of governmental control exerted on design and building practices. Fire, plumbing, mechanical, and general building codes limit or mandate the materials to be used in construction; setback and side yard requirements determine how buildings may be placed on lots; street plans and subdivision platting requirements determine the orientation of buildings; and in some communities, regulations based on historic, aesthetic, or simply locally agreed upon considerations determine the very appearance of the buildings themselves.

This web of direct controls has four sources—private agreements and local, state, and federal government. Land use controls are traditionally locally mandated, although there is a trend in American law to put control of certain areas (often designated "critical areas") under state control or to subject them to state review. Building codes began as local documents, and many cities still have their own building codes, usually based on one of several model codes. Legislation enacted in 1976 has directed several federal agencies to cooperate on the development of a national energy conservation code for buildings that is to be adopted by state or local governments. The development of that national standard—known as the *B*uilding *E*nergy *P*erformance *S*tandard (BEPS)—is detailed in a later chapter.

As noted above, there is a tie between privately developed consensus standards and codes and governmentally mandated regulations. Many of the building codes make explicit reference by name and number to tests or standards or procedures developed by one of the private groups mentioned above. Therefore, changes in the privately developed documents can have an enormous effect on publicly enacted law; likewise, direct governmental regulations can influence the direction in which private codemaking, testing, or standard-setting groups direct their resources. The relationship between private and public groups will no doubt change in the field of energy regulation for buildings, although it is too early to predict the exact direction of the change.

Building Codes

Any discussion of the regulation of energy use in buildings must take building codes into account. Approximately twenty states have state-promulgated codes; hundreds of substate jurisdictions are responsible for codes in the remaining states.[22] Building codes are found in every one of the most populous states of the nation; the construction of the vast majority of American buildings now takes place under either a state or a local code. Although it is hard to find exact figures, one knowledgeable expert estimates that 75 to 80 percent of Americans live where there are building codes in force and that 90 percent of all buildings constructed are subject to code control.

Approximately 60 percent of the jurisdictions with building codes have adopted them from one of the three primary model code groups. These groups are the Building Officials and Code Administrators' International (BOCA), the International Conference of Building Officials (ICBO), and the Southern Building Code Congress International (SBCC). A fourth model code, issued by the American Insurance Association (AInA), is not widely employed, although it was the first model code introduced (in 1905).

Building Officials and Code Administrators International. BOCA, with headquarters in Chicago, draws its membership primarily from cities in the northeastern United States. Active members include all cities, towns, townships, and other governmental units responsible for building code administration that have adopted the BOCA code. Usually, a building code official is designated as the voting representative of an active member, while individual active members are persons employed by a government that is not a BOCA member. Membership (and thus voting on code changes) is proportional. Jurisdictions with populations of less than 50,000 are entitled to two representatives, those with populations up to 150,000 have four representatives, and those with populations greater than 150,000 have six representatives.

BOCA's Model Code Program prepares and publishes the *Basic Code*, which includes a series of specialized documents (mechanical, plumbing, and the like). BOCA also cooperates with the other model code groups in the preparation of the One and Two Family Dwelling Code. In addition to the documents comprising the *Basic Code*, BOCA offers a number of services: it will interpret code provisions in particular cases, train local officials, evaluate materials and practices, and assist in matters not covered in the *Basic Codes*.

International Conference of Building Officials. ICBO's *Uniform Building Code* is used widely in the West and to a lesser degree in the states of the north central region. ICBO has designated eight categories of members. Only members of Class A—governmental units or departments involved in code administration—are entitled to designate representatives, vote on changes in the code, hold office in the organization, and serve on committees. In ICBO, voting is not proportional; one representative casts one vote.

ICBO's basic code, the *Uniform Building Code*, and its related documents are published every three years. A group of reviewers produces annual supplements to keep the code current between major revisions. Proposed code changes, which may be submitted by anyone, are published in ICBO's monthly periodical, *Building Standards*, and are reviewed by the Codes Changes Committee. At its annual meeting, ICBO's Class A membership acts on proposals that the Changes Committee recommends.

The Southern Building Code Congress International. "Southern," as the SBCC is often called, has strongest acceptance in the states evoked by its name. Southern's governing body, the Code Congress, is composed of government representatives who vote without regard to the size of the political unit represented. The Congress administers a group of model codes, known as the Standard Codes. These codes cover buildings and housing, plumbing, fire prevention, swimming pool construction, excavation, gas, and mechanical matters. Over 2,500 governmental units in twenty-five states have adopted one or more of the Standard Codes.

With its full-time staff located in Birmingham, Alabama, Southern provides a variety of services to its members. Southern interprets codes, checks plans, reports on new products and practices, and helps jurisdictions to establish code enforcement programs.

Code Adoption

Although the codes are written and updated by persons employed by local and state governments in code administration and enforcement, codes adopted by the four model code groups alone have no force whatsoever in law. Codes gain force only when adopted by a state, regional, or local government body. Obviously, such a process is open to pressures from local interests, a fact that is reflected in the numerous local amendments common to all the national codes. Sometimes changes are rooted in climatic conditions peculiar to a given locale. Other local conditions sometimes also lead to curious twists. For example, for a short period, Chicago's building code required that bricks used in the city have square holes as opposed to round holes (used virtually everywhere else). Chicago brick manufacturers who inserted square holes in the bricks to fire them properly thereby gained an advantage over out of town makers using the more common round hole. This example of local private influence represents an extreme, but it also illustrates the susceptibility of building codes to forces wholly unrelated to the health and safety considerations that were the original justification for their adoption.

Sometimes, the latest edition of a model code may not be in force in a jursidiction that accepts the code. Charles Field and Steven Rivkin, in their excellent study of building codes, *The Building Code Burden*,[23] report that only 16.6 percent of 554 cities included in a study on code revisions had adopted the latest changes in the code; fully 18 percent of those jursidictions had not revised their codes for more than five years! Thus, even a model code group that keeps current with changes in energy conservation standards and regulations cannot guarantee that any of its member jurisdictions will follow its advice and example.

Coordination Among the Model Codes

The Council of American Building Officials (CABO) makes an attempt to keep the model codes fairly uniform. The Board for the

Coordination of Model Codes (BCMC) of CABO exists to locate discrepancies among the three major codes, to eliminate differences when they are located, and to make sure that new items are handled uniformly before they become part of each code.

Code Type

Codes may be classified as "prescriptive codes," "performance or true budget codes," or "component performance codes." Prescriptive codes enumerate in explicit detail those construction features that a building must contain to pass code inspection. In the case of the thermal efficiency of the building shell, for example, a prescriptive code would specify that attic insulation must be of a certain type and thickness, that windows must be of a certain maximum size and must be double or triple glazed. Performance codes, on the other hand, merely set levels of quality or achievement that a structure must meet in order to pass inspection. A performance code for energy might specify that no more than Y BTUs are to be used in heating a structure of a certain size under a specified set of weather conditions. Component performance codes are a combination of these two principles. Instead of taking a whole building approach to energy consumption within a structure, the performance is examined building section by building section. On the other hand, within each component such as a wall, a roof, or a window unit, no exact recipe is given for meeting the performance standard. For example, a component performance standard on energy might direct the designer that the roof should transmit no more than X BTUs per hour with a given temperature differential between inside and outside.

Preferences for one type of code over another reflect professional differences and disagreements about the proper balance to be struck between code elegance and the ease with which the provisions of a particular code can be met. On one hand, the architectural profession prefers a pure budget approach. They argue that an energy budget gives the designer leeway in selecting design and design-insulation combination options to minimize energy consumption and that variety itself promotes innovative thinking. On the other hand, members of the engineering profession prefer a component performance standard that specifies the expected performance levels of each element of a building without requiring that the complex calculations of total building energy consumption be made. A third important group, the small contractor and the small building code inspection department, generally would prefer a more prescriptive type code, with its clear lists of what will and what will not be acceptable.

Although it is hard to reconcile the competing wishes of the architects and the engineers, to some extent the model code groups have tried to meet the needs of this third group—small builders and small building code departments—by agreeing on a single, easy to use code. This code, the *One and Two Family Dwelling Code*, is designed to reflect unanimity among the code groups on particular building practices. More than unanimity, it is designed to present the information in almost a "cookbook" fashion. To assure conformity among the code groups on particular building practices to be included in the "cookbook code," most amendments to the code come only after the three major model code groups (BOCA, ICBO, and SBCC) have formally adopted similar requirements. (The American Insurance Association, producers of the National Building Code, participated in the formulation of the original version of the *One and Two Family Dwelling Code*, but has not participated in the amendment process and is no longer formally consulted.) This simple code is administered by the Model Code Changes Committee of CABO. The committee reviews proposed code changes and makes recommendations to the four code groups, each of which has a committee responsible for overseeing the amendment process. These committees review CABO's work and make their own recommendations. CABO then fashions amendments on the basis of this process.

Unfortunately, there seems to be little forward motion on improving the energy conservation provisions of the *One and Two Family Dwelling Code*. Changes to that code take about ten months to one year to process into final form. Each year, there is a February deadline for making suggestions for new changes. Although as of the deadline in 1977 there had been no energy conservation changes submitted for inclusion, since then a few were submitted that should appear in the 1979 version of the code.

Interstate Cooperation

One other actor should be mentioned in this array of private organizations that deal with building codes. This group is the National Conference of States on Building Codes and Standards (NCSBCS, commonly called "NixBix"). Unlike the model code groups, which produce technical codes, and CABO, which tries to make certain that model codes are consistent, NCSBCS exists to exchange information among the administrators of building codes about administrative solutions to adoption and enforcement. Thus, NCBCS is most concerned with the administrability of codes, rather than their technical content. (NCSBCS is also involved in the enforcement of federal mobile home construction and safety standards.) NCSBCS has been an important actor, as we will see in Chapter 3, in changing the Energy Conservation Standard developed by the heating and cooling engineers into a code.

Attitude of Private Code-Related Groups
Toward Federal Intervention

The code groups have traditionally been concerned that any federal standard, operating through the building code mechanism, might not reflect sufficient attention to the question of enforceability. Some building officials suspect that a federal standard would be too complex and would place overwhelming burdens of interpretation and enforcement on some communities. This fear has some grounds. Building officials are often overworked and/or underpaid because governmental funds are often inadequate. Their jobs grow more demanding as they are called upon to inspect more aspects of building construction under increasingly unfamiliar conditions or standards. Many building inspectors are persons retired from the construction industry itself and do not have the training required to interpret sophisticated building energy regulations. Moreover, many inspection departments depend upon building permit fees for a large portion of their operating budgets. If building construction declines sharply, as it did during the economic slowdown of 1972-1974, departments must cut back funding. Finally, because the standards are becoming more complex, building code officials increasingly fear that they will be sued by property owners if they turn down a building because of code violations. In the words of one CABO official, this has made many inspectors "gun shy." A complex, federally written code, particularly one unaccompanied by extensive training materials for the inspectors, is an invitation to lawsuits, or so many officials feel.

All of these forces impelled the voluntary code groups to try (unsuccessfully) to head off mandatory federal action. Although they originally hoped that workable, voluntary codes would be sufficient to make unnecessary mandatory codes imposed from above, federal law now contains a requirement for such an energy code. However, the question is still open: sanctions for the federal code cannot be brought to bear unless Congress agrees. Thus, it is likely that the views of the building code community will be aired at least one more time before the federal government preempts the field of energy conservation for buildings.

Federal Standards for Property

The HUD Minimum Property Standards. The building codes discussed so far in this chapter are exclusively in the domain of state and local governments. Although there is not yet a federal energy building code per se, the federal government does influence a substantial amount of the construction in this country through the Minimum Property Standards (MPS) developed by the Federal Housing Administration within the federal Department of Housing and Urban Development.

Any housing constructed with the financial assistance of the federal government—including Federal Housing Administration-guaranteed housing, Veteran's Administration loans, Farmers Home Administration guarantees, and various kinds of urban renewal—must comply with the MPS developed and administered by HUD. The MPS consists of three volumes, dealing with various types of housing—one and two family dwellings, multifamily housing, and care type housing. The wide application of these three sets of standards makes them an important factor in American construction. Yet estimates vary as to the exact number of units affected by the MPS. Even compiling figures on the number of houses in a given year financed or insured under federal programs would not answer the question. The most reliable estimates suggest at least 25 percent or more of all housing built complies with the MPS; some have suggested that even this figure is too low. Many builders are said to build in accordance with the MPS to be certain that their construction will be eligible for federal financial assistance. Such compliance is clearly prudent, since at the time of building, the identity of purchasers and the kind of financing those purchasers will choose is unknown.

Although the current editions of the standards are several years old, revisions are common. For instance, the standards for one and two family dwellings are contained in a 1973 edition, but portions of the basic volume have been revised on at least four occasions since then. Most individual revisions deal with a number of sections in the primary document, while a number of the recent revisions have touched energy conservation issues. For example, the first revision to the MPS for one and two family dwellings, issued in July 1974, contained a number of standards related to conservation. The revision referred to the goal of energy conservation in its section on building insulation, mentioning in its discussion of insulation the need "to assure conservation of energy" and setting out performance criteria for ceilings, walls, and openings such as windows. To minimize the problem of heat loss from air infiltration, the first revision called for caulking and weatherstripping around the windows and doors "to reduce infiltration of undesirable outdoor elements." On the basis of these (and other) changes in the 1974 revision, HUD's Minimum Property Standards Branch has estimated that homes built after the revisions were made could on average use 15 percent less energy than those homes built before the revisions. Further revisions are on their way for the MPS, revisions that some observers believe could make them among the tightest currently enforceable standards available.

The MPS are an important force in the housing field for reasons beyond their mandatory or prudent application for federally aided buildings. They are also important because they are used as a reference by some builders, who rely upon the detailed explanations they contain on all aspects of buildings. A companion volume, *The Manual of Acceptable Practices*, also enjoys wide use by builders desiring detailed instructions. Although compliance with the manual is not mandatory, the handbook does contain information on energy conservation practices. Its section on climate, for example, contains recommendations relating to tree preservation and the use of trees as sun traps to heat buildings during the winter. Unfortunately, however, the manual's recommendations on these energy-related subjects are quite general, and they do not carry the force of law.

The Special Case of Mobile Home Regulations. Mobile homes have become increasingly important sources of shelter. Census Bureau statistics for 1975 show that there were 212,700 mobile home shipments that year as compared to 892,000 housing starts of privately owned homes. But mobile homes are not regulated by states; rather, federal regulation is preemptive. Therefore, discussion of this important form of housing from the point of regulation by state and local governments is out of place in this volume. However, mobile homes are an interesting case study of the relationship between government and private regulation. They provide a strong contrast to the National Association of Homebuilders (NAHB), which expends considerable resources fending off federal regulations of all kinds (including energy conservation features). Unlike the NAHB, the trade association of the mobile home manufacturers has worked vigorously for increased regulation of their product. Thus, a word about the history of their regulation is worthwhile. Moreover, from an energy conservation point of view, mobile homes are a tempting target because they are frequently exposed on all sides, including the bottom. They may also be unshaded and made of heat-conducting metal, and they are frequently purchased primarily because of their relatively low initial cost.

Beginning in the 1960s, the Manufactured Housing Institute (MHI) began to encourage states to adopt compulsory regulations covering mobile homes. Consequently, when federal standards for the industry became a real possibility, the institute did not attempt to defeat them. In 1974, federal mobile home standards were enacted that preempt state regulation, thus assuring the uniformity in regulation long sought by the MHI.[24] Mobile homes will ultimately be regulated under the federal energy conservation standards as well.

Conclusion

In this discussion of building code and mobile home regulations, the large number of actors with different interests and fields of expertise has been emphasized. A reader new to this field is fully justified in being confused both about which group does what and about where apparently overlapping jurisdictions or duties are reconciled in practice. The complexity of the system, with its tradition of "touching every base" through the consensus process, assures stability, general agreement in the final goals and methods selected, and careful consideration of the difficulties inherent in any change. But the process is ponderous and slow. It is conservative, since strongly held objections can prevent major changes. And it is complex. This quick tour of the regulatory and voluntary building code sources shows only too clearly that making a "simple" change in the provisions of an existing code is not an action taken in a vacuum.

As a practical matter, it is unlikely that this voluntary system of producing codes and other regulatory materials will soon be replaced. The volume of work that takes place outside of the government is large, and with governments pressed to cover necessary services, it is unlikely that undertaking a service already provided by others will be popular. Even if government were to step in to displace the code groups, as a practical matter, many of the interests those groups now represent would also have to be considered in making the government-written code a success. But this is not to suggest that the government shouldn't take an interest in the process when large matters of public policy such as energy conservation are at stake and the voluntary groups appear to be moving too slowly. Threat of governmental action may be an effective prod. Research to support the proposed public policy against misplaced concerns should be undertaken. Most important, government should participate actively in the ongoing process to make certain that compromises truly reflect public as well as private input. Mere participation by the code administrators of a state or locality is not enough, since they may fail to represent broader interests of the public; what is convenient for the building code department may not always be right for the public!

In the same way, citizens interested in making changes must be willing to immerse themselves in technical details and must ask to join the commenting groups that propose and decide upon the public policy. Citizens ought not be dissuaded from asking basic questions simply because the situation looks hopelessly complicated. Ultimately, citizens must educate themselves so that they can argue effectively with elected officials from their jurisdiction. This education can be the most effective form of pressure on the private code groups, since unless the elected officials adopt the changes proposed by the code groups, those changes will have no effect in law.

INTEREST GROUPS AFFECTING BUILDING DESIGN

Literally hundreds of groups have an interest in the way buildings are constructed. One need only look at home-decorating magazines to see the advertisements pushing aluminum siding, wooden windows, vinyl-clad door frames, asphalt roofs, and the like to understand the enormous force of commercial pressures to build one kind of a building rather than another. Not all of these groups affect building energy use directly, and few commercial groups—other than insulation manufacturers and suppliers of other products that conserve energy directly—have an economic interest in energy conservation. Energy conservation may be a selling point for one model or another of a line of equipment or appliances, but for most manufacturers, the particular model chosen at a certain price range matters little.

In contrast, some groups either yield to professional biases or have an active economic incentive to favor one kind of conservation over another or to oppose certain types of conservation. Buggy whip makers don't favor freeways; baseboard electric heater makers don't like energy regulations comparing their products to heat pumps. There is probably no way in which effective, efficient, and fair energy conservation legislation can be enacted that will not harm certain economic interests. Slow changeover periods to allow complete depreciation of invested capital, the gradual tightening of standards, and programs that concentrate on education rather than on regulation all help slow or ease the burdens of change but nothing can make change painless for everyone.

Some interest groups take well-defined and oft-vented positions on energy conservation issues. Listing only four of the dozens of groups that are interested in the building process gives some flavor of the pressures that are brought to bear on decisionmakers in the building arena.

- *The American Institute of Architects.* The AIA is the representative of the organized architecture profession, a profession that prides itself on a history of innovative design that has made American buildings copied throughout the world. The AIA favors building energy conservation programs that permit maximum freedom to the design professional who wishes to experiment with building spaces. In energy terms, this means that architects desire flexibility to control energy use within the building, without tying the designer down to limitations on the energy usage of any given component or section of the building. This control would permit an architect to conserve energy in one part of the building only to use it lavishly in some other part. The AIA has been a vigorous proponent of performance or true budget type energy conservation standards and an opponent of both presecriptive type standards and component specification standards.

- *National Association of Home Builders.* The NAHB argues in favor of keeping the initial cost of homes down so that its member-builders will have more customers. NAHB contends that regulations add to the price of the house and that the buyer should be able to choose whether to buy a house with a larger kitchen or one more bedroom and to add the other features later or, as an alternative, to save longer for a house that has the now-required features built in from the start.

- *Masonry Institute.* In certain state proceedings considering the adoption of energy conservation standards, the Masonry Institute opposed the particular standards being proposed. Apparently the institute feared that the heat transmission co-efficients of masonry were such that it would be placed at a competitive disadvantage to other structural materials if the standards were adopted. On the other hand, the institute has proven itself an ally of those who are interested in passive solar design. Since masonry is a good storage medium for sunlight streaming in through a south window, any standard that encourages passive storage of the sun's heat has a ready champion.

- *Glass Manufacturers Association.* In a few states, chapters of the GMA feared the energy conservation standards because glass transmits heat better than well-insulated walls, and certain of the energy conservation building standards therefore limit the percent of wall area that may be covered by glass openings. As in the case of the Masonry Institute, solar energy is favored.

This list could clearly be expanded in a variety of directions: the building owner's associations have views on energy conservation features, as do the manufacturers of heating and cooling equipment and the unions representing the laborers installing that equipment. The important point to note within the context of state or local regulation of energy conservation is that the presence and varying relative strengths of these interests (and many more not mentioned here) make it hard for an outsider to predict which conservation approaches will be successful within a given jurisdiction. In one state the contractors may be powerful, in another the lending institutions; the shape of the final legislation will always reflect at least in part the interests of the groups that make their voices heard.

But one group is conspicuously absent from the list provided above; this group is largely missing from the debate generally. It is, of course, the public, including homeowners, building operators, and tenant associations. These consumers of the products of the businesses and service organizations mentioned above are in one way even worse off than consumers generally, since they do not even have the benefit of independent, impartial rating services like *Consumer Reports*. Information concerning housing or building operations is difficult to come by, and the regulations under which buildings are built are obscure and seemingly the sole province of other forces in society. It is little wonder that the prospective homebuyer falters in his or her role as energy conservationist in the home or office. The increasing costs of energy will help focus attention on the problem; and improved understanding of the manner in which the regulatory system is working (or not working) will help him or her influence the final regulatory products. But ultimately, the consumer is dependent upon wise regulations, fairly administered and evenly enforced. Without the local, state, and federal governments to monitor the regulatory process, no one consumer can hope to influence such an abstract, technical, and arcane a business as energy conservation in building design and operation. The importance of carefully designed laws and regulations cannot be overstated.

CONCLUSION

This chapter has considered the influences of five forces on the way American buildings are built—the natural factors of climate and landscape; what lending institutions can do to soften the blow of higher first costs associated with energy-conserving building features; the limitations that materials, labor skills, and buyer expections impose on swift change; the regulatory framework (particularly the model code groups and the federal MPS); and finally, the influence that various pressure groups exert on the way energy policy is made. These forces and groups will appear again and again in the pages of later chapters. As they are examined in more detail in this book, readers should consider how the seemingly diverse interests of these groups could be brought together and how members of the public and informed government agencies can improve the processes of decisionmaking.

We know that in the real world, buildings are complex systems in which various parts work cooperatively together in order to determine the final energy consumption. Yet in the following chapters, this complexity may be obscured; relationships between ventilation and heating unit size may not be obvious, because each of the various components has been pulled out of context in order to examine it more closely. In exactly the same fashion, this chapter has taken various influences out of context for the purpose of examining the roles each plays. In the real world they too are part of a complex shifting reality. It is the subtlety and interrelated nature of the building process that makes it both fascinating and frustrating to change.

NOTES

1. Victor Olgyay, *Design with Climate: Bioclimatic Approach to Architectural Regionalism* (Princeton, New Jersey: Princeton University Press, 1963), pp. 53–54. Copyright © 1963 by Princeton University Press. Reprinted by permission of Princeton University Press. Another excellent study of the influence of climate on building design and urban form is Ralph Knowles, *Energy and Form: An Ecological Approach to Urban Growth* (Cambridge, Massachusetts: The MIT Press, 1974).

2. See, Patrick Hughes, *A Century of Weather Service: 1870–1970* (New York: Gorden & Breach, 1970). The National Climatic Center, located in Ashville, North Carolina, provides weather data to persons needing answers to specific questions.

3. American Society of Heating, Refrigerating and Air-Conditioning Engineers, Inc., *ASHRAE Handbook—1977 Fundamentals Volume.* This handbook is revised every four years on a cycle. In addition to the *Fundamentals Volume,* the other three parts of the *Handbook,* each one of which is revised every four years, are *Applications Volume* (last revised 1978), *Equipment Volume* (last revised 1975), and *Systems Volume* (last revised 1976).

4. Leckie et al., *Other Homes and Garbage* (San Francisco: Sierra Club Books, 1975), pp. 10–12.

5. See, e.g., the federal floodplain and mudslide regulations in 24 C.F.R. 1909.2-1910.4, which set out the standards that communities must follow if they wish to be eligible for federal insurance programs.

6. Corbin Crews Harwood, *Using Land to Save Energy* (Cambridge, Massachusetts: Ballinger Publishing Company, 1977).

7. For example, there is considerable evidence that homes built with attention to the role of the sun in heating and cooling cost no more than conventional homes to build and save considerable money to operate. Owens-Corning's Arkansas House, an energy-conserving design, cost less to build than a conventional house of similar design. Homes in Davis, California, which has an innovative energy building code, are not higher priced. Considerable savings come because smaller heating and cooling equipment can be used in buildings that are designed to conserve energy.

8. Kennethy J. Thygerson, "Inflation's Legacy is a Shrunken Housing Market," *Savings and Loan News*, March 1976, pp. 36–37.

9. David Rosoff, quoted in *Energy Update* (Skidmore, Owings & Merrill) II, no. 3 (September-October 1976): p. 2.

10. John R. Emshwiller, "Cost of Keeping Warm Poses a Real Hardship to Millions of the Poor" *The Wall Street Journal* (Eastern ed.) March 21, 1979, p. 1, col. 1.

11. The Long Island Savings Bank Centenergy 76 (pamphlet), p. 1.

12. Statement of Thomas J. Owen on behalf of the U.S. League of Savings Associations before the Senate Commerce and Interior Committees concerning S. 2932, The Energy Conservation Act of 1976, February 26, 1976.

13. 12 C.F.R. 541.14 (c).

14. 12 C.F.R. 545.6-1 (a) (5).

15. 12 C.F.R. 545.6-1 (a).

16. American Bar Association, Committee on Savings and Loan Associations, Section of Corporation, Banking, and Business Law, *Handbook of Savings and Loan Law*, Chicago: American Bar Association, 1975), p. 30.

17. Information on Seattle Trust and Savings Bank from personal communications. In an article in *The Washington Post*, February 4, 1978, pg. D21, the director of marketing of the Seattle Trust stated about the program, "It's been phenomenal." He stated that since July 1976, 695 loans worth more than $30 million had been made on energy-efficient homes. See also testimony of president of the Seattle Trust, J.C. Baillargeon, July 20, 1976, Energy and Power Subcommittee of the House Commerce Committee.

18. "Atlanta Bank Cuts Rates on Energy-Savings Loans," *The Wall Street Journal*, February 3, 1977, p. 16.

19. Information concerning Brooklyn Union Gas from personal communication with Lester W. Gwaltney, director, Energy Conservation, Brooklyn Union Gas. "Con Edison Seeks Right to Lend Funds to Insulate Homes," *New York Times*, June 29, 1976.

20. The Conference Board, *Energy Consumption in Manufacturing,* A Report to the Energy Policy Project of the Ford Foundation (Cambridge, Massachusetts: Ballinger Publishing Company, 1974), p. 523.

21. Ivan J. Tether, *Government Procurement and Operations* (Cambridge, Massachusetts: Ballinger Publishing Company, 1977).

22. There is a trend toward more statewide building codes. For an excellent discussion of codes, see Steven Rivkin and Charles Field, *The Building Code Burden* (Lexington, Massachusetts: Lexington Books, 1975). For a survey of energy building codes, see Robert M. Eisenhard, *Building Energy Authority and Regulations Survey: State Activity* (Washington, D.C.: National Bureau of Standards, Office of Building Standards and Codes Services, March 1976).

23. Rivkin and Field, *supra* note 22 at 46, table 3-3.

24. National Mobile Home Construction and Safety Act of 1974, 42 U.S.C. 5401 *et seq.*

Chapter 3

Improving the Thermal Efficiency of the Building Envelope

Better insulation of all buildings has become a national energy conservation goal. The Federal Energy Conservation and Production Act of 1976[1] directed the federal government to develop building energy performance standards that will, among other things, increase the amount of insulation used in most new buildings. Many states with building code authority are already improving the sections of their codes that deal with insulation in order to qualify for federal money being allocated under the Energy Policy and Conservation Act.[2] Private organizations, notably the American Society of Heating, Refrigerating, and Air-conditioning Engineers, Inc., and the American Institute of Architects, have developed standards and methods that will cause designers to make thermal improvements in buildings. Finally, even utility companies have begun to finance or even to install insulation for their residential customers.

Against this background of relatively uncoordinated activity, is it possible for a state or local government to become active in the process of developing a rational, cost-effective, and technically based program to encourage or to require increased insulation? There is no simple answer to this question. On the one hand, it is tempting to try to craft a relatively simple code that satisfies local needs and local climate. Unfortunately, as this chapter will point out, a simple code is no simple matter. Not only is there the web of laws and organizations that is detailed in the last chapter and this one, but there are real practical and technical difficulties in developing a good energy conservation code. An effective building energy conservation program must take into account differences in buildings. Large commercial buildings have problems of thermal efficiency quite unlike those of small commercial or residential buildings. Older buildings can be difficult to improve, and first cost barriers must often be removed to encourage capital investments. Other barriers to a broadbased insulation program are institutional, not physical: when, for example, a renter pays for utilities, the landlord has little motivation to improve the building structure to save energy, while the tenant lacks the ownership incentive. As a practical matter, then, a state or a locality will have a very difficult time developing its own energy-conserving building code. Most parts of the country will have to rely on the energy codes that are being developed by the code organizations or by the federal government. This chapter explains the codes that have been or are in the process of being developed, so that more rational choices can be made by states considering whether to adopt one of the national codes or to try to make a more stringent state or local code.

To take all these problems into consideration, this chapter is divided into three sections. The first sets down the principles of insulation and some of the terminology. The second considers programs to improve insulation in both new and existing residential structures. The third briefly discusses similar programs for larger buildings (including large apartment houses), both new and existing.

INSULATION: THEORY AND PRACTICE

The theory of insulation is simple: some materials, such as aluminum or brick, transmit heat easily while others, such as wood or plastic foam, transmit heat slowly. A good insulator impedes the movement of molecules, keeping their energy from being transmitted; the movement of molecules is called heat. The wooden handle on a pot with a copper bottom spares the cook a burn because wood is a good insulator.

The physical principle that explains building insulation is that dry, still air transmits heat poorly. Therefore, building insulation is made to trap the maximum amount of dry air in small pockets. The pockets prevent the trapped air from moving (by convection), and thus heat movement is retarded. Several common materials are used for building insulation—glass fibers formed into mats, rock minerals formed into fluffy masses, and rigid plastic foam are three common forms. Fiber, fluff, or foam is placed between wall surfaces, above ceilings, under floors, and in other places where a difference between the inside and the outside temperature permits heat to move from the warm side to the cool side. The insulation retards the movement of the heat.

Because the materials used for insulation vary in their resistance to heat transfer, methods of indicating heat transferability have been standardized. What scientists speak of as the "U value" of insulation is the amount of heat (in BTUs) transferred in one hour through one square foot of a given material from the air on the warm side to the air on the side 1°F colder. The lower the U value of a given building section, the more it resists heat transfer; low U values indicate good insulation properties. This makes sense intuitively, since the fewer BTUs of energy that move through a material, the more heat will stay where you want it to perform useful work.

The measure of resistance to heat transfer used in commerce is the "R value." Since U values tend to be small decimal numbers, they are hard to differentiate quickly. R values, which are the inverse of U values (R value = 1 divided by the U value), express in a simpler to understand form the same information provided by U values. High R values signify high insulation value. No matter what the material used, insulation with identical R values (or identical U values, for that matter) has the same insulation properties. Table 3–1 illustrates the way in which R values for each component are added together to arrive at a composite R value for a wall. The right-hand column shows the dramatic improvement in thermal efficiency that can be gained by adding about three-and-one-half inches of insulation batting (an R value of about 11).

In addition to wall and ceiling insulation, storm doors and storm windows have some insulating value. Doors and windows transmit heat more easily than walls or ceilings both because the materials of

Table 3–1. Effect on R Values of Adding Insulation to a Wall

	Wall Without Insulation	Wall With R–11 Insulation
Outer layer (air film, siding, building paper, sheathing)	R-2	R-2
Enclosed air space	R-1	R-0[a]
Insulation	R-0	R-11
Inner layer of wall (interior wall material, air film)	R-1	R-1
Total	R-4	R-14
Wall heat flow value (U=1/R total)	1/4=0.25	1/14=0.07

[a]Air space not credited to insulated wall because it has been replaced by the insulating material.

Source: Jeffrey C. Cohen and Ronald H. White, Citizens for Clean Air, *Energy Conservation in Buildings: The New York Metropolitan Region* (Washington, D.C.: Environmental Law Institute, 1975), p. 7.

which they are made resist heat less well than walls and because they are thinner than the structural elements. Since they open and close, they also permit heat to escape through cracks, a problem dealt with in Chapter 5. Insulating windows to the same degree as walls is impossible, and thickening doors enough to insulate them significantly may be aesthetically displeasing. Therefore, storm doors and windows, sealed double- and triple-glazed windows, and vestibules will utilize the insulating properties of still, dry air. Storm doors, vestibules, and storm windows, depending on their design, may also reduce the amount of air leaking into the structure, a subject also discussed in Chapter 5.

Since human activities generate moisture, one final part of building construction, the vapor barrier, deserves attention. Breathing, cooking, showering, and washing all put humidity into the air. In the winter, vapor pressure (the tendency of any vapor to distribute itself evenly throughout an area) will attempt to force moisture generated inside a building through the walls to the outside. When humidity is low, water vapors will gradually pass through any permeable barrier (such as the wall of a building) until the amount of moisture inside and outside equalizes.

Unless it is properly dealt with, the moisture driven by vapor pressure can seriously affect the structure of a building. Just as a glass of iced tea sweats in the summer, the water vapor in the air of a heated structure will liquify as it is cooled. As the moisture passes through insulation, it will condense into water (or ice) on the cold side. The condensate that forms can destroy the insulation, rot the structure of the building, and stain the interior or exterior paint. To prevent the passage of moisture through the walls, the installation of a vapor barrier is necessary. Vapor barriers, commonly made of plastic sheeting or aluminum foil, are placed on the warm side (inside) of the structure. Tightly sealed, they keep the interior moisture from migrating into the insulation and from condensing to water. Properly installed, they also serve to prevent the flow of air into and out of the structure.

Unfortunately, no item inside a building is without its complications. There is some concern among building professionals that excessively moisture-sealed homes may also cause structural problems. The Department of Energy has recently funded Princeton University's Center for the Environment (the institutional home of the "Twin River Studies" on energy use in townhouses) to study problems of moisture, moisture passage, and vapor barrier placement.[3]

These three elements—insulation, storm doors and windows, and vapor barriers—represent the most important means of improving the thermal performance of a building shell. Combined with proper design, proper orientation, the use of shading and windbreak features to keep solar and wind effects working with the building, efficient heating and cooling equipment, and tight construction to prevent air infiltration, insulation is an integral part of an energy-efficient building.

Savings Possible Through Proper Insulation

If cost and beauty were of no account, it would be possible to insulate buildings so that little heat passed into or out of them. But beyond some level, it would cost more to make buildings more conserving than it would to pay the periodic costs of the energy that might have been saved. The building owner should instead calculate the cost of installing various amounts of insulation, including, of course, the cost of the future interest foregone on his money, and tabulate the value of the fuel savings possible over the total life of the building. The owner should then install enough insulation to minimize the joint cost of the insulation and future fuel. Because those future savings will not have the same economic impact as present savings, the owner must discount future savings to their present worth. The wise building owner will also try to estimate the probable rise in energy costs during the period for which the discounting is to be done. Only if the money saved in the future is equal to or greater than the cost of the insulation chosen will the owner make the insulation investment. Thus, a correct assessment of the proper amount of insulation needed for a particular building must include detailed knowledge of design weather conditions, the costs of buying and installing insulation, and correct estimates of future fuel prices. For small buildings, including residences, the design weather conditions are average minimum temperatures for the city as a whole (or some larger area, in many cases). For larger commercial buildings, solar load, wind speed, and prevailing wind direction are also taken into account. Because of the care and precision required for large buildings and because the cost of design and construction and the annual operating expenses are both large, the annual heating and cooling load calculations are usually handled by professional engineers.

For small and large buildings alike, future fuel costs are a crucial factor. Most energy specialists believe that building owners currently underestimate the future costs of fuel. These underestimates wrongly persuade owners to install less insulation than they should because the future energy costs look smaller than they will in fact be. Studies have also shown that individuals making economic decisions tend to downplay inflation and to severely underrate future costs.[4] Such miscalculations push the insulation decision toward too little insulation.

Another factor also obstructs energy conservation—the way that we calculate utility charges in this country. As we will see later in this book, utilities use an average cost for figuring the price their customers must pay. The average is between expensive new power-generating facilities on the one hand and inexpensive (usually older) generators on the other. Thus, the price paid is a composite, lower than it would be if consumers knew what their new additional consumption would cost the power company to supply. In our market economy, most other goods and services are priced at their marginal product cost. Because the marginal cost for energy of all kinds is now almost universally higher than the average cost charged by utilities, utility bills are lower than they would be if they were priced in the way that almost all other goods and services are. Even in the face of high fuel costs and uncertain oil prices, such misleading pricing practices prompt many to decide not to insulate their homes or offices, because fuel seems so deceptively cheap.

Taking all of these factors into account, what can one say about the energy cost savings that proper insulation will make possible? Elsewhere in this book, examples drawn either from computer models or from actual experience are mentioned. But a few examples are appropriate here:

- Chevron Research Company commissioned a report prepared by George A. Tsongas, a professional engineer with Portland State University, on energy conservation modifications for several houses in the Pacific Northwest.[5] For one Portland house, Tsongas calculated the amount of energy that would be saved, the cost of the additional insulation, and the payback period for a number of changes, including installing the insulation. Savings were calculated on the assumption that only the listed modifications would be made. More to the point, the calculations showed how soon the investment would pay for itself (payback period) and, given the dollar amount of energy saved, the rate of interest (rate of return) a savings bank would have to pay to the homeowner (ignoring his income tax on the interest) to equal the savings from the energy conservation investment. Put another way, as long as home improvement loans are available at lower rates of interest than the rate of return shown in this table, consumers can make money by borrowing money to make the

Table 3-2. Representative Conservation Savings

| | *Possible Improvements and Savings* | | |
Possible Improvement	*Cost in $*	*Payback Period (years)*	*Rate of Return (percent)*
Ceiling Insulation, Rock Wool, 8" Blown in	$172	6.3	17.6
Wall Insulation, 3½ UFC Foam	$488	5.8	21.0
Drapes, Roller Shades Reduce Window U Value by 25 percent for Single Glazing	$305	9.9	7.3

Source: Chevron Research Company, "Home Energy Conservation Demonstration Project," Richmond, California. December 1975, p. 13.

improvement (assuming designs and weather conditions similar to those used by Tsongas). A truncated version of Tsongas's table is given in Table 3-2.

- A study conducted by Jeffrey C. Cohen and Ronald White, funded by the National Science Foundation, looked at the energy savings that would be possible in the New York Metropolitan Region if the state undertook three actions at once.[6] The strategies were (1) immediate application to all new residential construction of the HUD thermal insulation standards for one and two family homes; (2) immediate initiation of a vigorous retrofit program for insulating existing single family homes; and (3) immediate application of a modified GSA energy budget to all new commercial construction. The study showed that adopting these three policies would result in substantial savings. Although the HUD standards control air infiltration as well, energy savings in the residential sector come almost entirely from insulation, and the results displayed in Table 3-3 therefore indicate the economic importance of proper insulation.

Homeowners interested in calculating the savings that installing insulation and adopting other energy conservation measures make possible can find detailed practical advice in two publications prepared by the federal government. The shorter, simpler pamphlet, "Making the Most of Your Energy Dollars in Home Heating & Cooling," is published by the National Bureau of Standards. A more comprehensive booklet, which includes do it yourself instructions for

Table 3-3.   Energy Savings in 1985

Building Type	Consumption Assuming Current Average $(BTU \times 10^8)$	Reduced Consumption Level $(BTU \times 10^8)$	1985 Rate of Savings[a]		
			$(BTU \times 10^8)$	Barrels of oil (million)	$ (million)
New single family	958,014	583,518	374,496	6.56	110.2
New multifamily	287,800	228,413	59,387	1.04	17.4
New commercial	626,250	278,500	417,750	7.10	113.3
Existing single family: 10 percent retrofit by 1985	349,274[b]	254,017	95,255	1.7	28.6

[a]For all residential, No. 2 oil: 136,000 BTU/gallon; $.40/gallon.
For commercial, No. 4. oil: 140,000 BTU/gallon; $.38/gallon.

[b]Shows only what consumption level for 10 percent of housing stock would be in 1985.

Source: Jeffrey C. Cohen and Ronald H. White, Citizens for Clean Air, *Energy Conservation in Buildings: The New York Metropolitan Region* (Washington, D.C.: Environmental Law Institute, 1975).

installing common energy-saving improvements, is "In the Bank . . . Or Up the Chimney: A Dollars and Cents Guide to Energy-Saving Home Improvements."[7] Since the federal government has offered to make the printing plates for these publications available for any organization that wishes to print, distribute, and use the materials, they would also be valuable additions to a state-run educational program.

One final complication needs to be considered. The economic calculations that are made to determine the level of insulation justified by the savings accrued may indicate that more insulation is needed than current construction techniques permit. In the case of a house, for example, ceiling insulation is almost always justified. But where the slanting roofline of a home touches the tops of the walls, only a small amount of space in which to install insulation is available. Likewise, conventional walls may not be thick enough to permit installing an economically justified amount of insulation. New insulation materials may help alleviate this problem. For example, urea formaldehyde foam insulation has a thermal conductivity of about one-third that of rock wool and so requires less space than equally effective insulation materials. (Unfortunately, foam insulation is more expensive than other forms and requires proper, professional application techniques for successful results.)

One approach to meeting the space problem in new construction was taken by a builder and a manufacturer of insulation. To permit the use of more insulation, numerous changes were made in the standard design of a small house. The wall insulation was extended into the attic, where it could meet flush with the ceiling insulation. The corners were designed to be insulated snugly, and wall construction was modified to increase the amount of space for insulating from four inches to six inches. In addition, the crawl space was insulated, the window area was reduced, and a truss sytem was designed to permit the installation of twelve-inch ceiling insulation to the edges of the walls. Finally, one-inch duct liners were installed around heating and cooling ducts, and those ducts were installed inside the heated and cooled space.

The builder and the insulation company estimate that compared to homes constructed in the Little Rock, Arkansas, area that merely comply with the federal Minimum Property Standards, the well-designed and well-insulated homes showed a 73.6 percent savings in energy for heating and cooling and an average cost reduction for total energy use of 46.7 percent. The company's report shows that the homes, which contained humidification and dehumidification systems, electronic air filters, power attic ventilation, and increased acoustic insulation, cost less to build than homes with conventional design and insulation features. Fewer pieces of wood are used in the construction of such homes (343 versus 590 in a conventional home), less material is needed (2,050 board feet versus 3,254), wiring is simpler, electrical service can be reduced, and construction time can be as much as five days less than that required by a conventional home. The savings associated with this better insulated home vary with different designs or in different regions, but such savings will always be considerable.[8]

Insulation alone seldom plays the central role in the energy savings of a large office or commercial building that it can in a home. In such large buildings, the interplay of various design and mechanical features combine to determine energy efficiency. A building may have a warm interior with little or no added heat because the people and the lights heat it up; on the perimeter of that same building, the sunny side may be warm while the shaded sides are cold. As the sun shifts during the day and over the course of the seasons, the requirements for heating and cooling shift accordingly. Buildings in moderate climates commonly have larger cooling requirements than heating requirements on a cold but clear, sunny day.

REGULATIONS NOW
UNDER DEVELOPMENT

A discussion of the physical aspects of insulation leads naturally to the development of regulations covering insulation. As noted in Chapter 2, numerous groups are working on regulations for both old and new buildings, and the federal government now has a role in the process as well. As Chapter 2 states, building standards can be one of three types—prescriptive (standards that give detailed instructions for meeting the standard), component performance (standards that list the parts of the building, such as the walls or the ceiling, that must meet certain standards of thermal efficiency, but do not specify the method for accomplishing that performance), or performance or "true budget" (standards that set an overall energy consumption level for each type of building and climate, but which contain no guidance or details as to how the energy consumption budget should be achieved). This section will consider the two more modern approaches, component performance standards and true budget standards. The trend in building regulation has long been away from prescriptive standards in all fields; they are particularly inappropriate in the field of energy regulation because they assume the existence of a settled technology and building construction process, not one that needs to be changed. Energy conservation in buildings needs to be stimulated, not stifled.

Development of ASHRAE Standard 90-75:
Component Performance.

The most influential energy conservation code currently available is the Standard 90-75, developed by the American Society of Heating, Refrigerating, and Air-conditioning Engineers, Inc. Both the process followed in its development and the standard itself merit discussion.

The former president of ASHRAE, Roderick R. Kirkwood, described the early development of the standard in an address given in 1974.[9] In 1973, while the oil embargo was still a fresh national concern, the National Conference of States on Building Codes and Standards had asked the National Bureau of Standards (then the secretariat of NCSBCS) to develop the technical background necessary for the development of a legislative standard for new building efficiency. According to Kirkwood, the concern was for a technically based standard that would prevent the problems of interpretation and veracity associated with a large number of differing local codes.

The National Bureau of Standards formed a team and, assisted

by consultants, prepared a draft of the document that was transmitted to NCSBCS on February 27, 1974. The National Bureau of
Standards suggested in its cover letter to the document that the
standards were unsuitable for immediate enactment, but that they
would provide the basis for a legislative type standard. ASHRAE sub-
sequently undertook just such a task. Initially, it was expected that
ASHRAE would be able to transmit the document to the American
National Standards Institute (ANSI) for adoption by the end of
1974. Adoption by ANSI would mean that enactment of the standard into law would be greatly eased. That expectation proved wildly
overoptimistic. The various drafts of the document were difficult to
prepare, and even the most widely circulated draft proved controversial. The review procedures were extensive: among othe reviewers,
the federal government convened an interagency task force to provide review and comments for inclusion in the final draft. The final
draft was approved as an official ASHRAE standard on August 11,
1975. The decision was made at that time not to submit ASHRAE
Standard 90-75 directly to ANSI for adoption, but rather to filter it
through the adoption procedures of the model code groups and
states, gaining support as it went. The revision of the standard,
Standard 90-75R, is now being submitted to ANSI and to public
review, so that it may concurrently be accepted as an ASHRAE and
an ANSI standard. The first cycle of comments on Standard 90-75R
closed in March 1978; in early 1979, ASHRAE planned put it out for
its second public review.

The ASHRAE standard received strong support from the fact that
the federal government needed a completed energy conservation
standard to give to the states to fulfill the mandates of federal law.
Under the Energy Policy and Conservation Act (EPCA),[10] states
were offered federal money for carrying out energy conservation
programs but receipt of this money was conditioned on meeting
several mandatory requirements. Thermal standards for buildings
was one of the mandatory requirements. Section 362(c)(4) of EPCA
states that

> Each proposed State energy conservation plan to be eligible for Federal
> assistance under this part shall include—
> (4) mandatory thermal efficiency standards and insulation requirements
> for new and renovated buildings (except buildings owned or leased by the
> United States).

The final guidelines issued by the Federal Energy Administration
called on the states to adopt thermal insulation standards at least

consistent with ASHRAE 90-75 or, in the case of new residential buildings, consistent with ASHRAE or with the HUD Minimum Property Standards. The provisions were to be in place and ready for implementation with respect to all buildings by January 1, 1978.[11] Many states, wishing to obtain the funds that EPCA provided, simply adopted some form of Standard 90-75 by reference as a supplement to existing building codes. The movement to Standard 90-75 has been further enhanced by the fact that the major building code groups have begun or completed the process of accepting the standard as part of their own codes.

As any reader familiar with building code standards understands, the ASHRAE document is a standard, not a code, and therefore differs greatly from traditional building codes. The standard does not describe how its particular provisions are to be administered; indeed, it would be difficult for a building inspector using its provisions to determine whether a building complies with the code. For this reason, the United States Energy Research and Development Administration (ERDA) contracted with the National Conference of States on Building Codes and Standards (NCSBCS), the model code groups, and the National Academy of Code Administration to develop a model energy conservation code based on ASHRAE Standard 90–75 and suitable for adoption by the model code groups and by state and local building code agencies.

This code, the model *Code for Energy Conservation in New Building Construction*,[12] was developed and promulgated so that it could be used by states wishing to comply with the EPCA requirements for an ASHRAE 90-75 type energy-conserving building code. To help implement the code, the ERDA contract also required the contractors to develop training materials and to conduct courses to train building code officials to enforce the model energy conservation code. These training courses are designed to be conducted in four series: Series 000 consists of a short (perhaps little more than one hour) course for elected officials and other persons who need an introduction to the model energy conservation code and may need an explanation about the need to conserve within the building sector. Series 100, an eighteen-hour program, is designed to teach building inspectors how to assess a building without having to understand all of the technicalities that may lie behind the code. Series 200, a twenty-one-hour series, is designed to convey information about the ASHRAE 90-75 code to the plan examiners and code officials who must decide whether a building design passes muster. Graduates of this course should be able to deal with all conventional building designs. Series 300 is a more complete course for the sophisticated design professional and for plan examiners and code officials who need to know how to work with every building type, including the most complex structures. NCSBCS tested the courses, and the materials are now available from NCSBCS or from the Department of Energy.[13]

Because of the importance of Standard 90-75, it is worth describing its provisions, at least generally. Standard 90-75 is divided into eleven sections. Sections 1 through 3 deal with "Purpose," "Scope," and "Definitions." The standard covers:

> new buildings that provide facilities or shelter for public assembly, educational, business, mercantile, institutional, warehouse and residential occupancies, as well as those portions of factory and industrial occupancies which are used primarily for human occupancy, such as office space. Unless otherwise stipulated, the term buildings, as used in this Standard, includes mobile homes and manufactured buildings.[14]

Standard 90-75 does not cover buildings that use minimal amounts of energy (less than one watt per square foot) or those that are neither heated nor cooled.[15]

The stated purpose of the standard is as follows:

> The requirements of this Standard are directed toward the design of building envelopes with adequate thermal resistance and low air leakage and toward the design and selection of mechanical, electrical, service, and illumination systems and equipment which will enable the effective use of energy in new buildings.[16]

The substantive directions of Standard 90-75 are found in Sections 4 through 11. The standard permits buildings to conform to its directions in three different ways:

- Sections 4 through 9, which are discussed more fully directly below, provide a detailed listing of the acceptable thermal characteristics of the exterior envelope and the equipment (the heating, water, lighting, and electrical distribution systems).

- Section 10, "Energy Requirements for Building Designs Based on Systems Analysis," permits a building designer to disregard the requirements of Sections 4 through 9, as long as the designer can demonstrate the deviations "will result in annual energy consumption equal to or less than that resulting from compliance with these criteria."

- Section 11, "Requirements for Buildings Utilizing Solar, Geothermal, Wind or Other Non-Depleting Energy Sources," permits a building designed according to the requirements of Section 10 to use more energy than a building designed according to the prescriptions of Sections 4 through 9, provided that the additional energy comes from a nondepletable source. "Nondepletable" is defined as "Sources of energy (excluding minerals) derived from incoming solar radiation, including photosynthetic process; phenomena resulting therefrom including wind, waves and tides, lake or pond thermal differences; and energy derived from the internal heat of the earth, including nocturnal thermal exchanges."[12]

Sections 10 and 11, which establish a type of energy budget, are considered in Chapter 7 of this book, which deals with design features for energy conservation.

ASHRAE Standard 90-75, Sections 4 through 9. The ASHRAE standard does not make easy reading for a layman unversed in heating, cooling, and ventilating terminology and descriptive matter. The following descriptions are intended to indicate the matters covered by those sections and to suggest the general approach that the standard takes.

Section 4: Exterior Envelope Requirements. This section deals with the minimum thermal requirements of the exterior walls, windows, and other components of buildings for two different classes of buildings. Paragraph 4.3 applies to one and two family residential dwellings and to low-rise, multifamily residential buildings not exceeding three stories. Paragraph 4.4 applies to all other buildings. Paragraph 4.5 discusses air infiltration into any type of building and is dealt with more thoroughly in Chapter 5 of this book.

For both the smaller buildings (so-called "Type A" buildings) and for larger buildings ("Type B" buildings), the regulations contained in Section 4 are expressed in terms of combined thermal transmittance value and stated as maximums. As applied, the standards become progressively more stringent as the climate gets colder (more precisely, the U values of the building elements must be lower as the annual number of degree days rises). A formula for calculating the combined U value of a wall that contains unbroken walls, windows, and/or doors is also included in this section.

Section 4 establishes heat transmission limits for buildings on a component-by-component basis; it establishes thermal transmission limits for the walls, the roof, and the floor. The standard assumes for design purposes that the interior temperature is kept at 72°F in the winter and 78°F in the summer; if the temperature is kept lower in the winter or higher in the summer, the energy savings possible will be greater.

Section 5: Heating, Ventilating, and Air-Conditioning (HVAC) Systems: This section tells professional designers how large a heating or cooling unit to install, what ventilation rates to allow for, and how to insulate the ductwork of the heating and cooling system. The section assumes that "normally clothed people are engaged in sedentary or near-sedentary activities." Specifically excluded are such unusual situations as hospitals, computer rooms, and (surprisingly) supermarkets.

Section Five directs the designer to design for 72°F in winter, with a maximum relative humidity of 30 percent; in summer, the design temperature is 78°F. Ventilation requirements are set at the minimum value specified in ASHRAE's earlier Standard 62-73, "Natural and Mechanical Ventilation." This section makes the use of thermostats for heating and cooling mandatory and specifies that, where humidity is artificially added to the air, energy must not be used to increase relative humidity to over 30 percent in winter or to below 60 percent in summer.

Use of terminal reheat systems—a system that chills all the air in a building to the lowest temperature demanded by any of the building's occupants so that other persons might reheat the air to the temperature they desire—is discouraged. A mere description of this system, which usually relies on resource-intensive individual resistance heating coils for reheating, underlines its inherent inefficiency! As an alternative to terminal reheating, Section 5 encourages cooling with outdoor air and recommends that, wherever possible, energy that would otherwise be thrown away (such as the heat discharged by an air-conditioning system) be recaptured for use somewhere else in the building. Finally, the section establishes standards for insulating the heating and cooling ducts of the dual system.

Section 6: Heating, Ventilating, and Air-Conditioning (HVAC) Equipment. This section establishes performance standards for heating, ventilating, and cooling equipment and tells how to document compliance with these standards.

Section 7: Service Water Heating. This section covers the efficiency standards for water heating.

Section 8: Electrical Distribution Systems. This section requires that electrical distribution systems have a power factor (a measure of efficiency) of not less than 85 percent, and it limits the voltage drop for the outlet farthest from the main distribution point to 5 percent. It further requires that cleaning personnel have available individual switching for lighting and that switching systems be available for turning lights on and off according to variations in the outside light.

Section 8 explicitly recognizes that paying for one's own electricity tends to make one more careful, and the section states: "In any multi-tenant residential building, provisions shall be made to separately determine the energy consumed by each tenant. Where local codes and regulatory agencies permit, each tenant shall be made financially responsible for the energy he uses."[18] Only hotels, college dormitories, and other transient facilities are excluded from the provisions of this paragraph.

Section 9: Lighting Power Budget Determination Procedure. This section, drafted by the Illuminating Engineering Society, establishes a method for limiting the energy used for lighting. It is dealt with more thoroughly in Chapter 4.

Critique of ASHRAE Standard 90-75. A number of design professionals, including some who support the concept of a component performance standard such as Standard 90-75, have been dissatisfied with the actual standard as it emerged from the consensus process. By its very nature, the consensus method produces standards that do not demand much more than business people in the field can attain. Consensus standards tend to be reasonable from the point of view of those affected; to meet consensus standards for buildings, builders need not choose the very best that currect technology has to offer.

The most often expressed criticism of ASHRAE Standard 90-75 is that it is too liberal, particularly as it applies to residences. A study conducted by the Arthur D. Little Company of ASHRAE Standard 90-75 on energy consumption indicated that:

The unweighted average reduction in annual energy practices across the four locations investigated were as follows:

Single-Family Residence	— 11.3%
Low-Rise Apartment Building	— 42.7%
Office Building	— 59.7%
Retail Store	— 40.1%
School Building	— 48.1%

ASHRAE 90 may be seen as less effective in reducing annual energy demand in the detached single-family residence than in the larger residential and nonresidential buildings. This lower effectiveness may be explained in part by the moderately high overall thermal efficiency assumed for the conventional residences. However, the ASHRAE 90 modified residences in both the Northeast (New York City), North Central (Omaha) locations met the standard with single glazing and a minimum reduction in glass area.[19]

An energy conservation standard that permits single family homes to comply without improved window units appears on its face to be too liberal. Nonetheless, the ASHRAE standard represents a step in the correct direction for energy conservation, even if it is far too cautious. Virtue need not hurt to be effective, but it seems clear that the consensus process failed to squeeze enough fat from building energy use. Further revisions of ASHRAE Standard 90-75 have been made. Standard 90-75R adds Section 12, which deals with resource utilization factors and makes various technical, tightening changes. One can hope that, prodded by national performance standards and by the rising costs of energy, ASHRAE will continue to push the expected performance level far higher.

A second criticism of Standard 90-75, voiced after it was first released, was that the standard failed to deal explicitly with different kinds of energy sources. Electricity was treated exactly like natural gas, which was treated like oil. Yet there are differences among these fuels that the mathematical conversion to equivalent BTUs obscures. Electrical generation, for example, requires about three units of fossil fuel for each unit of electrical energy produced. Even comparing oil to natural gas is no simple matter, since one is commonly believed to be a declining source fuel and the other is imported at a high price. By treating each energy source equally at the meter or at the boundary of the building site, ASHRAE Standard 90-75 originally failed to give the potential consumer sufficiently complete resource energy information to make an intelligent decision. The suppliers of fossil fuel energy (natural gas, oil, and coal) quite naturally felt that electricity suppliers might gain an advantage in competition if the resource intensiveness of electricity were not pointed out to the prospective consumer. Fossil fuel merchants know that the price of electricity, which is higher per BTU than the price of fossil fuels, should make plain the relative costliness of electricity in primary energy sources, but they feared that the person contemplating the purchase of a building-space-conditioning system might not have such information at hand during the design stage.

Unfortunately, price or resource intensity alone do not decide the value of a fuel to the country. National security, desire to protect domestic industries, effects on inflation, income distribution effects—these are only a few of the factors that go into making a national fuels policy. Yet without a national fuels policy, ASHRAE's drafting committees had little guidance in evaluating the relative importance of those factors that do not currently appear in the price of energy. However, in response to the criticism, ASHRAE developed a new Section 12, "Annual Fuel and Energy Resource Determination," that is designed to disclose to the ultimate owner of the building the type and the amount of primary fuel that building operations will use. A draft of the new Section 12 was issued in August 1976 and, after a period of review, was approved by the ASHRAE Board of Directors in February 1977.

The purpose of Section 12 is to specify "procedures for calculating and tabulating the estimated quantities of fuel and energy resources required to meet the annual needs of a proposed building project." The procedure includes (1) tabulating the quantities of each form of energy required at the building to satisfy the building system needs (fuel and energy supplied to site), then (2) translating the energy delivered to the site into the amount of total resources devoted to supplying that energy by multiplying each type of delivered energy by the appropriate resource utilization factor.[20] The resource utilization factor (RUF) relates the amount of energy delivered to the boundary of the building site to the amount of natural resources actually consumed in making and delivering that energy. Resource consumption does not include the energy used in extracting the primary energy source, so applying the resource utilization factor does not produce "net" energy. Moreover, Section 12 explicitly states that the resource utilization factor omits "consideration of the availability, social, economic, environmental and national interest issues associated with the fuel and energy resources consumed." For those factors, ASHRAE is considering use of resource impact factors (RIFs) as an additional multiplier. Readers interested in the mathematical methods used for calculating the RUF for each type of fuel are referred to the article by Harry H. Phipps, a member of ASHRAE's committee for developing Section 12,[21] which is reprinted as an attachment to Section 12 of 90-75, although it is not an official part of the standard. The important point to remember is that Section 12 does not prescribe the sources of energy that the building owner should use; it merely requires that the owner be made aware of the resource consequences of his decision.

Standards for Existing Buildings:
ASHRAE Standard 100-P Series

ASHRAE convened six working committees to draw up standards for existing buildings. This set of standards, known as the 100 Series, was not available in final form as this volume was written. However, from drafts, some general comments can be made. The standards will cover six types of buildings: 100.1 will be for low-rise residential, 100.2 for high-rise residential, 100.3 for commercial, 100.4 for industrial, 100.5 for institutional, and 100.6 for public assembly buildings. These building types are found in most major building codes. Standard 100.1-P will look at energy conservation retrofitting from the viewpoint of the homeowner, taking his or her problems into account. Standards 100.2 through 100.4 will require the building to be audited, a "phantom" building to be constructed complying with Standard 90-75, and the real building to be altered to bring its energy consumption as close to the phantom building as possible. The standards are expected to be available early in the 1980s.

Development of Federal Performance Standards: True Budget

Federal law now mandates development of an energy code based on performance standards. The Energy Conservation and Production Act (ECPA), Title III, directed the secretary of the Department of Housing and Urban Development, after consultation with the administrator of the Federal Energy Administration and the secretary of Commerce (under whose jurisdiction the National Bureau of Standards lies), to develop and promulgate performance standards for new buildings. Jurisdiction for development of the standards was later passed to the secretary of Energy, although in fact initial development was redelegated to HUD. According to ECPA, a "performance standard" means "an energy consumption goal or goals to be met without specification of the methods, materials, and processes to be employed in achieving that goal or goals, but including statements of the requirements, criteria and evaluation methods to be used, and any necessary commentary."[22] Performance standards are to "take account of, and make such allowance or particular exception as the Secretary determines appropriate for, climatic variations among the different regions of the country."[23] The federal standards for both residential and commercial (including federal buildings and industrial buildings) must be promulgated in proposed form no later than August 14, 1979. Once promulgated in proposed form, they are to be reissued in final form no later than February 14, 1980. They must then become effective "within a reasonable time, not to exceed 1 year after the date of promulgation."[24] Thus, if deadlines are met, the standards would take effect on February 14, 1981. In addition, the secretary may extend the deadline an additional six months, until August 14, 1981. In fact, under presidential directive, this process was first speeded up so that standards were to be proposed in February 1979. Problems developed in meeting that accelerated deadline, and even the statutory deadline itself was missed.

According to the act, both Houses of Congress must pass a resolution approving the imposition of sanctions against the states for failing to adopt the federal standards. The statute says that Congress must find that the sanctions are "necessary and appropriate to assure that such standards are in fact applied to all new buildings."[25] Thus, although the entire federal process of development, comment, and promulgation of energy-conserving performance standards can take place, until Congress approves the potential imposition of the sanctions, there is little incentive for the states to adopt the standards. According to the act, if the federal government took the entire time allotted to it for the development of the final standards (including the six month delay noted above) and Congress took the time available to it under the act to approve the sanctions, the standards might not become mandatory—if they do at all—until 1981.

The sanctions specified in the act are extremely strong. If Congress decides to apply them, no federal financial assistance (including loans from banks and other lending institutions that are federally regulated or insured) may be given for construction of new buildings unless the state (or locality) has building standards that meet or exceed the federal standards and unless the particular building to be financed does as well. (The entire problem of what is a standard that "meets or exceeds" the federal standard is a further complication. The state of computer modeling of buildings is such that this question may well turn out to be a technical nightmare.) The federal government can waive compliance with the federal performance standard if there is a finding that the "new building is to be located in any area in which the construction of new buildings is not of a magnitude to warrant the costs of implementing final performance standards."[26] The state must request such a ruling from the secretary; the secretary can revoke a finding once made if "the amount of construction of new buildings has increased in such area to an extent that such costs are warranted."[27] Thus, federal standards can be relaxed when an area is subject to only sporadic building and reapplied if growth increases. The standards are so strong that there is serious question whether Congress will have the political will to impose them.

Description of the Federal Building Energy Performance Standards. The final version of the performance standards mandated under ECPA had not been released at the time of the writing of this volume.

However, an Advance Notice of Proposed Rulemaking is available that describes the process by which the proposed standards have been developed and the likely form of the standards to be promulgated.[28] This section describes the Building Energy Performance Standards, how they were developed, and criticisms of them based on the version in the Advance Notice of Proposed Rulemaking.

Research on the project began in May 1977, with a contract from HUD to the American Institute of Architects Research Corporation (AIA/RC). AIA/RC was instructed to collect data on the energy performance of buildings that had been designed after the Arab oil embargo of 1973-1974. Because the standards necessarily will have to apply to buildings at the design stage—since the code officials will only have the drawings and blueprints to work with in approving or disapproving construction—AIA/RC looked at a sample of buildings that had been designed, but not built, after the embargo. The sample included 1,661 buildings, selected from cities larger than 250,000 people. The sample was picked to include various building use types, such as day care centers, food markets, single family detached houses, motels, high-rise apartments, mobile homes, and the like. The sample was selected so that the buildings fell within seven climate zones defined according to heating and cooling degree days.

Because the standards must apply to buildings that are just being designed, AIA/RC used a computer program to calculate the amount of energy per square foot per year used by each building use type in each of the seven climate zones. The computer program selected was the AXCESS program, owned by the Edison Electric Institute (EEI), an organization of private electric utility companies. AXCESS is proprietary, which means that the methods it uses to calculate energy use from plans is known only to EEI, not to users—not even to the government.

Based on the analysis of the data received and processed by AXCESS, AIA/RC was able to list building designs by climate region, in order of energy use. For example, the study showed that office buildings nationwide ranged from 26,000 BTUs per square foot per year up to 199,000 BTUs per square foot per year. The average (or more correctly, the mean) usage was 64,000 BTUs per square foot per year. The study showed this range of energy consumption in each of the seven climate regions for each building use type (although, of course, the range differed from type to type and from region to region). It was clear that the standards should not be set at the average, since that would result in production of a national energy standard that would only represent what builders and designers were already doing in 1974–1975. But the Department of Energy felt for the purposes of the Advance Notice that the standard should not be the very best that was being done during that period, because it might prove to be too difficult for some builders to reach that level of achievement. Therefore, it was decided that the initial standard should be in the range of the best 20 to 30 percent of the designs. (The exact figures had not been selected at the time this manuscript was finished, so the 20 to 30 percent figure is simply what the Advance Notice of Proposed Rulemaking suggests as a likely example.) For an office building, usage of 48,000 BTUs per square foot per year would place it in the best 20 percent of performers across the nation.

To test whether the standards would be reasonable, AIA/RC entered Phase II of the project. This phase consisted of taking 168 of the buildings that had been part of the original 1,661 building sample and training the design team that did the original building on elements of energy conservation design so that they could "redo" the building. The designers attended an intensive three day session in Santa Monica, California, in March 1978. During that session, an attempt was made to convey a large amount of information without prejudicing the redesigns in any way. The results of this effort are instructive. In general, the redesigns show that 80 percent of the redesigns—after only three days of instruction—were equal to or better from an energy consumption point of view than the best 20 percent of the relevant buildings in the original 1,661 building data base. Put another way, this brief education of the design professionals showed that simply making them aware of how to achieve energy conservation in building design allowed four out of five of them to improve the energy design of the building so that the redesigns were in the best one-fifth of similar building use types.

Design instructions given to the redesign teams for the Phase II project were modest in the extreme: they had to comply with the wishes of the client, so if the client desired to have a large north-facing window that lost heat rapidly, that window had to be included in the redesign. Active solar equipment could not be included in the redesign unless it had been in the original design, although passive solar design elements were part of the training sessions. First cost was to be held approximately to the first cost of the original building, so that use of energy-conserving designs and equipment that would pay back relatively quickly were discouraged.[29]

The success of the educational efforts in improving the energy performance of the buildings led one of the major participants in the research process to suggest that educational efforts should be used instead of regulatory methods. His views were not, however, accepted, and his participation in the development of the standards was terminated.

Criticism of BEPS. Detailed criticism of BEPS is not warranted at this point because the crucial steps of picking the exact level of the standard, the costs of complying with the standard, and the environmental benefits have not been analyzed or announced. However, on the assumption that the data in the Advance Notice of Proposed Rulemaking are representative of the standard as it will emerge, the following points are worth making:

- The process by which the standards were developed was regrettably closed. The statute required that a wide variety of interest groups participate in preparing the standards. Unfortunately, the government selected only the professional association of the nation's architects, which in turn set up a technical advisory group consisting of other design and building professionals. There was no representation by consumer groups, by advocates of solar energy development, by environmentalists, by rural or urban poor, or by ordinary middle class citizens who will be affected by the standards. This closed process probably has resulted in a less stringent standard than might otherwise have been developed. It surely tended to minimize the design role that passive solar energy could have played.

- The standards depart from the performance standard route in dealing with residences. The residential section of the standards is a direct adoption of the Thermal Performance Guidelines developed and promulgated by the National Association of Homebuilders. Under those Thermal Performance Guidelines, the builder figures on a component-by-component basis how much insulation, how much glazing, and so forth, is "worth it" to the homeowner. "Worth it" is defined as a seven year payback period. (There is some indication that the proposed standard will adopt the Minimum Property Standards rather than the Thermal Performance Guidelines.)

- The climate zones picked by the AIA/RC do not take into account sunlight, humidity, or wind. Moreover, they stretch nationwide, so that, for example, both Maine and parts of northern New Mexico are in the same climate area. Because microclimates—local variations in wind, sun, and humidity— make so much difference in the performance of a building, a better approach might have been to develop a methodology for calculating energy performance standards for each building type, then let the local governmental unit fill in the local climate data and find out the local building standard.

- The Goal of BEPS as written seems to be to develop standards that are well within the reach of all builders. The words of the statute and the general feeling of the country seem to be that building energy performance standards, if they are worth doing at all, should pull the industry along, rather than simply set easily attainable standards. Recall that the standards are set, tentatively, at a level that at least 20 to 30 percent of designers were already meeting in 1974-1975. Since that time, it is highly likely that designs have continued to improve as educational efforts among the profession have grown to meet the needs of a new energy conscious time. Thus, we are in the anomolous position of developing standards that will apply in the 1980s, yet are based on design practice common in 1974.

- The standards, as available now, do not deal with the cost effectiveness of energy conservation. The data base upon which they rest (the materials collected by the AIA/RC) did not include the cost information. As repeatedly emphasized in this book, energy conservation is simply using money wisely: buy enough energy conservation so that the future savings in fuel are worth it to you. Yet the BEPS are drawn entirely from building practice as it existed in the mid-1970s, rather than trying to see what is economically possible.

- Implementation of the standards has been separated from the development of the standards. This means that some of the really difficult questions, such as whether the standards as written will work in practice, have been set aside. In particular, there is no evidence that the government has considered phasing in the standards gradually as with the automobile efficiency standards. Under a phase-in strategy, the government would announce in advance the level of the standards over the next five to eight years, each year being increasingly tight. This would give the building industry time to develop new construction techniques and new building components that will be ready when called for by the standards.

One may hope that some of these broad deficiencies, together with a host of more detailed criticisms, will be corrected before the standards are promulgated formally in late 1979.*

*The Department of Energy released proposed regulations for the federal Building Energy Performance Standards late in November, 1979. The proposed standards, which may be obtained by writing to the Department of Energy, Office of Building and Community Systems, Washington, D.C. 20545, respond in part to the criticisms voiced in the text. Additional changes may also occur before final regulations are promulgated.

Relationship Between ASHRAE 90-75 and
Federal Performance Standards

The current set of federal directives to states on energy conservation standards for buildings points in two different directions. On the one hand, under the regulations originally promulgated by the Federal Energy Administration under Section 362(c)(4) of the Energy Policy and Conservation Act, a state must adopt ASHRAE Standard 90-75 or the HUD Minimum Property Standards (or better) to qualify for federal assistance in carrying out its energy conservation program. On the other hand, Title III of the Energy Conservation and Production Act, passed less than eight months after the EPCA legislation was passed and long after it was clear that the FEA was going to use Standard 90-75 for the EPCA plans, instructs states to adopt the performance code just described. Basically, state governments have been instructed to enact one set of standards and then, some years later, to enact another set of standards based on a completely different philosophy. This philosophical bind is a product of a "holy war" between the architectural profession and the engineering and code enforcement groups: architects want a maximum amount of design freedom, while code officials want a system that is easy to work with. Unfortunately, states are caught in the crossfire. There have been some suggestions to strengthen ASHRAE, so that buildings built to that standard would meet the BEPS, or to put within BEPS a "cookbook" approach that would permit smaller builders to follow the explicit rules, confident that they were building a building that would conform to the more complicated performance standards. Reconciliation of the standards will no doubt occupy the time and attention of design professionals and federal building officials over the coming months.

Additional Standards Proposed or Adopted

Several other standards have either been proposed for national adoption or have been adopted in only one state. These are described briefly for those readers who wish to see different methodologies for approaching the energy performance question.

Ohio Modified Energy Budget Plan. This plan, described more fully in Chapter 7, is an attempt to answer the most common criticism of the energy budget method of building energy conservation: energy budgets, so the criticism goes, are fine in theory but lack any credible data base upon which to establish budget figures. The Ohio system does not try to set a budget for the building as a whole, but it does establish an upper limit either on the heating and lighting load or on the cooling and lighting load within the building, whichever is larger. The upper limit can be modified by a number of factors, including the building's occupancy classification, its area, and its height. The Ohio method avoids the complexity of a true energy budget. As detailed more fully in Chapter 7, the method may also lead to gross misestimates of correct energy usage in certain situations.

Texas Energy Conservation Manual. Texas' Energy Conservation in Buildings Act,[30] Section 7, requires the State Building Commission to "produce and publish an Energy Conservation Manual for potential use by designers, builders, and contractors of residential and non-residential buildings." Texas has no statewide building code, and the statute's reference to "potential" use explicitly makes the manual merely advisory. As the preface to the manual itself states, "This MANUAL is NOT A MANDATORY or COMPROMISE document. It is intended to encourage and promote the construction and use of energy conserving [buildings]."

The Texas manual recommends maximum consumption figures for different kinds of buildings in various locations in Texas. In addition, the manual contains a detailed form to assist users of the manual in meeting its suggestions.

Thermal Performance Guidelines: National Association of Home-builders. The National Association of Home Builders Special Committee on Energy asked the NAHB Research Foundation to develop a set of guidelines for voluntary use by NAHB's membership. In 1977, NAHB released *NAHB Thermal Performance Guidelines for One and Two Family Dwellings.*[31] As noted earlier, these NAHB guidelines appear in the Advance Notice of Proposed Rulemaking on BEPS as a suggestion for adoption as the federal standard for residences. The TPG are difficult to explain without having a copy in front of one, although the ideas that they use are not complex. However, there has been some criticism that the actual working out of the calculations is a more difficult procedure than many builders are willing to undertake.

Fundamentally, the TPG permit a builder to take a proposed house in a given city, determine the amount of various energy-conserving techniques that should be used in that house, and then determine whether the investment is economically worthwhile to the original purchaser. For making this final economic decision, the TPG assume a seven year payback, an annual increase in energy cost of 10 percent in current dollars, a finance interest rate of 9 percent, and average national costs for various energy-conserving improvements. The energy-conserving improvements considered by the TPG are limited to insulation of various parts of the building and installation of storm windows and doors. The TPG contain a list of "Additional Energy Conserving Techniques," but this list is merely the familiar list of good ideas, without any technique for evaluating whether a particular strategy should be followed in a given home. Thus, there is no provision for improving the home's thermal performance by careful attention to design, siting on the property, or any other method that uses nonmechanical energy or energy conscious design.

The TPG are a valuable step in an attempt to make the calculations involved in energy conservation simple to use for the residential builder. But they are conservative in the extreme and deserve a careful rethinking by NAHB to make them more rigorous.

Farmers Home Administration. The Farmers Home Administration (FmHA) has a separate set of insulation standards that apply to the rural homes built with FmHA assistance. Originally to be effective on March 15, 1978, they were temporarily blocked by a suit brought by the National Association of Home Builders. The FmHA standards are generally considered to be stricter than the Minimum Property Standards issued by FHA. The standards survived the NAHB suit and are expected to remain in force until the BEPS become effective.

THERMAL EFFICIENCY STANDARDS FOR RESIDENTIAL BUILDINGS

So far in this chapter, we have dealt with the way that insulation works and with the major suggested and proposed methods for changing those principles into actual regulation. The following sections relate this theoretical background to legal and regulatory strategies that are actually being tried at the state level. Since the problems of residential and nonresidential buildings are fundamentally different, as are the legal methods of enforcing or encouraging change in old and new buildings, this section will deal with both new and old residences and the next section will deal with both new and old nonresidential buildings.

Legal and Regulatory Strategies for New Residential Buildings

Many methods can be used to increase the thermal efficiency of new residences. All such strategies may be broadly classified as educational, economic, or regulatory. Economic strategies are more politically difficult to implement and to control than are educational strategies, and regulatory strategies are more difficult still.

Educational Strategies. Educational strategies may be either general or building-specific. General educational efforts are aimed at developing the knowledge of energy conservation features in that segment of the public apt to build or to buy homes or other buildings. Strategies specific to a given building are aimed at giving potential purchasers accurate information about the building that they are considering in order to influence a specific buying decision.

General Educational Efforts. Many states, along with the federal government, utility companies, insulation contractors and manufacturers, and makers of storm windows, among others, have launched extensive educational efforts. Bumper stickers that read "Don't Be Fuelish," switch plate covers that remind us that "Empty Rooms Love Darkness," energy conservation calendars, posters that list "600 Things You Can Do To Conserve Energy—Pick One and Do It!"—all are the trappings of an often witty campaign against waste. In addition, advertisements for double- and triple-glazed windows are features in home improvement magazines, and home insulation materials manufacturers now provide free ceiling insulation instruction kits.

Unfortunately, it is difficult to gather evidence proving that general education—even when it contains quite specific information on what energy conservation features to look for in a new home—has actually motivated buyers to make economically sound choices. Even though these programs have so far had little measurable effect, they deserve continued support. First, the effectiveness of educational strategies is always hard to measure. But more important, educational strategies are a relatively inexpensive, uncontroversial method of conveying information to the consumer about the changing nature of the energy crisis. Energy issues are kept alive in the minds of the consumer so that energy costs and consumption become one of the many factors that they consider when purchasing a home. Moreover, the continuing flow of information about energy conservation features may alert builders to their customers' possible interest in such features.

Sustained educational efforts are justifiable on other grounds as well. Fundamental changes in the way that homes look and operate may result from the decision to make energy conservation a national priority. Fewer windows, more opaque walls, overhangs, and fewer conveniences (because hidden insulation or improved mechanical features absorb capital saved from higher first costs)—these changes, as well as the economic and national advantages of choosing such features, will have to be explained to buyers. Unless they are, consumers may revolt and try to overturn governmental decisions to adopt vigorous incentives, penalties, or regulations.

Building-specific Energy Conservation Strategies. When people decide to buy newly constructed homes, they can estimate the operating costs of the houses they consider only with the utmost difficulty. There is no prior history of utility bills available for examination, and the builders themselves may be unsure of the consumption levels to be expected. But operating costs of new buildings are as relevant to purchasers as the costs of servicing mortgages or of paying taxes. In fact, in some places, homes with electrical resistance baseboard heating have winter electricity bills higher than the mortgage payments.

Is there a fair, administrable law that could provide as much information to the buyer as possible, without making unreasonable demands on the builder? One such strategy is to require an energy disclosure statement to be produced before a new house purchase is made. The disclosure statement—in effect an "efficiency label" for the house—would list the energy consumption of the major household equipment included in the sale price (the furnace, air conditioning, hot water heater, ventilating fans, and any other built-in appliances that use over a certain amount of energy per year). The disclosure statement would also list the R value of the major components of the house (or alternatively state its energy consumption per square foot) and would certify that the listed equipment and the energy efficiency of the house complied with existing state and federal regulations.

The more difficult question is whether the seller of the home should be required to state the probable dollar cost of operating the home. On the positive side, the dollar cost is probably the only figure that genuinely conveys to the potential consumer the information necessary to make an informed choice between two or more houses. While R values, EER (energy efficiency ratio) ratings of air conditioners, and other kinds of disclosure information mean little to the average person, an estimated utility bill hits home. On the negative side, the builders and designers of homes are understandably reluctant to certify energy consumption figures when actual consumption depends so much on how the occupants of the house live. If children leave outside doors open, estimates made in advance can be thrown off by an enormous amount. Builders may fear that if a disclosure statement estimates a certain dollar figure, an angry homeowner may try to sue if bills turn out to be higher. Because there are no standardized testing procedures for new homes, builders may also fear that their competitors will calculate energy costs in a self-serving fashion.

To partly meet the builder's objections, a state can develop a standardized, required procedure for estimating the expected energy consumption of a new house. This method might, for example, use the estimation forms contained in the energy conservation manuals developed by the Texas State Building Commission. These forms, which take building type, heating and cooling system type, outside climate conditions, and shading into account, require the person calculating the expected energy consumption to fill out a relatively simple form with information such as the square footage of the house, the area of each of the exterior walls, the area of glass and doors, the shading, the equipment efficiency, and so on. Many of these calculations can be made on the basis of tables that give average or representative figures for various items. Then, an annual energy consumption estimate for the building can be turned into a dollar figure by simply converting the BTUs involved to dollars.

Builders can then be required to furnish the results of such a calculation to buyers. To protect the builder from lawsuits based on later operational differences that result in higher energy costs, the form could explicitly state that the figure constitutes an estimate only and not a warranty. The builder would be liable for misestimations only if erroneous or misleading calculations were entered on the form itself. No statutes have yet set out this suggested method, although the city of Troutdale, Oregon, has an ordinance that requires builders to label each new home only with the amount of insulation installed during the construction. Such a label is helpful, but far from comprehensive.[32] Here is the text of a possible model statute that incorporates this relatively comprehensive plan:

Section 1. This act may be cited as the Energy Conservation Disclosure Statement Act of 19XX

Section 2. Purpose. The legislature finds that purchasers of new residences currently have no practical way to discover in advance the amount of energy that will be consumed in operating a particular residence and that the lack of such information seriously impedes the operation of the free market by denying to such purchasers an important and relevant item of information. The legislature further finds that methods of calculation exist or can be developed that will permit builders to estimate the energy-operating costs of new residential buildings without placing an undue burden upon those builders. The legislature further finds that this state and the nation as a whole face an energy crisis and that improvements in new residential buildings can contribute substantially to conserving energy needed for the health and public safety of the citizens of this state.

Section 3. **Definitions.**

New Residence. Any building receiving a building permit after final promulgation of the Energy Estimation Methodology pursuant to Section 6 of this act, which is used or intended to be used principally for dwelling purposes; multifamily dwelling units with more than three stories are not subject to the provisions of this statute.

Ultimate Purchaser. Any person who purchases a new residence whether for use by himself or for rental by others.

Section 4. **Disclosure Statement.** It shall be unlawful for any person to offer to sell a new residence to an ultimate purchaser after [an appropriate date] unless the ultimate purchaser receives an Energy Disclosure Statement prior to the time that the contract to sell or irrevocable option becomes legally binding according to the general contract law of this state.

Section 5. **Energy Disclosure Statement.** The Energy Disclosure Statement shall consist of disclosure of the following items:

(i) The energy consumption and the efficiency rating of the furnace, the air-conditioning unit(s), the hot water heater(s), and any other appliance required to be labeled pursuant to the provisions of the federal Energy Policy and Conservation Act, 42 U.S.C. Sections 6291 *et seq.*, as amended, whether or not the appliance price is separately listed in the sales contract. The energy consumption and efficiency ratings shall be in the form required to appear on the appliance label mandated by the federal Energy Policy and Conservation Act as amended.

(ii) Either (a) the R value of the ceiling, each of the exposed walls, the foundations, and any other living space bounded in any direction by unheated or uncooled space, or (b) the energy consumption in BTUs per square foot per year, certified by a professional engineer licensed to practice in this state.

(iii) A listing, calculated according to the methodology developed pursuant to Section 6 of this act, disclosing the estimated dollar costs for the energy required in the operation of the new residence.

Section 6. **Energy Estimation Methodology.** Within [appropriate number of] months following the enactment of this act, the [appropriate state agency] shall develop and promulgate in accordance with the terms of the [state's Administrative Procedure Act, if any] a methodology for calculating the estimated dollar costs for the energy required in the operation of new residences covered by the terms of this act. The methodology shall take into account the climate for the city or region in which the new residence is located; the floor, wall, window, door, and other appropriate areas of the new residence; the effect of siting, orientation, shading, and design factors on energy consumption; the use of efficient space conditioning, hot water heating, or other household equipment; and such other considerations as the [state agency] shall deem to be relevant. No less frequently than each year during the month of December, the [state agency] shall promulgate fuel cost figures, based on the best available materials at that time, to be used to calculate estimated energy costs for a new residence. The [state agency] shall promulgate by [date] a form to be used in disclosing the information required to be provided to the ultimate purchaser pursuant to this act, and use of the promulgated form shall be mandatory. The [state agency] shall attempt, to the maximum extent possible, to make the methodology for filling out the mandatory form simple and clear, so as to lessen the administrative burdens placed on the seller.

Section 7. **Effect of the Energy Disclosure Statement.**

(i) The information disclosed in the Energy Disclosure Statement on the form provided by the [state agency] shall not constitute a guarantee or a warranty of performance at the calculated level, and the seller shall not be liable for breach of contract because of any statement made in the Energy Disclosure Statement;

(ii) substantial miscalculation, concealment, misstatement, or other action taken with the intent of understating the energy consumption of the new residence shall be unlawful. For the purposes of this section, a miscalculation or misstatement amounting to [percentage] below the correctly calculated figure, as certified by the [state agency] shall constitute prima facie proof of willful intent to understate the energy consumption of the new residence.

Section 8. **Penalty.** Failure to deliver an Energy Disclosure Statement shall make the seller liable for a fine of not less than

$_____ nor more than $_____ . Failure to calculate or state correctly the figures on the statement, where intent can be shown as stated in Section 7 of this statute, shall make the seller liable for a fine of not less than $_____ nor more than $_____ . Each new residence offered without a statement or with a statement incorrectly calculated or stated shall constitute a separate offense.

A system of energy disclosure statements for new residences can make energy conservation features visible to the purchasers, so that some reasonably accurate estimation of utility bills can be included in the purchase price calculation. An energy disclosure statement law can also assist the operation of the free market system by providing information to buyers in a clear format enabling the prospective homeowner to compare new houses with the confidence that all the calculations are made on the same basis.

Another method that states can develop to get building-specific information on new residences is to offer to inspect, at cost, new homes for energy efficiency. Dr. Robert Socolow, one of the Princeton University investigators of energy usage in the planned community of Twin Rivers, New Jersey, termed such inspections "house calls."[33] A walk-through inspection of a new house, together with examination of the inside and the outside with an infrared (heat) detecting device, can give a prospective purchaser of a home some indication of the care that had been taken in its construction and in the design.

A state might want to consider offering such a service, for a fee, through its technical extension service, through building departments, or through some new agency developed for the purpose. A demonstration project might later be taken up by existing private home inspection services.

Economic Incentives or Removal of Economic Barriers. A second method for increasing the thermal efficiency of new residences is to provide a financial incentive (such as a cash refund or a credit on the state tax) or to lift some financial burden by, for example, cutting real estate taxes on the cost of adding energy-conserving features to buildings.

Since economic incentives are politically popular among those who stand to benefit from the payments, potential homeowners, builders, and lending institutions, among others, might all be expected to support legislation creating financial incentives. Unfortunately, energy conservation incentives tend to lower the utility bills only of those who exercise foresight in making energy conservation investments. But incentives for purchasers of new homes, for example, must be paid for by those already owning houses, by those buying older houses, and by those who, because they have limited incomes, have no prospect of buying homes. Thus, those who develop incentives must keep fairness in mind.

An additional difficulty with providing incentives for energy conservation in new homes is that such incentive legislation cannot be written upon a clean regulatory slate. Almost every jurisdiction in this country has some kind of building regulations, and many jurisdictions have or soon will have building regulations that deal explicitly with energy conservation for new buildings. The federal Energy Policy and Conservation Act offers financial incentives to the states to adopt energy-conserving building standards based on either ASHRAE Standard 90-75 or a stricter model; this option will, in effect, make even more new buildings subject to energy conservation regulations. With such mandatory legal regulations already in force, legislators will find it difficult to frame a financial incentive that rewards those who go further than the requirements of the regulation, without rewarding those who put in far more insulation or shading than economically justified energy conservation alone warrants. In short, the problem is to provide some incentive to go beyond the law without rewarding those who merely comply with the law's minimal requirements. Because even Standard 90-75 allows builders to comply with its component performance standards in hundreds of ways, drawing a statute that distinguishes between what is required and what is beyond is no easy task; to draw a statute that also separates necessary and optional costs in a way that fairly and accurately determines an incentive payment may be so politically difficult that it will not be done.

Just because economic incentives may be hard to draft in the presence of regulations that address the same goal does not mean that some barriers that add to the cost of constructing energy-conserving buildings should not be removed. One such barrier is the extra taxation that may result from energy conservation purchases and investments. Insulation, efficient equipment, awnings, storm windows, caulking, and the like all bear a sales tax in most states. They also become part of the basis for calculating the value of the house for real estate tax assessment purposes. A number of states have specifically exempted solar energy equipment from the sales tax and from property tax assessments. An example is the following statute from Indiana, which was the first state to pass such an exemption:

Section 1. The owner of real property which is equipped with a solar energy heating or cooling system may have deducted annually from the assessed valuation of the real property a sum which is equal to the lesser of:

(1) the remainder of (i) the assessed valuation of the real property with the solar heating or cooling system included, minus (ii) the assessed valuation of the real property without the system; or

(2) two thousand dollars ($2,000).

Section 2. The owner of real property who desires to claim the deduction provided in this chapter must file a certified statement in duplicate with the auditor of the county in which the real property is located. In addition, the owner must file the statement on forms prescribed by the state board of tax commissioners, and he must file the statement between March 1 and May 10, inclusive, of each year for which he desires to obtain the deduction. Upon verification of the statement by the assessor of the township in which the real property is located, the county auditor shall make the deduction.[34]

Solar heating and cooling systems have not proved easy to define. Are passive solar systems (e.g., a large south-facing window with a black floor) solar heating systems, subject to the deduction? As noted above, the difficulty is even greater for energy-conserving features of a house. One federal bill introduced to provide financial assistance for solar and energy conservation devices simply listed four eligible devices (insulation, heat pumps, devices or improvements to increase furnace efficiency, and clock thermostats). This cookbook approach has the virtues of simplicity and the vices of failure to deal with the most important changes and innovations.

A second, more subtle flaw in a system that depends on rebates on property tax is that many homeowners would rather "let sleeping dogs lie" when it comes to arousing the interest of the property tax assessor. In areas where property assessments are behind (either in frequency or in market valuation), an owner has little incentive to call attention to his or her property.

The difficulties of defining conservation, differentiating between what is required and what is extra, and administering such legislation all suggest that state financial incentives to improve the thermal efficiency of new residences may not be a workable strategy. Those financial incentives that can be easily identified—such as the removal of sales tax from specified items and the exemption of energy conservation materials from property tax assessments—tend to involve amounts of money too small to hold much appeal as incentives. Although changing the price of a good slightly will permit a few people at the margin to alter their buying choices, the few dollars of sales tax or property tax saving pale in significance against the total price of a house.

Direct Regulation for Energy Efficiency in New Residences. Educational strategies and incentive strategies appear relatively weak in the present battle to upgrade the thermal efficiency of buildings. So much could be done to improve homes right now, without adding significantly to their first cost, that direct regulation through building codes and energy efficiency codes makes most sense. Many theorists dislike direct regulation because it allows those regulated no choice. Though individuals can exert their choices when economic assessments are used or in the free market, different persons with different value judgments about their own best interests are not permitted to do with less of some other good in exchange for more of the good that is being regulated. For example, a rich old man might want to keep his fire burning in the middle of summer with the air conditioner running and is willing to incur the extra expense of simultaneously heating and cooling his house. If we were to regulate that behavior, he would not be able to burn the fire, even if burning that fire meant a great deal to him. Economists argue that the operation of the market will, ideally, sort out conflicting desires and will provide the best mix of goods and services to meet human desires to the greatest extent possible. Regulation, so the argument runs, can interfere with this system.

In principle, the economic argument is true; certainly in the long run the operation of the price system will press us to build better residences and buildings of all types—if, that is, the market operates rationally, correctly, and freely and if the flow of information is unrestrained. Unfortunately, rational, correct, free housing markets are rare, if they exist at all. Fortunately, many recent improvements in building technology are sure to save energy in a clearly cost-effective manner. Consequently, there seems to be little reason not to regulate, even though there will occasionally be inequities involving individuals whose preferences conflict with the value judgments contained in the regulation. Wise regulation will minimize the number of times that the law mandates what many people do not want.

The materials that have been presented in the earlier part of this chapter and in Chapter 2 have described sufficiently the building code and energy efficiency code strategies that can be used at the state level to mandate energy conservation in new buildings, including residences. No complete compilation of building code provisions for energy conservation is included in this book. The pioneer collection of codes, published in March 1976 by Robert M. Eisenhard of the National Bureau of Standards, detailed pending and enacted legislation through November 25, 1975.[35] Many states have adopted or are still adopting building codes in order to obtain the money offered by the federal government under the Energy Policy and Conservation

Act. In Appendix A to this chapter, a compilation as of February 15, 1978, prepared by the National Institute of Building Sciences, is reprinted. Also reprinted as Appendix B is a list of state officials who can give more detailed current information. Readers interested in the situation in their own state should write or telephone the officials listed.

Public Utility Commission Regulations. One kind of regulation for energy conservation circumvents the usual building code procedure entirely and makes the provision of a necessary service—gas or electricity—dependent on meeting certain energy conservation standards. This approach has been tried in New York State. In December 1972, the New York State Public Services Commission (PSC) began to take evidence on the energy conservation measures in the service territory of the Consolidated Edison Company of New York, Inc. Hearings continued until August 1973. On January 31, 1974, the presiding commissioner recommended that the use of electricity in newly constructed buildings in the Consolidated Edison service territory be prohibited unless:

(i) in all residential structures and in small commercial buildings (not over two stories), the structures contain insulation conforming to minimum standards set by the Commission; and

(ii) in large commercial buildings, approval of a local government body is obtained for a program for energy conservation in the design of the building prepared in accordance with standards set forth by the Commission.[36]

In June 1974, the state legislature passed a law requiring the State Building Code Council to prepare and present an Energy Efficiency Construction Code by December 1, 1974.[37] In light of that law, the full PSC declined to accept the insulation recommendations of the presiding commission, although the PSC found that "the record in this proceeding confirms, beyond question, the need for energy conservation construction standards including minimum insulation requirements in New York State."

In 1976, the issue was once again in front of the Public Service Commission of the State of New York. At that time, the commission adopted a set of building regulations for new buildings with electric heat and for conversions to electric heat. The regulations, amended in October 1976, also supercede earlier PSC regulations governing gas-heated residences. According to the provisions of the order in Case Number 76-16, meeting the provisions of the standard is "a precondition for all new electric service; and also the expansion of

existing electric service for the purpose of providing electric heat."
This standard thus also applies to oil-heated homes, because new oil-
heated homes require electric service.

The text of the regulations adopted by the New York PSC can be
obtained from the commission in Albany. Briefly, they set minimum
insulation standards for various components of the building. Unlike
the ASHRAE Standard 90-75, they do not treat the component as
a whole, so that window area is not as limited under the New York
standard. Nor is the heat transmission limit on a building component
dependent on the number of degree days, as in the case of the
ASHRAE standard. Enforcement of the New York standard is not in
the hands of the building code department, as it will be when a
standard is adopted by states or localities as part of the ordinary
building code. Instead, utilities are permitted to rely on certifications
of compliance signed by the builder and by the owner of the building. The certification contains an acknowledgement that service is
subject to cutoff if the building is later inspected and found not to
be in compliance. The PSC opinion urged utilities to undertake inspections of a sample number of residences subject to the new regulation.

Although the New York standard is not as complete and as well
thought out as the ASHRAE standard, it does contain real teeth—
fear that the building will not be provided with electricity if the
standards are not met. This enforcement technique might well be
adopted by states, even those that choose to follow one of the
national standards rather than standards developed locally.

Legal and Regulatory Strategies for
Existing Buildings

Governments and private agencies have worked vigorously to develop standards for new residences; those actions have been detailed
above. But the fact remains that there are far more existing residences, and no program of energy conservation can be complete that
ignores the potential for improving those homes and apartments. The
following sections deal with programs that address those housing
units already in place. Once again, this discussion is divided into
three categories—educational, incentive-oriented, and regulatory
programs.

Educational Strategies. The general educational strategies that
focus on new residences apply equally to existing residences. Since
homeowners already know the range of their own utility bills—
perhaps only too well!—they have a direct incentive to make changes

if such changes appear sensible, important, and affordable. General educational tools may include pamphlets, night courses at local colleges on calculating potential energy savings, and do it yourself instruction pamphlets. Unfortunately, these general educational strategies do not tell the homeowner very much about the specific case he or she is most interested in—his or her own home. What makes sense in one home with good insulation doesn't make sense in another that must attend to weatherstripping first.

In view of the incredible variety of homes and locations, the most interesting educational programs have attempted to be building-specific. One early federal demonstration program, Project Conserve, tested two different approaches to making homeowners aware of energy conservation possibilities. The first approach was based on a computer-analyzed questionnaire. The homeowner filled in a relatively simple form, answering twenty-nine questions about the size, heating, windows and doors, and insulation of his home. The completed questionnaire was to be mailed, postage paid, to the Federal Energy Administration. Within a few weeks, the government mailed back an analysis of the thermal efficiency of the house, including specific recommendations for home improvements that ranged from no cost options such as turning the thermostat lower at night to potentially costly improvements such as insulation. The report contained contractor installation costs and do it yourself estimates for each recommendation. Also included was an estimate of the savings potential and the payback period associated with each recommended action. Adding insulation, storm windows and doors, and caulking and weatherstripping, as well as adjusting thermostat settings, were all included in the recommendations.

The second method used by Project Conserve was the Home Energy Savers' Workbook. This workbook provided homeowners with a step-by-step method for making energy audits of their own homes. Using simple calculation methods, owners could determine the potential dollar savings for various improvements. In addition, the workbook provided instructions both for finding a contractor to make such improvements and for making them without professional help.

Project Conserve was first tested in a number of cities. In 1975, Massachusetts and New Mexico were selected to test the questionnaire program, and all or parts of Connecticut, Rhode Island, New York, Pennsylvania, Maryland, South Carolina, West Virginia, Ohio, Illinois, Tennessee, Nebraska, and Utah were selected to participate in a program based on the workbook. Federal assistance of $1.6 million was provided to these fourteen states. In Massachusetts, questionnaires were mailed to all 924,000 single family homeowners in the state, and supplies of questionnaires were made available to banks, grocery stores, and other places. Newspaper, radio, and television advertisements, a toll-free telephone line, a mobile infrared scanning truck (called "Red Rover") for the colder months, and volunteers were used to further publicize the program. As of the end of July 1976, 139,000 homeowners (15 percent) had returned questionnaires. Testing of the questionnaire program in New Mexico began in late 1976; testing of the workbook programs was conducted during the winter of 1976-1977.[38]

The Red Rover mobile infrared scanning truck was particularly successful in improving awareness of the potential for energy conservation. As it drove along a street, Red Rover scanned the passing houses to detect the escape of heat through poorly insulated walls or ceilings or through cracks around doors and windows. The scanning produced a color picture of a house, showing the loss of "invisible" heat in tones ranging from yellow (high loss) to red (medium loss) and blue (small losses). Apparently the drama of seeing color pictures that showed the invisible was a particularly rewarding "selling" technique for energy conservation. The success of the Red Rover in Massachusetts suggests that such a service might be underwritten by a state, perhaps combined with walkthrough energy audits that provided homeowners with ideas for weatherproofing and energy proofing their own homes and with a clear picture of the costs and benefits of taking the recommended actions.

One energy conservation tactic that has not been turned into a widespread program is the education of consumers on the energy costs of their own actions. In the Twin Rivers, New Jersey, study of energy consumption in a planned unit development of townhouses,[39] some consumers were given daily feedback on their individual energy use. They were also told how that use compared with prior usage. The daily analysis was simply posted on a board outside the consumer's kitchen window. Obviously, such a labor-intensive method of providing information to the consumer is possible only in a research project. But utility companies could provide a somewhat similar service to all consumers.

In most areas, utilities store billing records for individual customers in computers so that payments can be calculated on a "level payment plan." Utilities also have access to information concerning weather, degree days, the energy usage of homes within the service territory, and other data that would make comparisons valid and meaningful. Utility computers could be programmed to provide information on each bill showing the number of units of the fuel (kilowatt hours or therms) used in the billing period per degree day compared to the number of units used during the previous year in the same billing period. The bill could also tap the computer to find out how the customer's energy usage per degree day compared with the energy usage of all other consumers within a given geographical area (perhaps a zip code area). This information might force a household to question why its usage of energy had risen in the past year or why it was using more than other households in its billing class and geographical area. Combined consumption analysis and billing could either be adopted by the utility acting with permission of the state's public utility commission or mandated by action of the public utility commission itself.

Taken together, these educational strategies (and others) can have a positive effect on energy usage. Unfortunately, Americans' recent success in ignoring the energy shortage suggests that educational efforts alone will fail to motivate enough owners to take even economically self-serving measures. To be sure, the results of the initial pilot tests of Project Conserve look promising. In Topeka, Kansas, 17.5 percent of those receiving questionnaires responded, and 45 percent of the respondents said that they would follow through on one or more of the recommendations given. In Danbury, Connecticut, 24.8 percent responded, and 85 percent of the respondents said that they planned to take some action. But these figures, released by the Federal Energy Administration, do not indicate whether highly effective measures with relatively high first cost (such as ceiling insulation) were selected or whether no cost actions such as adjusting thermostats were counted. The defect of education programs—that they can motivate some, but not all, who would benefit—suggests that additional measures would be worth pursuing as a part of state policy.

Economic Incentives and Removing Barriers to Energy Conservation for Existing Homes. For some time now, plans to provide economic incentives for retrofitting older homes with additional insulation have been in place. These include insulation programs financed through utilities, credits or tax remissions for additional insulation, and direct grants to elderly or low income citizens.

Utility-financed Insulation. As mentioned in Chapter 2, a number of states and utility companies now have programs to finance insulation for their customers. The first program of this type was proposed by the Michigan Consolidated Gas Company in 1973. The Michigan program began when the then chairman of the Public Service Commission of Michigan made the chance observation that the snow on his roof melted faster than the snow on his neighbor's roof. His neighbor, an engineering professor at Michigan State University, had put in six inches of ceiling insulation because his heating bills were rising so fast, a move that indirectly triggered the adoption of a state-wide program.

Under the program as it was finally developed, an interested customer receives a free, illustrated thirty-two page "how to" book on home insulation. If the customer wants a contractor to install insulation, the gas company provides a cost estimate. The gas company offers financing, and when the work is completed, it gives the customer a three year warranty that covers defects in workmanship and materials. After making a 20 percent down payment, customers can pay immediately, or in three equal installments, or over a period of three years. For the first two options, no service charge is levied; the annual interest rate associated with the three year option is 12 percent.

A key feature of the Michigan plan has been the gas company's vigorous advertising program. The company launched a seven week advertising program in over one hundred newspapers; it also placed television spot announcements during evening news shows on five stations for four weeks and bought numerous thirty-second radio spots. Approximately 130,000 copies of the do it yourself handbook were mailed to Detroit residences, 125,000 copies were supplied to insulation retail outlets, and 6,700 copies were distributed in response to customer requests during the first two months.

During 1974, over 42,000 homes were insulated. During 1975, an additional 35,000 homes were insulated. In 1976, the utility estimated that about one-quarter of the homes that could be insulated had been insulated under the program at that point. Both the gas company and the Michigan Public Service Commission felt that many more people were motivated to insulate their homes than these figures show, but simply did not report their actions.[40]

Since the introduction of the Michigan program, a number of other states have also begun such programs. The Public Service Company of Colorado has handled some 14,000 insulation jobs under its program, which seeks to bring the attic floor insulation to an R-30 level. The company will provide financing for up to thirty months at 9.5 percent interest. Savings in energy consumption have been about 15 percent, corrected for degree day differences.

Northern States Power Company has retrofitted 150,000 houses. Washington Natural Gas Company has insulated 8,000 attics and 1,800 sidewalls. Detroit Edison finances for up to four years at 11 percent and recommends ceiling insulation of R-44.[41]

Readers interested in learning about more of these utility-sponsored insulation programs should obtain a copy of a June 1978 report prepared for the U.S. Department of Energy, *Utility Sponsored Home Insulation Programs.*[42] That study summarizes programs in great detail, giving strengths and weaknesses of the programs as perceived by the utilities and their customers.

Perhaps the most innovative program in concept is one passed by the Montana Legislature in 1975. Unfortunately, the program envisioned by the legislature never materialized in fact, because of lack of interest on the part of the utility companies. According to the Montana law,

(1) A public utility providing electricity or natural gas may install or pay for the installation of energy conservation materials in a dwelling. The utility may agree with the occupant of the dwelling that the occupant shall reimburse the utility for its expenditure in periodic installment payments added to the occupant's regular bill for electricity or natural gas. The utility may charge interest not exceeding the equivalent of a rate of seven percent (7%) per year on the declining balance of the sum advanced.

(2) A public utility lending money under this section may compute the difference between interest it actually receives on such transactions and the interest which would have been received at the prevailing average interest rate for home improvement loans, as prescribed in rules made by the public service commission. The utility may apply the difference so computed as a credit against its tax liability for the electrical energy producer's license tax . . . and for the corporation license tax . . . .[43]

Although the law does not define the exact meaning of "energy conservation materials" as used in the statute, the phrase "energy conservation purpose" is broadly defined: "one or more of the following results of an investment: reducing the waste or dissipation of energy, or reducing the amount of energy required to accomplish a given quantity of work." Thus, the Montana law permits utilities, at no cost to themselves, to lend money to occupants of dwellings for a wide variety of energy-conserving investments, not limited to insulation. The loan to the consumer is highly attractive during times when home improvement loans are 11 to 12 percent or more.

Unfortunately, the public utility companies have not chosen to pass these benefits along to their rate payers. One large utility in the state stated in late 1975 that such programs faced "poor public reception." Moreover, the company had "misgivings" about financing purchases for customers when traditional lenders had funds available. Another lender stated that there is "no reason for (the utility) to try to undercut the banks by offering competing service at lower rates."[44]

The shortsightedness of these attitudes is clear. Study after study has demonstrated that investments in conservation actions such as insulation are far more cost-efficient than investments in new generating capacity for utilities. Although there might be some valid state policies against subsidizing home insulation programs as the Montana law does, the reluctance of the utilities in that state to pass the benefits offered by the legislature on to the citizens is surprising.

Another innovative plan for utility involvement in home insulation is the program started by Pacific Power & Light Company in Oregon. PP&L's program, "Oregon Energy Saver Plan," has four parts: first, PP&L will provide a no cost home energy audit to customers; second, PP&L will arrange for the installation and inspection of any weatherization measure it recommends; third, PP&L will loan the consumer the money for the weatherization measures at no interest cost to the homeowner; and fourth, PP&L will only demand that the loan be repaid at the time the home is sold or transferred. The utility figures that it will cost each customer in its system about $1.10 per month for the program, but the cost of the program is only about half what new plant construction would cost.

At the time that the plan was submitted for approval, PP&L estimated that it would cost $75,000 and take five years to complete. However, the company planned to save a projected 64,000 kilowatts of new generation plant capacity, an amount equal to about twice PP&L's annual Oregon residential load growth. The program was an instant success. Within four weeks of offering it to the public, the utility received 2,500 requests for the energy audit. Soon after the PP&L program was announced, Portland General Electric started a similar program; Puget Sound Power & Light Company, Washington Water Power Company, and PP&L in Washington all asked for permission to carry out a similar program in Washington State. Filings were also made in other Pacific Northwest states.

This PP&L plan is truly a creative response to the need for a program that is perceived by the public as being fair, yet gets the utility involved in "generating" energy more cheaply than from central station power plants. Unfortunately, the National Energy Act will forbid any new plans of this sort being used unless waivers are granted.[45]

Innovative Plan for Utility Involvement in Insulation Programs. Two additional programs have been suggested for involving utilities either directly or indirectly in encouraging homeowners to insulate. The first, called the "conservation gas" plan, seeks to encourage utilities to use their investment capital for insulation rather than for new natural gas supplies. The second, an "entitlements" plan, uses the utility as a broker between homeowners and industrial users, with the industrial users making investments in home insulation in return for the right to purchase the natural gas that is saved by those investments.

CONSERVATION GAS PLAN. It is a commonplace observation that the price of energy is going up. In the case of natural gas in particular, some experts believe that new supplies will not be available when they are needed. Natural gas is commonly sold in units of one million cubic feet (abbreviated Mcf). When natural gas is sold between states, its price is regulated by the Federal Energy Regulatory Commission (the new name for the Federal Power Commission, with slightly different powers). Natural gas is commonly sold in contracts extending over a long period of time (although the trend is toward shorter term contracts). Because the price of natural gas has risen so sharply over the last few years, some older contracts are still at relatively low prices, while new gas at higher prices is now only a fairly small (though growing) part of the mix. This market structure makes the price of natural gas sold to the local utility a mixture of various gas prices plus the cost of transporting that gas to the city gate.

This digression into how natural gas prices are set is important because it demonstrates that the economic incentives that press upon the gas company buying new gas are different from the incentives that operate on the ultimate consumer of natural gas in the household or business. The gas utility sees that new gas may cost it around $2 per Mcf, that gas from Alaskan fields may cost around $5 or more per Mcf, and that synthetic natural gas from coal may cost more than $7 per Mcf.

Suppose that the gas utility could find additional supplies of gas that cost it less than $2 to buy. Obviously, the utility would be insane to purchase more expensive gas, and if the utility bought that cheaper gas, all of the utility's customers would benefit from the cheap source. Where is such cheap gas available? It is available when the utility prevents waste by its customers: an Mcf saved is an Mcf found. Saving the gas suggests that the utility should take the capital that it would spend on new gas supplies and apply it to improving the efficiency of customer use. They should continue to make these investments in the customer's property up to the point that it becomes more expensive to save an Mcf of gas by further insulation, caulking, furnace retrofit, or clock thermostats than it does to supply an Mcf of new gas. Happily, the natural gas that is saved by insulating even your neighbor's residence benefits you on your bill.

Because the utility does not have to go out to buy the new, more expensive gas, your bill will go up more slowly than it would otherwise, even if your house is not insulated under the program. (Of course the person whose house is insulated by the utility gets the benefit of the gas saving and the benefit of the lower gas rates, so there is undoubtedly substantial advantage to the persons getting insulation.)

This conservation plan differs from the many insulation plans that have been described above because the individual utility customer whose residence is insulated would not pay the cost of that insulation directly. Instead, the public utility company might set up an insulation subsidiary to do the insulation, and the expenses that were paid to the insulation subsidiary would be treated for rate-setting purposes as though they were the price of new gas purchased. Thus, it would be spread among all customers, rather than being paid directly by the homeowner receiving the insulation. This obviously means that some customers who purchased their own insulation before the program began will be angry; even those who have not purchased insulation may be angry, because they will have to wait their turn to have the gas company insulate them. These are both public relations stumbling blocks to the implementation of the plan. However, a series of calculations made by the Federal Energy Administration, using actual data supplied by three natural gas utilities, helps set the problem of "paying for your neighbor's insulation" in the proper context. Comparing, as a reference case, the purchase of increasing amounts of new gas against a conservation case of implementing the conservation gas plan, the FEA figures show that: "when the conservation case is compared to the reference case, the average space heating bill declines for virtually every class of consumer, even those whose residences are fully insulated."[46]

Again according to the figures developed by the Federal Energy Administration, the potential for savings under this plan is enormous:

Assuming full national implementation by 1984 of the three conservation measures (insulation, clock thermostats, and furnace improvement) to the extent physically feasible, and assuming a 100 percent penetration by all gas utilities for all residential heating customers, it is estimated that natural gas savings in 1985 would amount to 1.2 trillion cubic feet per year. This amount would be the energy equivalent to: 130 percent of the annual deliveries estimated to come from the North Slope of Alaska, 13 high-BTU coal gassification plants (250 million Mcf per day), 39 major electric power plants (1,000 megawatts), (or) 575,000 barrels per day of imported oil.[47]

The conservation gas plan is not free from regulatory or legal difficulties, and it would take the action of regulatory commissions, state legislatures, and Congress to solve those problems. But these difficulties are surmountable if the will to overcome them and to adopt the proposal is present.

NATURAL GAS ENTITLEMENTS PLAN. A second innovative plan for encouraging energy conservation investments in the homes and small business of the nation is to permit those customers wishing to purchase more gas for their use to pay for it by making conservation investments for other people, then using the gas those other people saved. This entitlements plan begins with the observation that many large manufacturers are currently operating under "interruptable" rates for energy. This kind of rate permits a utility company to cut the industrial plant from the system when there is a gas or electricity shortage. In return for this less secure supply of gas or electricity, the industrial customer pays a somewhat lower cost for the energy it purchases. The arrangement is exactly analogous to a standby fare on a plane, assuming the standby fare is less. In some recent winters, interruptable customers found, to their discomfort, that interruptions were frequently necessary and that the utility refused to supply "firm" (that is, noninterruptable) gas to them. In parts of the nation, this meant that factories had to close, tossing workers out of jobs.

Suppose that the large industrial customer could go to hundreds or thousands of small users of natural gas and make them the following offer: I will pay for the installation of energy conservation improvements in your building if, in return, you will give me the right to buy the energy that those improvements save. This would be an offer that neither party would be likely to refuse. Small building owners would beneft because they would get insulation free, would use less energy each month, and thus would lower their monthly bills from the utility. Industrial customers would obtain gas, unobtainable to them in any other way, while at the same time paying fairly low rates for that gas because it would be derived from inexpensive conservation, not expensive new supplies.

The immediate practical difficulties of implementing this plan will occur to anyone. It is unlikely that a major industry, interested only in the business of making its own product, would wish to take on the job of talking residential and small commercial customers into accepting this plan. Nor would the industry have access to records necessary to know how much gas was being saved and therefore available for its own use. Finally, the industry would not have the power to divert that gas saved from the consumer in whose building the conservation improvements had been made to the industry that had paid for the improvements. However, the utility company—with its records and its penetration into each home—

would have the information, the method, and (with proper regulatory permission) the ability to make gas saved by a customer available to another customer. The utility company could act like a broker, bringing the buyer and the seller together.[48]

Effect of the National Energy Act of 1978. In late 1978, Congress passed the National Energy Act; one of its parts, the National Energy Conservation Policy Act (P.L. 95-619), deals extensively with the role of utilities in energy conservation programs for residences. At the time of this book's preparation, no final regulations were available under the act, so only the bare outline of the act is given here, with the caveat that readers must check the latest regulations of the federal Department of Energy. The act establishes a requirement that public utilities above a certain size (selling more than ten billion cubic feet of natural gas or 750 million kilowatt hours of electricity each year) provide energy conservation assistance to their residential customers. Any customer who lives in a building with up to four units is eligible for the services, so long as the building is not a "new building," covered by the Building Energy Performance Standards. Basically, the act requires each utility to provide to eligible customers the following items:

- A suggested list of energy conservation measures and an estimation of how much money can be saved using each measure. (The act lists items that must be mentioned by the utility, but the Department of Energy can add to the list.)

- Energy conservation measures that can be implemented without capital investments (i.e., operational changes) and their associated savings.

- A description of the additional services that the utility will offer to the customer. These additional services are:
  + Providing on-site energy audits,
  + Making arrangements for having suggested items installed,
  + Making arrangements for financing suggested changes,
  + Providing lists of approved suppliers and contractors offering energy conservation measures (the lists are compiled by the state, not by the utility), and
  + Providing lists of approved institutions offering credit for energy conservation measures (the lists are developed by the state, not the utility).

For the most part, the act forbids utilities themselves to provide energy conservation services or loans to their customers. However, there are several exceptions to this general prohibition:

- Utilities may modify furnaces to increase their efficiency,
- Utilities may sell clock thermostats,
- Utilities may install load management devices for the energy form supplied by the utility, and
- Utilities may make loans for those items it can sell under the act (furnace modifications and load management devices), so long as a loan does not exceed $300.

There are a few cases in which a utility may engage in more extensive energy conservation activities of the kind described earlier in this chapter. Basically, these exceptions to the general prohibition "grandfather in" those utilities that actually had ongoing programs at the time of the passage of the act. If the utility was actually carrying on newly prohibited activities or if it had planned to do so and had broadly advertised or taken other action, then the utility's own plan could continue, subject to the state conservation plan. Finally, if on November 9, 1978 (the date of the act's passage), the state had on its books a law or regulation that required or explicitly permitted broader conservation activities by the utility, the activity could continue, not subject to the act or the requirements of the state plan. In addition, DOE can waive the prohibitions of the act if the utility petitions for waiver and demonstrates that it will charge fair and reasonable prices and if DOE finds in addition that there will be no unfair or anticompetitive practices.

The act permits the governor of each state to extend generally the same plans to home-heating suppliers that are not utilities (such as heating oil distributors). The requirements are similar to those that apply to utilities.

As noted above, the states will be required to develop state plans for carrying out the utility energy conservation programs. Any state that fails to promulgate such a plan will have a plan provided by the federal Department of Energy.

The act requires the federal government to make a series of studies in connection with energy conservation services provided to residential customers:

- The Federal Trade Commission must report to Congress by January 1, 1982, on how utilities and home-heating suppliers (if governors extend the program to them) are performing and the effect of their activities on competition and supplies.

- The Department of Energy must study the problem of apartment buildings and make recommendations for legislation.

Obviously, this summary of the provisions of the act only begins to sketch out the possible conflicts between the federal government and states and utilities that want to expand services to customers along the lines suggested earlier in this volume. The provisions of the act seem to reflect a deeply held suspicion of utilities. It remains to be seen whether or not the tightly circumscribed arena now left for utility action on residential energy conservation will be sufficient. It is entirely possible that in its zeal to protect the public from rapacious actions, Congress has neutralized the one set of institutions capable of truly innovative energy conservation programs.

State Agency Grant and Loan Programs for Energy Conservation. It is entirely possible for the state government itself to take an active part in financing the improvement of energy conservation in existing homes. For example, the Minnesota Housing Finance Agency provides both loans and grants for energy conservation purposes. The MHFA program has local programs in St. Paul, Minneapolis, and Duluth and a statewide program for any part of the state. In addition to the state program, local programs are conducted by municipal housing and redevelopment authorities in each of the three cities. Let us deal first with the city program, then with the state program itself.

St. Paul Program.   The city of St. Paul makes grants and loans available to homeowners. The city has a system to assist homeowners in getting quality workmanship. Once an application is reviewed and accepted, the city assigns an advisor who provides lists of acceptable contractors (licensed, bonded, and insured) to the owner and evaluates the work. Once the work is done, the city inspects it and issues a check. Health and safety hazards must be repaired; in addition, insulation, foundations, and storm windows can be installed or repaired. Most of the funds are restricted to target areas of the city; the rest can be expended anyplace within city limits.

The program is funded by sale of local bonds (of which $2.5 million worth have been sold). The program staff estimates that it will be able to finance about 1,200 to 1,500 loans and grants per year.[49]

Minneapolis Program.   The Minneapolis program is similar to the St. Paul program. Loans are available up to the full equity in the property. There is a maximum family income limit of $19,250. The city program is financed through a sale in 1974 of $10 million in bonds; approximately $1 million remains.[50]

Minnesota Housing Finance Agency Program

GRANT PROGRAM. This program was enacted to permit lower income Minnesotans who own property to repair and improve it. To qualify for the program, the following conditions must be met: (1) the owner must occupy the property; (2) the home must be no more than a two family structure and in compliance with zoning and land use guides; and (3) annual adjusted gross income must be $5,000 or less, and the gross value of the owner's assets must be no more than $25,000, excluding personal property and the property being improved. The grants are limited to $5,000, and special emphasis has been placed on energy-saving home improvements; all homeowners are encouraged to upgrade inadequate insulation, weatherstripping, and caulking. The grant must be repaid in full if the owner moves, sells, or transfers the property during the first three years; thereafter, in the fourth year only 75 percent need be repaid; in the fifth year, only 50 percent; in the sixth year, only 25 percent; and by the seventh year, the full grant is forgiven.

The program has been going for three years. Approximately 2,700 grants a year have been made, with approximately $9 million expended. Of that approximately $9 million, over $2 million per year has been used for insulation and heating improvements. Average insulation costs per home are about $460; average heating improvements are about $850.

LOAN PROGRAM. The Minnesota Housing Finance Agency also has an energy conservation loan program with more liberal family income requirements. To qualify for this program, the homeowner must (1) own the property being improved; (2) have an annual adjusted gross income of not more than $16,000 per year; and (3) be a reasonable credit risk. The property being improved must be (1) at least fifteen years old, or require correction of items hazardous to health or safety, or be in need of energy conservation improvements; (2) be used mainly for residential purposes; (3) contain no more than six dwelling units; and (4) comply with all local zoning ordinances and other land use guides. The interest on the loans is calculated by dividing the recipient's annual adjusted gross income by $2,000; an income of $9,000 to $10,000 would qualify for an interest rate of 5 percent. The repayment period is fifteen years for a single family residence, twelve years for a multifamily residence. The loan principal is limited to $15,000 for a single family dwelling and to $25,000 for properties with six dwelling units.

According to Minnesota officials, the loan program is divided into phases of approximately six months each. The program has now completed seven phases. Insulation loans began at about 4.7 percent of the loan funds and have reached as high as 19.5 percent of the funds. Improvements in the heating plants average around 6 percent of the funds expended. Unfortunately, there are no figures available on the improvement in energy consumption that the Minnesota program has made possible for those using its services.

These direct grant and loan programs cost the state relatively little. Local housing and redevelopment authorities, banks, and savings and loan associations handle the administrative work of originating the loans, while the grants are handled by the state or local agency itself. The Minnesota program includes grants to lower income and older citizens as a priority item. A model of energy conservation programs that offer low cost loans and direct grants, the Minnesota program deserves to be emulated.[51]

Federal Programs.   In addition to Minnesota's program and those of other states, the federal government has a number of long-existing programs to assist low income persons. Three programs are of particular interest. One is operated by the Community Services Administration (under the Economic Opportunity Act of 1964), another is the weatherization program operated by the Department of Energy (under the Energy Conservation and Production Act of 1976), and the third is the Section 504 program operated by the Farmers Home Administration (under the Housing Act of 1949). Before the National Energy Act of 1978, these three programs had slightly different requirements and benefits. The National Energy Act requires the three programs to become more standardized, allowing grants for caulking; weatherstripping; replacement of furnace burners with substantially more efficient burners, flue dampers, or other devices to increase efficiency; spark or electronic pilot lights; clock thermostats; insulation; water heat insulation; storm doors and windows and other modifications to windows; and any other device that DOE certifies is eligible. In order to qualify for a grant, recipients must be at or below 125 percent of the official poverty level. Expenditures of up to $800 per dwelling unit are allowed, of which up to $100 may be used in ways to make the weatherization more effective, to pay for delivery of workers and materials to the site, and to pay for supervision. Labor must be either volunteer or furnished under the provisions of the Comprehensive Employment and Training Act (CETA), although exceptions are permitted in rural areas. Finally, the amount authorized in prior years for these programs is increased. Other federal programs are slightly increased to provide weatherization for public housing or low and moderate income multifamily housing.

The National Energy Act also made changes in the rules of the various federal housing assistance programs and the various publicly mandated private secondary market entities. These include authorizing the Federal National Mortgage Association and the Federal Home Loan Mortgage Association for the first time to purchase home improvement loans when they are made for energy related improvements. In addition, the Federal Housing Administration is permitted to insure loans for up to 20 percent over its "maximum" for solar-equipped homes.

The Department of Housing and Urban Development is required to study whether federal legislation is necessary and feasible to promote energy conservation standards for existing residences. A report on this subject is due to Congress at the end of 1979.

Although state or federally financed assistance programs can encourage energy conservation actions by citizens, the government cannot afford to absorb a significant portion of the total cost of the improvements it recommends. Therefore, while poorer and older citizens should continue to receive grants and subsidized loans, other means—including the actions taken by citizens without the encouragement or assistance of the government—will play the largest role in retrofitting older homes.

Direct Regulation for Energy Efficiency in Existing Residences. Rather little effort has been made to force improvements in existing residences through direct regulation. Laws forcing an important class of voters to expend large amounts of money understandably are politically unpopular. Direct regulations affecting homeowners have typically had what lawyers refer to as a "grandfather" clause, one that permits existing uses and abuses to remain. For example, regulations prohibiting use of natural gas for decorative outdoor gas lights (an extravagant use of a declining resource) typically have permitted existing lights to remain; all they actually prohibit is the connection of new outdoor lights. The National Energy Act will actually phase these lights out.

The grandfather clause in most regulatory statutes grows out of political horse sense, common sense, and constitutional considerations. Regulations requiring large numbers of citizens to spend money are politically hard to enact. That's the political horse sense.

The existing uses of any commodity are likely to be so diverse that a law must either be unwieldy enough to take such variations into account or provide for an administrative bureaucracy to resolve conflicts between the general goals of the legislation and the particular claims of those affected by it. That's the common sense. The constitutional concern that favors inclusion of a grandfather clause is the fear that overregulation by the state may constitute a "taking of property," which, according to the Fifth Amendment to the United States Constitution, is permissible only if the government pays for the property taken.

The constitutional lore on the so-called "takings issue" is enormous. Because the issue applies most directly to land use regulation, readers interested in finding more about the issue in the context of energy are encouraged to read another book in this series, *Using Land to Save Energy*, by Corbin Crews Harwood. The description herein relates only to the question of whether required improvements on existing residences constitute such a degree of regulation that they become a taking, for which the government must pay.

In the context of existing houses, grandfather clauses are nonsense, since the very purpose of the legislation is to force change. Countless cases uphold the right of the state to require that various, often expensive, additions be made to buildings. Most of these cases have dealt with rooming houses and apartment buildings—state government has traditionally protected tenants and lodgers, since they are preseumed to be unable to bring market or political pressures to bear upon the landlords. For example, in *Queenside Hills Realty Co. v. Saxl,*[52] a lodging house built in 1940 in compliance with all applicable laws became subject to a requirement passed in 1944 that a sprinkler system be installed in all existing lodging houses. The United States Supreme Court upheld the retroactive application of this expenditure, saying, "[I]n no case does the owner of property acquire immunity against exercise of the police power because he constructed it in full compliance with the existing laws." But because courts recognize that retroactive application of building requirements imposes difficult practical problems, they do require a greater showing of need than they would require in cases where the expense involved is less. The rule appears to be that regulations may be valid if it appears that the public welfare demands retroactive application. However, the power is circumscribed by the facts of each situation, particularly that affected property owners should not suffer unreasonable exactions.

The test of avoidance of unreasonable exactions seems to be a kind of cost-benefit calculation performed by the courts as they consider mandatory regulations presented to them. An old New York case, *Health Department v. Rector, Etc., Trinity Church*, makes this cost-benefit consideration explicit. In upholding a regulation requiring tenement houses to have a supply of water to each floor, the court cautioned that "no one would contend that the amount of the expenditure which an act of this kind may cause, whether or without a hearing, is within the absolute discretion of the legislature."

These cases show that laws requiring retrofitting existing homes with energy conservation features are probably constitutional, provided that certain guidelines are followed. First, the regulations must mandate additions that have a clear relationship to the purpose of saving energy and that are demonstrably effective for that purpose. Studies analyzing the cost savings that such improvements make possible are helpful in upholding such regulations, particularly if based on weather collection data within the state. Second, the regulations should permit building owners to be excused from complying with the regulation if they can show that for their particular residences, the general regulations are not cost-effective. Thus, an owner of a brick home with a finished attic should be able to show that to add wall and ceiling insulation he would have to rip out plaster and undo a finished attic and that the economic savings would not justify the expense. Third, the homeowner should be given a reasonable time in which to comply and should be able to choose from alternative methods of saving energy so as to maximize energy conservation while minimizing expenses.

The problem of when to impose the retrofitting requirement must also be tackled. If the law requires that all houses in a state be retrofitted within a certain time, contractors will be overloaded and will raise prices if qualified workers and appropriate materials are in short supply. One suggested solution to this problem was introduced twice in California, but it failed to become law. Under the California approach, houses had to meet energy conservation standards at the time of sale or other transfer of ownership. Originally, the party acting as the escrow agent in the transaction was to be responsible for enforcing the statute. The title companies, which do a large escrow business in California, objected to this additional burden. The second version of the legislation required that, before transferring the title to the house, homeowners obtain from a licensed contractor a certificate stating that their attics were insulated according to the standards to be promulgated by the Commission of Housing and Community Development. The legislation states:

On or after January 1, 1977, the attic spaces of all residential dwellings shall meet or exceed energy insulation standards before a change in title to the dwelling can be recorded. The county recorder shall not record a change of title to a residential dwelling unless a statement of adequate energy insulation is recorded with the title showing that the dwelling meets or exceeds the energy insulation standards in the attic space.

. . . .

On or after January 1, 1977, whenever any licensed contractor inspects a residential dwelling in connection with the sale, exchange, or transfer of title of the dwelling, he shall inspect the attic space of the residential dwelling for compliance with the energy insulation standards. If the licensed contractor finds after inspection that the attic space of the dwelling meets the energy insulation standards, he shall issue a statement of adequate energy insulation which shall be recorded with the county recorder by the owner. However, if the licensed contractor finds that the attic space of the dwelling does not meet the energy insulation standards, he shall report to the owner and potential buyers or transferees of a residential dwelling the extent to which the dwelling meets the energy insulation standards in the attic space and an estimate of required alterations or additions necessary to meet the energy insulation standards in the attic space.[53]

The California proposal has much to commend it, but it lacks flexibility. Individuals are not permitted to challenge the cost-benefit calculations in particular cases, unless the buyer files a notarized statement with the county recorder that the dwelling being purchased will be demolished within three years of purchase or is not intended to be used for human habitation as a dwelling within three years of the purchase.

Other methods have been suggested that grant additional time to homeowners to improve existing residences. Using the final digit of house addresses, housing authorities could draw lots to determine the yearly order in which home improvements must be completed, or neighborhoods in which compliance would be required, generally using the areas serviced by elementary schools (to concentrate the work within a geographical area and permit retrofitters to take advantage of the economies of mass production). Other means of avoiding a sudden bonanza for insulation contractors can also be devised. The research program to be undertaken by the Department of Housing and Urban Development under the National Energy Act on this subject may be helpful in suggesting other alternatives.

The Special Case of Landlord and Tenant in Existing Housing. Rental housing, in which the lease agreement makes meeting utility bills the responsibility of the tenant, poses special problems for those designing incentives to encourage energy conservation. The landlord has no incentive whatsoever to add insulation or other energy conservation improvements, because he does not directly benefit. (Of course he has a somewhat more desirable rental property because of the lower utility bills, but this benefit may be nominal, if not ficticious, where housing markets for rental units are tight or where the margin of profit is squeezed by other economic factors.) On the other hand, even the tenant who stands to save money by making apartment improvements does not want to put capital into property he does not own. Therefore, neither party does what would be good for both parties.

This impasse can be circumvented in several ways. The first and most direct method is simply to require that landlords bring rental properties up to the current standards of energy efficiency. As noted above, assuming that proper procedural safeguards are followed, courts have tended to enforce regulations strictly against apartment owners because of the supposed inability of tenants to protect themselves. Cases have upheld the installation of tubs and showers, fire escapes, central heating, hot water, safety devices for elevators, and many other health and safety items. If the legislature were to find that energy conservation was a matter of great public concern (because, for example, of its effect on the state's economy), a case could be made for the mandatory installation of insulation or other improvements to apartments. A law that required these improvements at the time of transfer of the property (as suggested in the preceeding section) might be one equitable solution to the problem.

A second method, one that would put the cost of the improvement on the persons enjoying the benefits, is to require the local public utility to install insulation, with the costs of the installation charged to the person paying for the energy. This makes the improvement more attractive to the landlord, since property improvements would not be paid for out of profits, and depending on the prior state of the apartment, the tenants might find that utility bills were not increased substantially because of the conserving effect of the insulation. Since utility companies keep detailed records and have already established contact with energy consumers, they would be able to cease adding charges for the insulation once it was paid for—an adjustment many tenants might not feel that their landlords could be counted upon to make.

Another method for handling the landlord-tenant problem is for a state to adopt either the conservation gas plan or the natural gas entitlements plan detailed earlier. In both cases, the owner of the building is indifferent to the fact that insulation is being added to the building since he or she does not pay for the cost of the installation. The current occupant of the rental unit, on the other hand, is delighted to have the insulation installed.

Unfortunately, no state has devised any satisfactory method for dealing with the landlord-tenant problem, so no existing legislation or regulations thoroughly treat the issue.

Thermal Efficiency Standards for Residential Buildings: Conclusion

The preceding sections have dealt with strategies and programs designed to encourage or to mandate installation of adequate insulation and other thermal efficiency improvements in both new and existing housing. The discussion has shown that, to date, no satisfactory program has emerged and that strategies for dealing with existing housing are especially needed. Yet existing housing provides the greatest opportunity for energy savings. Much of the housing still in use in this country was built before any insulation standards at all were in force. Housing "turns over" slowly in this country: 2 percent per year is a common estimate.

The reason for this failure to come to grips with the pressing need to develop strategies for retrofitting existing housing is not difficult to discern. Since the public lacks a strong awareness of the long term seriousness of this country's energy situation, politicians and officials are not motivated to negotiate the difficult first steps toward improved existing housing.

Although the standards that are currently being discussed fail to push the potentials for savings far enough, we have progressed in our efforts to make new housing more energy-efficient. It is a much simpler matter, legally as well as politically, to insist that the homes being built today comply with economically rational energy conservation standards. The major drive in the coming years must be to continue improving the energy conservation standards that are recommended for new housing, so that as technology improves and as the price of energy increases (thus changing the cost-benefit ratio of undertaking more and more energy conservation investments), the regulations continue to become stricter. The American Society of Heating, Refrigerating, and Air-conditioning Engineers, Inc., has already shown itself willing to revise its Standard 90-75; as more data accumulates on energy budgets, the figures that are based on that approach can become more exact and stringent. Similarly, BEPS should be revised to make it increasingly stringent. In all cases, legislatures should require that energy regulations be updated at least every two years. A clause to assist in this update is suggested here:

The Legislature hereby directs the [State Building Code Department] to prepare a report no less frequently than every two years, with the first report due [date] describing the operation of the energy efficiency code hereby adopted and to make recommendations for improving that code. The [department] is specifically directed to prepare detailed, specific suggestions for increasing the minimum figures contained in this code in response to rises in the price of energy and in response to improved data collected by [the department] or any other source concerning technological, economic, or other relevant information that would indicate that energy efficiency at a higher level than mandated herein is feasible or desirable.

THERMAL EFFICIENCY STANDARDS FOR NONRESIDENTIAL BUILDINGS

Motivating or requiring property holders to improve the thermal efficiency of large buildings is an even thornier problem than increasing the energy efficiency of the smaller, residential building. Large apartment buildings, although residences, have much in common with commercial structures, so they are treated in this section.

The complexities of the energy consumption patterns of large buildings stem from a number of factors. First, large buildings are heavily influenced by solar heating and by wind cooling. Glass office buildings in particular have enormous solar heat gains on one side during the morning hours that shift to the other side by the afternoon. Therefore, the heating and cooling equipment must be capable of treating the same space differently at different times of the day and the year. Second, loads on the building are not constant within a floor; in the winter, the perimeters of many large buildings are heated, while the interiors are cooled. Third, individual occupants of the building make different heating and cooling demands. Such differences do not always reflect human tastes. A computer room or a room full of copying machines can require enormous cooling capacity. It is usually impossible to plan for these loads at the time a commercial building is constructed. Fourth, large buildings require complicated mechanical equipment and sophisticated temperature control systems, so builders are tempted to select inexpensive-to-purchase-electric resistance heating coils that are expensive to operate, simply because they are easy to install (electrical wiring takes less space and less ingenuity to snake through a building than do air, water, or steam ducts). Efficiency is compromised in favor of simple, low cost heating, ventilating, and air-conditioning systems. Finally, in a large building, ventilation and lighting play much greater roles in energy consumption than in other types of buildings. If a building is sealed because the windows don't move, air must be mechanically introduced and transported to occupied spaces.

All of these factors, combined with the usual pressures on any owner to keep first costs low and to embrace the certainty that a conventional design affords, make energy conservation difficult in large buildings. Law and regulation cannot control these large energy-consuming buildings without careful, detailed study that takes into account the complexity of the structure intended to be regulated. Yet it is clear that large buildings need some regulation, since improvement is coming at a slow pace, and massive improvements are possible. The Arthur D. Little study of ASHRAE Standard 90-75 found that using relatively conventional energy conservation techniques resulted in energy savings of up to 59.7 percent in the computerized models of tall office buildings. An energy conservation demonstration building in Manchester, New Hampshire, constructed by the federal government, was designed to enjoy savings of over 50 percent. The redesigns done for the new federal performance standards show that on the average, energy improvements are 40 percent or more. These studies suggest that incentives or regulation, properly applied, can have an enormous effect on energy consumption for large buildings.

Because large buildings are so complex and because they come in so many sizes and shapes, the most rational strategies are those that maximize the choices of the persons designing the buildings. No single prescriptive solution should be forced upon designers; instead, a single result—the reduction of energy consumption—should be sought.

One of the most fruitful methods for increasing building designers' freedom is to adopt the true budget approach. This approach, along with the energy budget sections of ASHRAE Standard 90-75, the Ohio modified energy budget, the General Services Administration federal energy goal, the federal Building Energy Performance Standards, and other approaches, is discussed at greater length in Chapter 7. But as that chapter mentions, a present defect of energy budgets is the lack of credible data from which to construct a reasonable budget. Although the AIA/RC efforts in connection with the design of the Building Energy Performance Standard development (discussed earlier in this chapter) have begun to provide these data, the effort is far from trivial either in theory or practice. This short section deals with some of the methods that might be used in addition to an energy budget for saving energy in a large building.

Educational Strategies

Efforts to educate the public on energy conservation in large buildings are most appropriately directed at the design professional—

architect or engineer—who is responsible for the design and installation of the heating, ventilating, and air-conditioning systems. The complexity of those systems makes it impossible for the building owner to take an active role in technical decisions on the systems that the building should include. The complexity suggests that education directed to building owners should try to convince them of the wisdom of making somewhat higher capital outlays in order to lower long term costs.

The power of education to change designs is illustrated by the results of Phase II of the development process for BEPS. Recall that a large number of buildings were studied in the design stage. Then, 168 of those buildings (scattered around the country and diverse in intended use) were redesigned by the same architectural teams that had done them originally. The difference was that the teams were given a three day course in techniques of energy conservation design and told to pay attention to energy conservation in addition to the other demands made by the client. In general, four out of five of the redesigns were better than the top one-fifth of the original buildings. Put differently, three days' training produced redesign results that were better than 80 percent of newly designed American buildings.

State-run or -sponsored seminars for building professionals represent one method of sharing information about energy conservation techniques. State training can also be given by putting out bids for the construction of highly energy-conserving state office buildings so that at least some design professionals learn how to construct such buildings partially at public expense. This method gives the state a well-designed building as well as increased expertise in its own future contracting. Licensing examinations for contractors and builders that include sections on energy conservation design and construction will also force new design professionals to become aware of the range of energy-saving techniques available.

To the extent that suggestions cost little or nothing and have short payback periods when implemented, education is especially valuable to conservation. If professionals find methods for lowering building costs through energy conservation (by, for example, combining use of better insulation with the use of smaller, less expensive equipment) they will be likely to use them. If professionals can be convinced that some relatively low cost techniques pay for themselves in two to four years, they will be able to incorporate them in future designs and to demonstrate to their clients that the savings will quickly recoup the initial outlay. But to bring about major design changes that have somewhat longer payback periods or that entail future savings that are harder to guarantee, educational strategies will have to be supplemented by other incentives and regulations.

Owners of large buildings are extremely sensitive to the first cost of the buildings and will be able to calculate those costs fairly accurately; if any doubt surrounds the benefits associated with a new method, the standard method will probably be chosen instead. Thus, educating those in the commercial building field is important, but true innovation may need more.

Incentive Strategies

Because of the sensitivity of owners of commercial buildings to first costs, incentives (or disincentives) have a large potential for encouraging energy conservation. But because the total cost of making every cost-effective energy conservation improvement may be high within a state, incentives for encouraging energy conservation in large commercial office buildings may be politically unpopular. On the other hand, disincentives, although effective, must be tied to some standard so that the charge can be levied according to a measure of performance.

In a companion book in this series, *Tax Strategies: Alternatives to Regulation* by Joe W. Russell, a charge scheme for encouraging large buildings to comply with regulations is put forth. The strategy, based on an innovative system used in Connecticut for curbing pollution, calculates the cost to the building owner of meeting the standard. To the extent that the building falls below the standard, a charge that closely approximates the cost of taking the steps necessary to bring the building up to standard is assessed. This charge is levied in lieu of regulatory action or other penalties, and its effect is simple: since building owners must pay the charge anyway, they would be foolish not to use the money to improve the building to the standard. If they do, they save money in two ways: the charges are dropped and the costs of operating their buildings go down.

Loan programs, loan guarantees, relief from increased property tax assessments, and the array of other financial assistance programs discussed above in the context of residences may also be used for larger buildings.

Regulatory Strategies

The legal methods for regulating large buildings differ only slightly from those used to regulate small buildings or residences. Building codes, energy budgets, and design standards for shading, orientation, and placement are all considered in the regulation of both offices and homes. ASHRAE Standard 90-75 applies to large buildings as well as to small ones. In the section of the standard devoted to the building envelope, a particular subsection treats the design of large buidlings explicitly. In the same way, the Building Energy Performance Standards deal explicitly with large office buildings.

Present educational incentives and regulatory strategies all have a long way to go to fully account for the complexities of the energy system in a large building and to balance improved performance and economic payoffs. Even a good standard—whether component, performance, or true budget—must contain a mechanism for increasing its own stringency as technology improves and as energy prices rise.

CONCLUSION

In this chapter, we have considered most of the control strategies for improving the building envelope's resistance to heat transmission. Among the improvements that do not entail design changes, installing insulation and reducing air infiltration are probably the best ways to improve the efficiency of residences. For larger buildings, the situation is more complex, and insulation plays a different role in the entire system of energy conservation improvements.

Energy accounting is undeniably complex. More insulation may mean smaller heating and cooling plants; fewer lights will increase the need for heat from other sources in the winter and decrease cooling loads in the summer. The legal documents that control these interrelationships do not often make the relationships clear, but readers should be cautioned against tinkering with only one part of a regulatory system for controlling a complex physical entity. While this book isolates subsystems of buildings for the sake of convenience, readers and legislators must recognize that energy problems must be treated as a whole, at least when it comes to regulating building energy use.

APPENDIX A: States' Energy Conservation Standards for Buildings: Status of States' Regulatory Activities*

States	State Authority to Issue Energy Conservation Standards for Buildings Legislative	Other	Legislative Authority Pending	Authority Applies to Following Building Types Residential	Non-residential	Public	Energy Conservation Standards Mandatory Residential	Non-residential	Public	Enforcement: State and Local Governments Residential	Non-residential	Public	Technical Basis for Standards	Model Code— Adopted, Modified, or Considered	Remarks
Alabama	Yes	No	No	Yes	Yes	Yes	Yes	Yes	Yes	Local & State	Local & State	State	ASHRAE 90-75	ICBO	Legislation passed during 1978 session gives authority to state Building Commission to promulgate and enforce standards for all new buildings.
Alaska	No	No	No[a]												[a] State is evaluating ASHRAE 90-75R and will propose legislation in 1979 session. City of Anchorage has adopted and is implementing ASHRAE 90-75 standards.
Arizona	Yes	No	No	Yes	Yes	Yes	No[b]	No[b]	Yes	Local & State	Local & State	State & Local	ASHRAE 90-75	ICBO	[b] Recent legislation authorized development of performance standards for legislative review, with adoption of interim ASHRAE-based standards voluntary. Performance standards expected to be mandatory for all buildings. 1977 legislation applied to state buildings only.
Arkansas	No[c]	No	No[c]												[c] Legislation defeated last year. The residential requirements a factor in defeat. State Energy Office developing legislation for introduction in 1979. At present, details of legislation unclear.

State												State Standards— Residential: ASHRAE 90-75— Nonresidential		Comments
California	Yes	No	No	Yes	Yes	Yes	Yes	Yes	Local & State	Local & State	State & Local		ICBO	
Colorado	Yes	No	No	Yes	No	No	Yes	No	Local	Local	State & Local	ASHRAE 90-75	NCSBCS	
Connecticut	Yes	No	No	Yes	Yes	Yes	Yes	Yes	Local	Local	State & Local	ASHRAE 90-75	BOCA	State standards do not include all prescriptive standards of ASHRAE 90-75. State Building Codes Committee working on complete adoption of ASHRAE 90-75.
Delaware	No	(Yes)	(Yes)	(Yes)	(Yes)	(Yes)	(Yes)	(Yes)	(Local)	(Local)	(State & Local)	(ASHRAE 90-75)	(None)	Legislation passed Senate. Under consideration by House committee. Prognosis: Uncertain.
District of Columbia	No	(Yes)	(Yes)	(Yes)[d]	(Yes)	(Yes)	(Yes)	(Yes)	(Local)	(Local)	(Local)	(ASHRAE 90-75)	(NCSBCS)	[d]Does not apply to federal buildings. Anticipate approval by city council and Congress within next five months.
Florida	Yes	No	No	Yes	Yes	Yes	Yes	Yes	Local	Local	State & Local	ASHRAE 90-75 HUD MPS	SBCC	Developing performance code to be available for adoption.
Georgia	Yes	No	No	Yes	Yes	Yes	Yes	Yes	Local	Local	State & Local	ASHRAE 90-75	NCSBCS ICBO	State Building Administrative Board authorized to develop standards for legislative consideration; legislation passed by 1978 General Assembly effective July 1. 1978.

(continued)

*Published by National Institute of Building Sciences, 1730 Pennsylvania Avenue N.W., Suite 425, Wasington, D.C. 20006, ©1978: reproduced with permission.

States	State Authority to Issue Energy Conservation Standards for Buildings		Legislative Authority Pending	Authority Applies to Following Building Types			Energy Conservation Standards Mandatory			Enforcement: State and Local Governments			Technical Basis for Standards	Model Code—Adopted, Modified, or Considered	Remarks
	Legislative	Other		Residential	Non-residential	Public	Residential	Non-residential	Public	Residential	Non-residential	Public			
Hawaii	Yes	No	No	Yes	Yes (Over 10,000 sq. ft.)	Yes	Yes	Yes	Yes	Local	Local	State & Local	ASHRAE 90-75	ICBO	Legislation enacted in May 1978; standards to be incorporated into county codes by July 1, 1978.
Idaho	No	Yes[e]	No	—	—	Yes	No	No	Yes	Local	Local	State	ASHRAE 90-75	ICBO	[e]Authority applies to state-owned and educational facilities. Eighty-three percent of population covered by voluntary adoption of standards.
Illinois	No	Yes[f]	Yes	(Yes)	(Yes)	Yes	(Yes)	(Yes)	Yes	(Local)	(Local)	State & Local	ASHRAE 90-75	(State Code)	[f]Capital Development Board has adopted ASHRAE 90-75 Modified for state-owned or state-financed buildings, effective July 1, 1978.
Indiana	Yes	No	No	Yes	Yes	Yes	Yes	Yes	Yes	Local & State	Local & State	State & Local	ASHRAE 90-75	ICBO	
Iowa	Yes	No	No	Yes	Yes	Yes	Yes	Yes	Yes	Local & State	Local & State	State & Local	ASHRAE 90-75	NCSBCS ICBO	
Kansas	No	Yes[g]	No	Yes	Yes	Yes	Yes	Yes	Yes	Local	Local	State & Local	ASHRAE 90-75	ICBO	[g]Kansas Corporation Commission (a public utilities commission) authority to implement ASHRAE 90-75 in 80% of state extended to entire state by legislation, effective March 23, 1978.

State											
Kentucky	No	Yes[h]	(Yes)	(Yes)	(Yes)	(Yes)	(Local & State)	(Local & State)	(State & Local)	(ASHRAE 90-75)	(NCSBCS)
Louisiana	No	No	(Yes)	(Yes)	(Yes)	(Yes)	(Local)	(Local)	(State)	(ASHRAE 90-75)	(NCSBCS)
Maine	No	No	Yes[i]	—	—	Yes	—	—	State	ASHRAE 90-75	BOCA
Maryland	No	Yes	(Yes)	(Yes)	(Yes)	(Yes)	(Local)	(Local)	(State & Local)	(ASHRAE 90-75)	BOCA
Massachusetts	Yes	No	Yes	Yes	Yes	Yes	Local	Local	State & Local	ASHRAE 90-75	NCSBCS
Michigan	Yes	Yes[j]	Yes	No[j]	No[j]	No[j]	Local	Local	State & Local	ASHRAE 90-75	BOCA
Minnesota	Yes	No	Yes	Yes	Yes	Yes	Local[k]	Local[k]	State & Local	ASHRAE 90-75	ICBO

[h] Executive order authorizing Department of Housing to promulgate energy conservation standards must be confirmed by legislature in 1980 session.

Pending legislation assigns development, adoption, and enforcement of standards to Department of Natural Resources.

[i] Applies to all new state-financed buildings. Legislature established a study commission. Must recommend standards for consideration at next legislative session (January 1979).

Adoption of state building code voluntary. Proposed legislation would make ASHRAE 90-75 enforceable statewide.

[j] Opt-out provision in state building code. Only jurisdictions adopting state code subject to standards. Pending legislation would mandate use by all jurisdictions.

[k] Local entities required to establish enforcement mechanism by January 1, 1979.

(continued)

State	State Authority to Issue Energy Conservation Standards for Buildings		Legislative Authority Pending	Authority Applies to Following Building Types			Energy Conservation Standards Mandatory			Enforcement: State and Local Governments			Technical Basis for Standards	Model Code—Adopted, Modified, or Considered	Remarks
	Legislative	Other		Residential	Non-residential	Public	Residential	Non-residential	Public	Residential	Non-residential	Public			
Mississippi	Yes	No	No	Yes	Yes	Yes	Yes	Yes	Yes	Local & State	Local & State	State & Local	ASHRAE 90-75	State Code	Legislation passed during 1978 session. State Building Commission to develop standards to be approved by state legislature.
Missouri	No	No	No[l]												[l]Legislation died in general assembly; new legislation to be introduced in 1979 session.
Montana	Yes	No	No	Yes	Yes	Yes	Yes	Yes	Yes	Local	Local	State & Local	ASHRAE 90-75	NCSBCS	
Nebraska	No	No	No[m]												[m]Legislation died due to insufficient time to act; an interim study is expected to result in new legislation in next session.
Nevada	Yes	No	No	Yes	Yes	Yes	Yes	Yes	Yes	Local[n]	Local[n]	State & Local[n]	ASHRAE 90-75	NCSBCS	[n]Local governments required to establish enforcement mechanism by July 1, 1978.
New Hampshire	Yes	No	No	Yes	Yes	Yes	No	No	Yes	Local	Local	State & Local	ASHRAE 90-75	NCSBCS BOCA	
New Jersey	Yes	No	No	Yes	Yes	Yes	Yes	Yes	Yes	Local	Local	State & Local	ASHRAE 90-75	BOCA	

														Standards	Code Group
New Mexico	Yes	No	No	Yes	Yes	Yes	Yes	Yes	Yes	State & Local	State & Local	State & Local	ASHRAE 90-75	ICBO
New York	No	Yes[p]	Yes	Yes[p]	(Yes)	(Yes)	Yes[p]	(Yes)	(Yes)	Local[p]	(Local)	(State & Local)	Public Service Commission Standards (ASHRAE 90-75)	None (NCSBCS)
North Carolina	Yes	No	No	Yes	Yes	Yes	Yes	Yes	Yes	Local	Local	State & Local	ASHRAE 90-75	State Building Code
North Dakota	Yes	No	No	Yes	Yes	Yes	Yes[q]	Yes[q]	Yes[q]	Local	Local	State & Local	ASHRAE 90-75	ICBO
Ohio	Yes	No	No	Yes	Yes	Yes	Yes	Yes	Yes	Local	Local	State & Local	Ohio Standards	Ohio state-wide building code
Oklahoma	No	No	No[r]					No	No (Legislation mandatory)					
Oregon	Yes	No	No	Yes	Yes	Yes	Yes	No	No	Local & State	Local & State	State & Local	ASHRAE 90-75	ICBO
Pennsylvania	No	No	Yes	(Yes)	(Yes)	(Yes)	(Yes)	(Yes)	(Yes)	(Local)	(Local)	(State & Local)	(ASHRAE 90-75)	(BOCA)

[p] Public Service Commission promulgated (4/1/77) standards for 1, 2, 3, and 4 family dwellings. Enactment of pending legislation expected within weeks.

[q] Mandatory in jurisdictions that have building codes. In other areas standards are legally enforced.

If no local building code, statewide code applies. Since Ohio is home rule state, enforcement of statewide code limited.

[r] Legislation defeated in 1978 session. State may resubmit legislation in 1979.

Oregon Energy Conservation Board will recommend that the Structural Codes Advisory Board approve mandatory standard for nonresidential buildings. This can be achieved without legislation. Approval by September 1978.

Legislative prognosis: Good.

(continued)

State	State Authority to Issue Energy Conservation Standards for Buildings		Legislative Authority Pending	Authority Applies to Following Building Types			Energy Conservation Standards Mandatory			Enforcement: State and Local Governments			Technical Basis for Standards	Model Code—Adopted, Modified, or Considered	Remarks
	Legislative	Other		Residential	Nonresidential	Public	Residential	Nonresidential	Public	Residential	Nonresidential	Public			
Rhode Island	Yes	No	No	Yes	Yes	Yes	Yes	Yes	Yes	Local & State	Local & State	State & Local	ASHRAE 90-75	BOCA	
South Carolina	No	No	Yes	(Yes)	(Yes)	(Yes)	(Yes)	(Yes)	(Yes)	(Local) & State	(Local)	(State & Local)	(ASHRAE 90-75)	(SBCC)	
South Dakota	No	No	No[s]												[s]Legislation in 1977 defeated. State plans to introduce legislation in 1979 session.
Tennessee	Yes	No	No	Yes	Yes	Yes	Yes	Yes	Yes	Local	Local	State & Local	ASHRAE 90-75	NCSBCS SBCC	Legislation passed during 1978 session to become effective 1/1/79.
Texas	Yes[t]	No	No	—	—	Yes	—	—	Yes	Local	Local	State	ASHRAE 90-75	NCSBCS	[t]State buildings only. Under state Energy Conservation Plan, testing NCSBCS in several cities. Presently no plans to introduce legislation mandating statewide energy conservation standards for all buildings.
Utah	Yes	No	No	Yes	Yes	Yes	Yes[u]	Yes[u]	Yes[u]	Local	Local	State & Local	ASHRAE 90-75	NCSBCS	[u]Local governments can reject if they adopt standards that are equal to or exceed state standards.
Vermont	No	No	No[v]	Yes[v]	Yes[v]	Yes[v]	Yes[v]	Yes[v]	Yes[v]	—	—	—	ASHRAE 90-75	NCSBCS	[v]Legislation enacted (2/10/78) to study and recommend standards. Should result in legislation being introduced in 1979 session.

State									Enforcement			ASHRAE	Code	Notes
Virginia	Yes	No	Yes	Yes	Yes	Yes	Yes	Yes	Local	Local	State & Local	ASHRAE 90-75	Residential—Virginia Uniform State Building Code; Nonresidential—BOCA	
Washington	Yes	No	Yes[w]	—	—	Yes	—	—	Local	—	—	ASHRAE 90-75	ICBO	[w] Residential not to exceed three stories. Legislation on nonresidential will be introduced in 1979 legislative session.
West Virginia	No	No	—	No	No	—	—	—	—	—	—			Legislation defeated in 1978 session. State plans to introduce similar legislation in 1979 session.
Wisconsin	Yes	No	Yes	Yes	Yes	Yes	Yes	Yes	Local & State	Local & State	State & Local	ASHRAE 90-75	State Code	Regulations for community public buildings in effect; new regulations going beyond ASHRAE 90-75 take effect 7/1/78. Regulations for residential dwellings going beyond ASHRAE effective 12/1/78.
Wyoming	Yes	No	No[y]	Yes	Yes	—	Yes	—	—	State & Local	State & Local	ASHRAE 90-75	ICBO	[y] State plans to introduce legislation in 1979 session covering thermal efficiency standards for residential buildings.

LEGEND:

( ) — Actions Pending

ASHRAE — American Society of Heating, Refrigerating, and Air-conditioning Engineers, Inc.

ASHRAE 90-75 — "Energy Conservation in New Building Design"

BOCA — Building Officials and Code Administrators, International

ICBO — International Conference of Building Officials

NCSBCS — National Conference of States on Building Codes and Standards, Inc.

SBCC — Southern Building Code Congress, International

APPENDIX B: State Contacts*

State	Energy Policy	Standards Administration	Standards Enforcement	Building Codes and Standards
Alabama	Alabama Development Office State Capitol Montgomery, Ala. 36130 205-832-6960	Alabama Energy Management Board State Capitol Montgomery, Ala. 36130 205-832-5010	State Building Commission State Office Building 501 Dexter Avenue Montgomery, Ala. 36104 205-832-3404 (state buildings)	Director of Technical Staff State Building Commission State Office Building 501 Dexter Avenue Montgomery, Ala. 36104 205-832-3404
Alaska	Division of Energy Power and Development Department of Commerce and Economic Development 338 Denali Street Anchorage, Alaska 99501 907-274-8655			State Fire Marshal Department of Public Safety Pouch N Juneau, Alaska 99801 907-586-2946
Arizona	Office of Economic Planning and Development State Capitol Building, West Wing 1700 West Washington, 4th Floor Phoenix, Ariz. 85007 602-271-5371	Department of Administration 1700 West Washington Phoenix, Ariz. 85007 602-271-4029	Department of Administration (state buildings) and Local Governments	Division of Building Codes State of Arizona 1645 West Jefferson Phoenix, Arizona 85007 602-271-4072
Arkansas	State Energy Office 960 Plaza West Building Little Rock, Ark. 72205 501-371-1379	Same		Department of Local Services Suite 900, First National Bank Building Little Rock, Ark. 72201 501-371-1211

California	Energy Resources Conservation and Development Commission 1111 Howe Avenue Sacramento, Cal. 95825 916-322-3690	Same	Local Governments	Department of Housing and Community Development 921 Tenth Street Sacramento, Cal. 95814 916-445-4775
Colorado	Office of Energy Conservation Office of the Governor State Capitol Denver, Colo. 80203 303-839-2507	Energy Conservation Code Advisory Committee (residential) Board for Energy Efficient Building Standards (nonresidential) State Capitol	Local Governments	Division of Housing State of Colorado 1313 Sherman Street, Room 523 Denver, Colo. 80203 303-892-2033
Connecticut	Division of Energy Office of Policy and Management 20 Grand Street Hartford, Conn. 06115 203-566-2800	Energy Programs Management Division of Energy Office of Policy and Management 20 Grand Street Hartford, Conn. 06115 203-566-2800	Local Governments	State Building Inspector Public Works Department 525 State Office Building Hartford, Conn. 06115 203-566-4036
Delaware	Governor's Energy Office Townsend Building Dover, Del. 19901 302-678-5644	Energy Conservation Plan Office of Management, Budget and Planning Dover, Del. 19901 302-678-5621		State Fire Marshal P.O. Box 109 Dover, Del. 19901 302-478-4893

(continued)

117

*Published by National Institute of Building Sciences, 1730 Pennsylvania Avenue N.W., Suite 425, Washington, D.C. 20006, ©1978; reproduced with permission.

State	Energy Policy	Standards Administration	Standards Enforcement	Building Codes and Standards
District of Columbia	Energy Conservation Office Municipal Planning 14th and E Streets, N.W. Washington, D.C. 20004 202-629-2631	Office of Housing and Community Development Building and Zoning Regulation Administration 614 H Street, N.W. Washington, D.C. 20001 202-724-8943	Same	Office of Housing and Community Development Bureau of Building, Housing and Zoning 614 H Street, N.W. Washington, D.C. 20001 202-629-5050
Florida	State Energy Office Bryant Building, Room 301 Tallahassee, Fla. 32304 904-488-6764	Same	Local Governments	Bureau of Codes and Standards Department of Community Affairs 2571 Executive Center Circle, East Tallahassee, Fla. 32301 904-488-3581
Georgia	Office of Energy Resources Office of Planning and Budget 270 Washington Street, S.W. Atlanta, Ga. 30334 404-656-3874	State Building Administrative Board 166 Pryor Street, S.W. Atlanta, Ga. 30303 404-656-3930	Local Governments	State Building Administrative Board 166 Pryor Street, S.W. Atlanta, Ga. 30303 404-656-3930
Hawaii	Department of Planning and Economic Development P.O. Box 2359 Honolulu, Hawaii 96804 808-548-6914	State Energy Office Department of Planning and Economic Development P.O. Box 2359 Honolulu, Hawaii 96804 808-548-4080	Local Governments	Building Superintendent City and County of Honolulu 650 South King Street Honolulu, Hawaii 96813 808-523-4716

State				
Idaho	Office of Energy State House Boise, Idaho 83720 208-384-3258	State and Local Governments	Building Code Advisory Board Idaho Department of Labor and Industrial Services 317 Main Street, Room 400 Boise, Idaho 83720 208-384-2327	Bureau of Uniform Building Safety Idaho Department of Labor and Industrial Services 317 Main Street, Room 400 Boise, Idaho 83720 208-384-2327
Illinois	Division of Energy 222 South College Springfield, Ill. 62705 217-782-2811	Local Governments	Same	Capital Development Board Stratton Office Building, 3rd. Floor Springfield, Ill. 62706 217-782-2864
Indiana	Energy Group 7th Floor, Consolidated Building 115 North Pennsylvania Street Indianapolis, Ind. 46204 317-633-6753	Local Governments	Energy Conservation Division Administrative Building Council 215 North Senate Avenue Indianapolis, Ind. 46204 317-633-5433	State Building Commissioner Administrative Building Council 215 North Senate Avenue, #300 Indianapolis, Ind. 46204 317-633-5433
Iowa	Iowa Energy Policy Council 215 East Seventh Des Moines, Iowa 50319 515-281-4420	Local Governments	Office of Planning and Programming State Capitol Complex 523 East Twelfth Des Moines, Iowa 50319 515-281-3807	State Building Code Commissioner State Capitol Complex 523 East Twelfth Des Moines, Iowa 50319 515-281-3807
Kansas	Energy Office 2nd Floor 503 Kansas Avenue Topeka, Kansas 66603 913-295-2496	Local Utilities Commissions	Kansas Corporation Commission 4th Floor State Office Building Topeka, Kansas 66612 913-296-3325	Division of Architectural Services State Office Building Topeka, Kansas 66612 913-296-3811

(continued)

State	Energy Policy	Standards Administration	Standards Enforcement	Building Codes and Standards
Kentucky	Department of Energy Capitol Plaza Tower, 9th Floor Frankfort, Ky. 40601 502-564-7070	State Department of Housing Capitol Tower Building Frankfort, Ky. 40601 502-564-3626	Local Governments and State Fire Marshal	Department of Housing and State Fire Marshal Capitol Tower Building Frankfort, Ky. 40601 502-564-3626
Louisiana	Research and Development Division Department of Natural Resources P.O. Box 44156 Baton Rouge, La. 70804 504-389-2771	Department of Natural Resources P.O. Box 44396 Baton Rouge, La. 70804 504-389-2866	Department of Natural Resources and Local Governments	State Fire Marshal 8941 Jefferson Highway Baton Rouge, La. 70809 504-389-7409 and Local Governments
Maine	Office of Energy Resources State House Augusta, Maine 04333 207-289-2196	Commission on Energy Efficiency Building Performance Standards State House Augusta, Maine 04333 207-289-2196	State Department of Finance and Administration Bureau of Public Improvements Augusta, Maine 04333 207-289-3881 (state buildings)	Bureau of Public Improvements State of Maine Augusta, Maine 04333 207-289-3881
Maryland	Energy Policy Office State of Maryland 301 West Preston Street Baltimore, Md. 21201 301-383-6810	Department of Economic and Community Development 1748 Forest Drive Annapolis, Md. 21401 301-269-2701	Local Governments	Director, Codes Administration Department of Economic and Community Development 1748 Forest Drive Annapolis, Md. 21401 301-269-2701

State				
Massachusetts	Massachusetts Energy Policy Office McCormack Building, 14th Floor 1 Ashburton Place Boston, Mass. 02108 617-727-4732	State Building Code Commission McCormack Building, Room 1305 1 Ashburton Place Boston, Mass. 02108 617-727-6916	Local Governments	State Building Code Commission McCormack Building, Room 1305 1 Ashburton Place Boston, Mass. 02108 617-727-6916
Michigan	Energy Administration Michigan Department of Commerce Law Building, 4th Floor Lansing, Michigan 48913 517-374-9090	Michigan Department of Labor Bureau of Construction Codes 7150 Harris Drive Lansing, Michigan 48909 517-322-1798	Local Governments and Bureau of Construction Codes	Director, Michigan Department of Labor 309 N. Washington P.O. Box 30015 Lansing, Michigan 48909 517-373-9600
Minnesota	Minnesota Energy Agency Conservation Division 150 E. Kellogg Boulevard St. Paul, Minn. 55101 612-296-8894	Building Code Division 408 Metro Square 7th & Robert St. Paul, Minn. 55101 612-296-4639	Local Governments	Assistant Commissioner Department of Administration 50 Sherburne Avenue St. Paul, Minn. 55155 612-296-7037
Mississippi	Mississippi Fuel and Energy Management Commission Woolfolk Street, Office Building, Room 1307 Jackson, Miss. 39202 601-354-5792	State Building Commission P.O. Box 2108 Jackson, Miss. 39205 601-354-6326	Local Governments and State Building Commission	Mississippi Municipal Association 2301 Sun-N-Sand Building Jackson, Miss. 39202 601-353-5854
Missouri	Missouri Energy Agency Department of Natural Resources P.O. Box 1309 Jefferson City, Missouri 65101 314-751-4000	Building Code Authority	Department of Consumer Affairs, Regulation and Licensing	Director, Division of Mobile Homes State of Missouri Jefferson Building Jefferson City, Missouri 65101 314-751-2557

(continued)

State	Energy Policy	Standards Administration	Standards Enforcement	Building Codes and Standards
Montana	Energy Research and Conservation Office Route 310, Power Block 7 West 6th Avenue Helena, Montana 59601 406-449-3940	State Building Codes Division Capitol Station State of Montana Helena, Montana 59601 406-449-3933	Local Government and Building Codes Division	Montana Building Codes Advisory Council P.O. Box 6177 C.M. Russell Station Great Falls, Montana 59406 406-452-0791
Nebraska	State Energy Office P.O. Box 94841 Lincoln, Neb. 68509 402-471-2867	Same	Local Governments and State Energy Office	Office of Housing and Environmental Health Nebraska Department of Health 301 Centennial Mall South Lincoln, Neb. 68509 402-471-2541
Nevada	Department of Energy 1050 East Williams, Room 405 Carson City, Nevada 89710 702-885-5157	State Public Works Board 505 East King Street, Room 400 Carson City, Nevada 89710 702-885-4870	Local Governments	Nevada State Planning Board 505 East King Street, Room 400 Carson City, Nevada 89710 702-885-4870
New Hampshire	Governor's Council on Energy 26 Pleasant Street Concord, N.H. 03301 603-271-2711	Department of Public Works John O. Morton Building Concord, N.H. 03301 603-271-3731	Local Governments and Department of Public Works	Governor's Council on Energy 26 Pleasant Street Concord, N.H. 03301 603-271-2711
New Jersey	Department of Energy 1100 Raymond Boulevard Newark, N.J. 07102 201-648-2017	Department of Community Affairs Bureau of Housing Inspection P.O. Box 2768 Trenton, N.J. 08625 609-292-5984	Same	Division of Housing and Urban Renewal Bureau of Housing Inspection 363 West State Street Trenton, N.J. 08625 609-292-6415

State				
New Mexico	Division of Energy Conservation and Management P.O. Box 2770 Santa Fe, New Mexico 87501 505-827-2386	Construction Industries Commission P.O. Box 5155 Santa Fe, New Mexico 87503 505-827-2085	Same	Same
New York	New York State Energy Office Agency Building 2, 9th Floor Empire State Plaza Albany, New York 12223 518-474-1785	New York State Energy Office and Public Service Commission Agency Building 3 Empire State Plaza Albany, New York 12223 518-474-2528	Public Service Commission and Local Governments	Housing and Building Codes Bureau Division of Housing and Community Renewal Two World Trade Center New York, New York 10047 212-488-7080
North Carolina	Division of Policy Development Department of Administration Administration Building Raleigh, N.C. 27611 919-733-4131	Energy Office, Conservation Programs Department of Commerce P.O. Box 25249 Raleigh, N.C. 27611 919-733-4962	Local Governments	Deputy Commissioner Engineering Division Department of Insurance P.O. Box 26387 Raleigh, N.C. 27611 919-733-3901
North Dakota	Energy Coordinator Energy Management Office, Governor's Office 1533 North 12th Street Bismarck, N.D. 58505 701-224-2250	Office of the Secretary of State Bismarck, N.D. 58501 701-224-2900	Local Governments	
Ohio	Energy and Resource Development Agency State Office Tower 30 East Broad Street Columbus, Ohio 43215 614-466-3465	Board of Building Standards Department of Industrial Relations 2323 West 5th Avenue P.O. Box 825 Columbus, Ohio 43216 614-466-3316	Same	Building Commissioner Municipal Building High and Monument Streets Hamilton, Ohio 45011 513-868-5882

(continued)

State	Energy Policy	Standards Administration	Standards Enforcement	Building Codes and Standards
Oklahoma	Oklahoma Department of Energy 440 N. Lincoln Boulevard Oklahoma City, Okla. 73105 405-521-3941	Same		Engineering Department State Board of Public Affairs State Capitol Building, Room 306 Oklahoma City, Okla. 73105 405-521-2111
Oregon	Department of Energy 111 Labor and Industries Building Salem, Ore. 97310 503-378-8607	Department of Commerce Building Codes Division 401 Labor and Industries Building Salem, Ore. 97310 503-378-3176	Local Governments and Building Codes Division	Department of Commerce Building Codes Division 401 Labor and Industries Building Salem, Ore. 97310 503-378-3176
Pennsylvania	Governor's Energy Council 410 Payne-Shoemaker Building Harrisburg, Pa. 17120 717-787-9749	Building Energy Conservation Committee	Department of Community Affairs—residential; Department of Labor and Industry—nonresidential	Division of Industrialized and Mobile Housing State Office Building, Room 500 Harrisburg, Pa. 17120 717-787-9682
Rhode Island	Governor's Energy Office 80 Dean Street Providence, R.I. 02903 401-277-3370	State Building Commission 12 Humbert Street North Providence, R.I. 02911 401-277-3032	Local Governments and State Building Commission	State Building Commission 12 Humbert Street North Providence, R.I. 02911 401-277-3032
South Carolina	Energy Management Office Edgar A. Brown Building 1205 Pendleton Street Columbia, S.C. 29201 803-758-2050	Same	Local Governments	Division of Inspection Services 300 Gervais Street Columbia, S.C. 29201 803-758-2941

State				
South Dakota	Office of Energy Policy Capital Lake Plaza Pierre, S.D. 57501 605-773-3603		Board of Architectural and Engineering Examiners and State Engineers	State Engineer State Office Building #2 Pierre, S.D. 57501 605-773-3466
Tennessee	Tennessee Energy Authority 250 Capitol Hill Building 7th and Union Nashville, Tenn. 37219 615-741-2994	Same	Local Governments	Division of Fire Prevention 202 Capitol Towers Building Nashville, Tenn. 37219 615-741-2981
Texas	Texas Energy Advisory Council 7703 North Lamar Boulevard Austin, Texas 78752 512-475-5588 and Governors Office of Energy Resources 512-475-5491	State Board of Control P.O. Box 13047 Capitol Station Austin, Texas 78711 512-475-2323 (state buildings only)	State Board of Control (state buildings only)	Division of Housing Department of Community Affairs P.O. Box 13166 Capitol Station Austin, Texas 78711 512-475-3383
Utah	Energy Council 118 State Capitol Building Salt Lake City, Utah 84114 801-533-6491	State Building Board 124 State Capitol Salt Lake City, Utah 84114 801-533-5561	Local Governments	State Building Board 124 State Capitol Salt Lake City, Utah 84114 801-533-5561
Vermont	State Energy Office 110 State Street Montpelier, Vt. 05602 802-828-2768	Same		Commissioner, Department of Labor and Industries State Office Building Montpelier, Vt. 05602 802-828-2106
Virginia	State Energy Office 823 East Main Street Richmond, Va. 23219 804-786-8451	State Board of Housing 6 North 6th Street, Suite 202 Richmond, Va. 23219 804-786-7891	Local Governments	State Fire Marshal P.O. Box 1157 Richmond, Va. 23219 804-786-4751

(continued)

State	Energy Policy	Standards Administration	Standards Enforcement	Building Codes and Standards
Washington	State Energy Office 400 East Union, First Floor Olympia, Wash. 98504 206-753-2417	Same	Local Governments	Department of Labor and Industry General Administration Building Olympia, Wash. 98504 206-753-6307
West Virginia	Fuel and Energy Office Office of Federal-State Relations 1262-½ Greenbrier Street Charleston, W. Va. 25311 304-348-8860			State Fire Marshal State Capitol, Unit 1 1800 Washington Street, East Charleston, W. Va. 25305 304-348-2191
Wisconsin	Office of State Planning and Energy 1 West Wilson Street Madison, Wisc. 53702 608-266-6850	Department of Industry, Labor and Human Relations Safety and Buildings Division 201 East Washington Avenue Madison, Wisc. 53701 608-266-3151	Local Governments and Safety and Buildings Division	Safety and Buildings Division 201 East Washington Avenue Madison, Wisc. 53701 608-266-3151
Wyoming	Department of Economic Planning and Development Office of Energy Conservation Barrett Building Cheyenne, Wyo. 82002 307-777-7131	Fire Marshal's Office 720 West 18th Street Cheyenne, Wyo. 82002 307-638-6509	Same	Same

126

*Published by National Institute of Building Sciences, 1730 Pennsylvania Avenue N.W., Suite 425, Washington, D.C. 20006, ©1978; reproduced with permission.

NOTES

1. P.L. 94-385, enacted by Congress August 10, 1976, signed by President Ford August 14, 1976; amended by P.L. 95-70, July 21, 1977.

2. P.L. 94-163, enacted by Congress December 17, 1975, signed by President Ford December 22, 1975; amended by P.L. 94-385, August 14, 1976; P.L. 95-70, July 21, 1977.

3. Personal communication with Dr. Robert H. Socolow, Center for Environmental Studies, Princeton University.

4. The divergence between sound economic analysis and consumer behavior is discussed in the context of consumer purchases of energy-conserving appliances in Jerry A. Hausman, "A Model of Consumer Purchase and Utilization and Energy Using Durables: Calculating Individual Discount Rates from Observed Market Behavior." (Work supported by National Science Foundation, MIT Energy Laboratory, and the Electric Power Institute). Professor Hausman derives consumer discount rates that are substantially higher than those used in conventional engineering and economic analysis. Professor Hausman notes, "Energy conservation through improved technology may have difficulty succeeding if consumers do have such a high discount rate."

5. Chevron Research Company, Richmond, California, "Home Energy Conservation Demonstration Project," December 1975.

6. Jeffrey C. Cohen and Ronald H. White, Citizens for Clean Air, *Energy Conservation in Buildings: The New York Metropolitan Region* (Washington, D.C.: Environmental Law Institute, 1975).

7. "Making the Most of Your Energy Dollars in Home Heating & Cooling" (Washington, D.C.: U.S. Government Printing Office, #C13.53:8); "In the Bank . . . or Up the Chimney" (Washington, D.C.: U.S. Government Printing Office, Number 012-000-00297-3). Both are available from the Superintendent of Documents, U.S. Government Printing Office, Washington, D.C. 20402.

8. Owens-Corning Fiberglas Corporation, Insulation Operating Division, Fiberglas Tower, Toledo, Ohio 43659: "Energy Saving Homes: The Arkansas Story," Publication No. 4-BL-6958-C, June 1976.

9. See, "Proceedings of the Conference on Energy Conservation in Commercial, Residential, and Industrial Buildings" (Fawcett Center for Tomorrow, Ohio State University, Columbus, Ohio May 5-7, 1974), available from National Technical Information Service. Remarks are in "ASHRAE's Views on the NBS 'Draft Design and Evaluation Criteria for Energy Conservation in New Buildings'," p. 49.

10. P.L. 94-163, § 362 *et seq.*

11. 10 CFR 420.35, 41 *Federal Register* 8335, February 26, 1976; amended by 41 *Federal Register* 48325, November 3, 1976.

12. *Code for Energy Conservation in New Building Construction*, December 1977. Jointly Prepared by Building Officials & Code Administrators International, International Conference of Building Officials, National Conference of States on Building Codes and Standards, and Southern Building Code Congress International.

13. U.S. Department of Energy, *A Training Program for Energy Conservation in New Building Construction*, 4 vols. (December 1977). Available from National Technical Information Service, U.S. Department of Commerce.

14. ASHRAE Standard 90-75, § 2.1.1.

15. *Id.* at § 2.12.

16. *Id.* at § 1.2.

17. *Id.* at § 3.0.

18. *Id.* at § 8.6.

19. Federal Energy Administration, "Energy Conservation in New Building Design, An Impact Assessment of ASHRAE Standard 90-75," Conservation Paper Number 43B, p. 5.

20. The federal interagency committee convened to comment on a draft of Standard 90-75 developed the notion of the resource utilization factor and referred to it in the following terms:

> Thus the RUF may be defined as: A multiplier, applied to the quantity of energy delivered to the site, which provides quantitative estimates of the resources consumed in providing that energy. This multiplier accounts for the burdens of processing, refining, transporting, converting and delivering energy from the point of extraction to the building site.

See Harry H. Phipps, *ASHRAE Journal*, May 1976, p. 29.

21. Phipps, *supra*, note 20 at 28.

22. P.L. 94-385 § 303(9).

23. *Id.* at § 304(b).

24. *Id.* at § 304(a).

25. *Id.* at § 305(c).

26. *Id.* at § 305(a)(3).

27. *Id.*

28. Advance Notice of Proposed Rulemaking and Notice of Public Meetings, Title 10—Energy, Chapter II—Department of Energy, Subchapter D—Energy Conservation, Part 435—Energy Performance Standards for New Buildings. 43 *Federal Register* 54512 (November 21, 1978).

29. For an account of the development of the materials that underlie the BEPS, see Ray Rhinehart, "Baseline," in *Research & Design* (The Quarterly of the AIA Research Corporation) I, no. 4 (October 1978): 9 *et seq.*

30. Article 678i, Texas Civil Statutes.

31. National Association of Home Builders, *Thermal Performance Guidelines* (Wasinhgton, D.C., 1978). Copies are available from the National Association of Home Builders, 15th and M Streets Northwest, Washington, D.C. 20005, for $3.00.

32. Ordinance Number 228, August 10, 1976, Troutdale, Oregon. Available from Clerk, 104 Kibling Street, Troutdale, Oregon 97060.

33. See, R.H. Socolow, "Energy Conservation in Existing Residences: Your Home Deserves a House Call" (Paper presented at Energy Efficiency as a National Priority conference sponsored by Public Citizen, Inc., May 20, 1976, Washington, D.C.).

34. Indiana, Sen. Enrolled Act No. 223 S.L. 1974.

35. Robert M. Eisenhard, *Building Energy Authority and Regulations Survey: State Activity* (Washington, D.C.: National Bureau of Standards, Report Number NBSIR 76-986, (March 1976). See also, Patrick W. Cooke and Robert M. Eisenhard, *Building Energy Conservation Programs—A Preliminary Examination of Regulatory Activities at the State Level* (Washington, D.C.: Center for Building Technology, National Bureau of Standards, Report Number NBSIR 77-1259, June 1977).

36. New York State Public Service Commission, Case 26292, "Report on Energy Conservation in Space Conditioning," in *Recommended Decision of Presiding Commissioner* (Albany, N.Y., January 1974), p. 284.

37. New York State Laws of 1974, Chapter 824.

38. Federal Energy Administration, "Project Conserve Briefing Sheet" (n.d.).

39. For a report of this multiyear, multidiscipline project see the April 1978 issue of *Energy and Buildings* 1, no. 3, which is devoted entirely to reports on Twin Rivers. See also, R.H. Socolow, "The Twin Rivers Program on Energy Conservation in Housing: Highlights and Conclusions" (August 1978), available from National Technical Information Services. The articles in *Energy and Buildings* are published separately as *Saving Energy in the Home, Princeton's Experiments at Twin Rivers*, Robert H. Socolow, ed. (Cambridge, Massachusetts: Ballinger Publishing Company, 1978).

40. This account and other figures are drawn from a report to the Public Service Commission by Joel A. Sharkey. See also, reports filed monthly with the commission in compliance with Case Number U-4404.

41. *Insulation Reporter* (Published by the National Mineral Wool Insulation Association, 382 Springfield Avenue, Summit, N.J. 07901), December 1976–January 1977, p. 1.

42. See, *Utility Sponsored Home Insulation Programs* (Washington, D.C.: U.S. Department of Energy, Economic Regulatory Administration and Assistant Secretary for Conservation and Solar Applications, HCP/W1227-01, June 1978).

43. Chapter 548, Montana Session Laws 1975 (House Bill 663), effective July 1, 1975. See "Energy Conservation and The Law," in *ASHRAE Journal*, 18, no. 5, (May 1976): p. 18, for an account of this law.

44. Letter on file, Environmental Law Institute.

45. See, "Oregon Electric Customers Flock to Utilities' Free Lunch," *The Energy Daily*, Friday, September 1, 1978, p. 3.

46. William Rosenberg, "Conservation Investments by Gas Utilities as a Gas Supply Option," *Public Utilities Fortnightly*, January 20, 1977, p. 17.

47. *Id.* at 18.

48. For a description of this plan, see James J. Tanner, "Building an Incentive for Home Insulation," *Public Utilities Fortnightly*, October 21, 1976.

49. Information from Curt Miller, supervisor, Loans and Grants, St. Paul, Minnesota.

50. Information from Mark Campbell, finance officer, Housing Resources, Minneapolis Housing Redevelopment Authority.

51. Information from James Cegla, supervisor, Home Improvement Loan Program, Minnesota Housing Finance Agency Program.

52. Queenside Hills Realty Co. v. Saxl, 328 U.S. 80 (1946).

53. California Assembly Bill #724, February 6, 1975.

Chapter 4

Lighting Controls to Save Energy

In preelectricity days, the value of lighting conservation was a quantity easily measured. Melville, writing in *Moby Dick*, could admonish his readers: "For God's sake, be economical with your lamps and candles! not a gallon you burn, but at least one drop of man's blood was spilled for it."[1] With the advent of electric lighting, the connection between turning on a light switch and damage to man or his environment seems far more remote. Yet the link between excessive or unnecessary lighting and natural resource protection is just as strong now as it was in Melville's day. Building lighting consumes a significant percentage of the electrical energy generated in this country: in 1972, direct lighting in offices consumed around 30 percent of the total electrical energy input into buildings; for the nation, lighting is estimated to consume over 20 percent of generated electricity.[2]

Because there are few practical alternatives to electric lighting, building owners and state and local governments must look to strategies that eliminate the use of lighting at certain times, that make existing lighting more efficient, or that reduce the amount of lighting where present custom is excessive. These strategies are designed to make do with less, since there are few ways to do without. This chapter will identify current problems in the way we use lighting and will explain the policy and regulatory strategies available to states and localities to reduce the energy devoted to lights.

GENERAL METHODS FOR SAVING LIGHTING ENERGY

A number of current practices waste lighting energy. Because lights are so much a part of our daily world that we tend to ignore them, it is helpful to identify a number of those practices and to suggest alternatives.

Use of More Efficient Light Sources

Most homeowners are familiar with ordinary incandescent light bulbs and with tubular florescent lights. But many are unaware of the difference in efficiencies between the two types. Energy needed for lighting could be reduced by 70 percent by replacing incandescent with fluorescent lighting, which produces three times the light with the same amount of electricity. Moreover, additional savings are possible because incandescent lights also produce significant amounts of heat that must be removed during the hot months. (Of course, the advantage of that heat during the heating season is also lost, but air conditioning is generally more consumptive of basic resources than is heating.)

Even more energy efficient than incandescent or fluorescent bulbs are high intensity discharge lamps (HID), often used for outdoor area lighting or in gymnasiums. Other highly efficient bulbs are either in use or under development. For example, the Department of Energy gave substantial funding to the development of a bulb that screws into ordinary sockets but works by generating a radio frequency signal that sets up a magnetic field. This field excites atoms, causing a phosphor layer to glow. The so-called LITEK bulb is not yet perfected, and government funds are no longer devoted to the project, but commercial manufacturers are picking up the development of the device.

The possibilities for saving energy through increased lighting efficiency are suggested in Table 4-1.

Table 4-1. Approximate Light Output in Lumens Per Watt (Including Ballast).

Lamp Used as Light Source	Smaller Sizes	Middle Sizes	Larger Sizes
Low Pressure Sodium[a]	90	120	150
High Pressure Sodium	85	105	125
Metal Halide	65	75	95
Fluorescent	65	75	70
Mercury	45	50	55
Incandescent	17	22	24

[a]Interior applications of this efficient light source are very limited because of poor color rendition. The light output is a monochromatic yellow that transforms other colors to shades of grey. It should not be used in areas where it is necessary to distinguish color.

Source: "Optional Lighting Standards for Existing Buildings," adopted June 12, 1978 (CON-19B:01) by the California Energy Resources Conservation and Development Commission, p. 17.

Unfortunately, a number of the current alternatives to the incandescent light bulb have characteristics that make them undesirable in some circumstances. HID lamps cannot be used in applications where they are turned on and off repeatedly; fluorescent lights have a color that some find unappealing when compared to the yellowish incandescent light. But these are technical problems that can be solved; in some cases, it would be worth reeducating one's taste to achieve the savings possible. For example, if two 100 watt bulbs are replaced by one fluorescent source, over a period of 2,700 hours, 400 kilowatt hours of electricity will be saved, amounting to almost $17 in a year.[3] In Mecklenburg County, North Carolina, converting the light sources in one building from incandescent to fluorescent resulted in a savings of $5,910 for the life of the lamps and reduced electrical consumption by 14 percent.

Other success stories abound. In San Francisco, the Crowley Maritime Corporation spent an extra $130,000 on office furnishings that either incorporate lighting fixtures within them or maximize the use of available light. Lighting levels vary from task to task; photocells turn off lights when not needed. Instead of the conventional 5 watts per square foot allocated to lighting, Crowley uses 1.7 watts per square foot, and the burden on air conditioning is reduced, so that only about half the amount is used compared to other tenants in the same building. Because of individual metering, Crowley saves on its lease payments and expects to get back the extra expenses in seven years. Moreover, as an article in *Fortune* magazine points out, there is a hidden tax advantage as well. Because the furnishings are written off by Crowley in seven years, it can lower its taxes through depreciation and investment tax credit. Best of all, the benefit goes to Crowley rather than to the owner of the building.

ARCO's offices in Philadelphia, covering twenty floors of a large office complex, save 3,888,000 kilowatt hours per year over conventional designs; the cost savings is approximately $155,000 per year![4]

More Efficient Light Fixtures
The design of the lighting fixture (luminaire, in the language of lighting engineers) itself can influence the light efficiency. Well-designed luminaires direct the maximum amount of light to the task at hand. Placement of the fixture can influence how efficiently the light it produces reaches the work surface. Perhaps as important as design is regular cleaning and maintenance of the fixtures so that dust does not absorb the lighting energy paid for. This subject is

a difficult one for law to control, other than by enforcing regular cleaning schedules for government-owned buildings and educating consumers on the importance of cleanliness.

Lighting According to the Needs of the Actual Task

One of the greatest misuses of lighting is providing it at a uniformly high level without taking the lower lighting requirements of particular tasks into account. Offices are usually lighted to deal with the most visually demanding tasks (such as bookkeeping) even though most of the activity within the office is visually relatively undemanding. It is impossible when designing a building to know in advance the level of illumination required for work stations, but once a building is occupied, lower general lighting supplemented by task lights, grouping of similar tasks together, use of natural light through windows, and replacing ordinary on-off switches with variable level controls are possible ways to operate efficiently while minimizing the energy required for lighting. One development to be applauded—on energy conservation grounds, at least—is the development of "open offices" that provide soft general upward lighting on the ceiling and more intense desk lights (individually switchable) as required.

Use of Daylight Where Possible

There have been some experiments with reflective shutter designs that spread outside light onto the ceilings of offices and homes, providing a good general lighting level without the need for electric fixtures. These designs, when combined with variable level lighting (preferably automatically controlled), can save enormous amounts of energy.[5]

Improved Lighting Control Circuits

Matching lighting to the actual task being performed is difficult or impossible in the absence of proper control systems. Switching systems should be designed at the building construction stage to provide future occupants with the maximum number of points for turning individual lights on and off. A common practice has been to put an entire suite or floor of a building on one switch. This practice had been justified by the labor savings made possible through eliminating wiring and control switch installation during construction. A result of this initial economy is that a single late office worker has to turn on the lights in many offices—perhaps even an entire floor—just to have light in one office. The problem is similar for janitors, whose room-by-room travels are heralded only as they change floors. A simple solution to this problem is to put light switches in each office or small section of the open space; more sophisticated building designs can place lights under central control, with manual override for the single office that is used on an occasional night or weekend. Some computer-controlled office lighting systems even keep the custodial staff on schedule by switching on one section of lights long enough for cleaning, then switching on lights in a new area, turning off the lights in the cleaned offices. Finally, controls integrated with the outside daylight relate actual need to an objective standard.

Lighting Integrated With Other Building Systems

Although energy-savings modifications in a lighting system would appear to be uncomplicated and an unmixed blessing, lighting in large structures cannot be modified without considering the effect that modification has on the heating and cooling loads of a building. The most significant undesirable side effect of lighting is heat production during hot months. Some authorities suggest that when air conditioning is operating, each watt of lighting energy causes one-half watt of air-conditioning power to be consumed. The *Lighting Handbook*, published by the Illuminating Engineering Society, states that each watt generates 3.4 BTUs per hour.[6] Therefore, modifications in lighting must be coordinated with modifications in the heating and cooling systems.

Lower Levels of Illumination

In recent years, trends in lighting have suggested that Americans are becoming blinder. Tasks that formerly could be done under 70 footcandle illumination must now be performed under 100 footcandles, at least if the standards are to be believed. Fortunately, this trend is now being reversed. For example, the HUD Minimum Property Standards that apply to multifamily houses were revised to require less lighting in public areas. Conservation of energy was the basis for the changes, which in many cases reduced by one-half the minimum footcandles of artificial light. Table 4–2 illustrates the changes in the 1973 HUD standards made by the March 1976 revision.

Lower levels of illumination must be handled with care, so that there is sufficient light for the tasks to be accomplished without producing glare or shadows. Removal of existing lighting fixtures (or bulbs, where they are replaced with "phantom" or low level

Table 4-2. Changes in HUD MPS Lighting Standards.

	1973 Edition	*1976 Edition*
Lobby (general)	20	10
Dining	30	15
Corridors	20	10
Stairs	20	10
General Storage	10	5
Laundries	30	20
Garages (general)	10	5

bulbs for safety and conservation) may be the only immediate method open to existing buildings, but for new construction, or when extensive remodeling makes changes possible, flexible controls and multiple fixtures should be adopted.

LIGHTING CONTROLS REQUIRED BY THE ENERGY POLICY AND CONSERVATION ACT

The federal Energy Policy and Conservation Act (EPCA)[7] contains "mandatory lighting efficiency standards for public buildings" as one of the requirements for a state plan to be eligible for federal assistance. In addition to this mandatory requirement, EPCA suggests that states may place "restrictions on the use of decorative or nonessential lighting." The regulations issued by the federal government to guide states in developing lighting standards require that they be at least as strict as those contained in Section 9 of ASHRAE Standard 90-75. States are permitted to determine a building size below which the lighting efficiency standards would not apply, although the federal guidelines are silent on how that determination is to be made.

One further wrinkle of the federal guidelines implementing EPCA is worth noting. EPCA itself makes lighting standards applicable to "public buildings," defined in the statute as "any building which is open to the public during normal business hours." According to Section 362 (c) (1) of EPCA, mandatory lighting standards do not apply to "public buildings owned or leased by the United States." Therefore, EPCA-funded state programs reach solely to nonfederal buildings that are open to the public during normal working hours and that are above a certain size to be determined by each state. Smaller buildings and residences are not controlled.

It is interesting to compare the coverage of these lighting standards with the somewhat broader coverage of the thermal efficiency standards mandated by EPCA. Under Section 362 (c)(4), the thermal efficiency standards apply to all new or renovated non-federal buildings, including private residences. Finally, under the Building Energy Performance Standards now mandated by federal law, thermal efficiency coverage will apply to all new buildings. The reach of the lighting standards is much shorter.

Nothing within EPCA tells a state how small a building may be made subject to lighting controls; only common sense and administrative feasibility serve as limits. However, for constitutional reasons, states do not have the power to control property owned or operated by the federal government. The United States Government (General Services Administration) customarily follows local practices and building codes for convenience and consistency with local safety regulations, but this custom is circumvented (quite lawfully) as necessary.

ENERGY CONSERVATION
LIGHTING STANDARDS

Energy conservation lighting standards have proven difficult to develop in response to the federal mandate. The task is complicated because there is such a variety of visual requirements within buildings. Wristwatch factories have fundamentally different lighting needs from fish hatcheries; file rooms and drafting rooms differ in their needs from cocktail lounges and retail stores. This variety of genuine needs makes it difficult to develop a legal standard covering all situations.

One attempt to develop a lighting standard underlines the difficulty of the exercise. Section 9 of ASHRAE Standard 90-75 was drafted by the Illuminating Engineering Society and simply incorporated into the ASHRAE standard without revision. This section attempts to provide a methodology for determining the lighting power budget of a building. The lighting power budget is defined in Section 9 of ASHRAE Standard 90-75 as "the upper limit of power to be available to provide the lighting needs in accordance with a given set of criteria and given calculation procedures." In other words, Section 9 simply gives a methodology to be followed for finding the maximum number of units of electricity that can be used for lighting within a given building. The budget does not tell a designer how to design the lighting for a building; in fact, Section 9.2.1 states that "once the limit has been determined, the designer should strive to develop the actual lighting system . . . without exceeding the budget limit." Moreover, Section 9 does not apply to private residences (except in kitchens, bathrooms, and laundry areas), in apartments and other residential type space, or in theaters "where the lighting is an essential technical element for the function performed."

The methodology set out in Section 9 determines three figures. First, on a task-by-task basis, the area to be illuminated and the level of illumination are calculated. For areas where no specific tasks are performed, general lighting is to be one-third of the average task lighting. Next, the light sources and fixtures (luminaires) are selected. Using the data on the particular sources and fixtures and working with the lighting levels chosen as part of the first step, the total wattage of the lighting load is determined. To this total wattage, a designer can add medical and dental lamps, lamps used for highlighting art objects and items for sale in a store, and specialized lighting required by particular tasks such as color matching.

The procedures established by Section 9 of ASHRAE Standard 90-75 are difficult to describe adequately in a short section. The technique itself is relatively complex and is probably ultimately unenforceable in practice. For the most part, the section merely exhorts designers to follow good design practice and provides many opportunities for making exceptions to those few rules that are given. The comparative ineffectiveness of Section 9 in contributing to total building energy conservation is underlined by the Arthur D. Little report on the ASHRAE standard as a whole. Although Arthur D. Little admitted that, because of the nature of the calculations, it was difficult to do more than make an educated guess about the role of each section in lowering building energy use, the company did estimate relative effects,[8] as seen in Table 4-3.

From Table 4-3, it is clear that (except for retail stores) in no case does Section 9 contribute its share to reducing energy consumption in buildings. Of course, this test is only the roughest of guides to strictness. Nonetheless, the poor contribution that Section 9 makes to energy conservation in lighting commercial buildings suggests that other, tougher standards should be considered and adopted if and when available.

On the positive side, Section 9 of ASHRAE Standard 90-75 is a start at solving an admittedly difficult problem. It recognizes that careful design controls, including the encouragement of task-oriented lighting and sensible switching systems, can save energy. But a further refinement of the section is clearly needed if it is to be rigorous enough to force more innovative approaches to energy conservation in lighting.

Table 4-3. Effects of ASHRAE Standard 90-75 on Energy Used for Lighting.

Building Type	Percent of Building Energy Use Attributed To Lighting	Total Amount of Energy Saved Using 90-75 (percent)	Amount of Energy Saving From Using Section 9 (percent)
Residential	5	11.3	0
Low-rise Apartments	5	42.7	1.8
Office Buildings	17	59.6	6.3
Retail Stores	21	40.1	8.6
Schools	18	48.1	4.4

Source: Federal Energy Administration *Energy Conservation in New Building Design: An Impact Assessment of ASHRAE Standard 90-75*, Conservation Paper 43B (Washington, D.C: U.S. Government Printing Office, n.d.), from Table III-12.

OTHER APPROACHES TO LIGHTING ENERGY CONSERVATION

Mandatory lighting controls are now beginning to appear in state plans in response to the inducement of the federal funds available under EPCA. One early example is interesting because of the extension of public control that it implied. In Oregon, the low water runoff in the Columbia River basin affected the generation of hydroelectric power and produced an "electricity crisis" in 1973. In response, the governor issued an executive order banning the use of outdoor lighting and advertising lighting. The text of Executive Order Number EO-73-7 stated:

> that no person shall cause or permit display lighting. Display lighting is the use of artificial light for decorative purposes, or to direct attention to the providers of goods or services, or to illuminate or direct attention to:
>
> (a) Signs advertising goods or services or the providers of goods or services;
> (b) Displays of goods;
> (c) Objects or designs symbolic of commercial enterprises such as trademarks; or
> (d) Buildings or landscaping.
>
> However, where light is ordinarily used for purposes in addition to display lighting, display lighting includes only that use of light not reasonably necessary to accomplish the other purpose. Display lighting does not include the use of light necessary to identify the location of essential government services (e.g., fire and police), or health and communications services.

Although compliance with the executive order was apparently good because of public appreciation of the true emergency conditions, there was also substantial doubt whether the governor had legal powers to impose such lighting controls acting solely on his own authority without legislative support.

REACTIONS OF STATES TO EPCA REQUIREMENTS

The states are clearly having a difficult time providing innovative solutions to the mandate to develop mandatory lighting standards. The State Energy Conservation Plan submitted by Massachusetts, on file at the Department of Energy, is a good description of the dilemma states face:

> Although this [state] program will produce mandatory lighting standards, it is hoped that the program can be implemented with a minimum of regulation and enforcement. It is clearly not feasible to attempt standards that will encounter strong resistance from the commercial sector. The expenses that would be encountered in enforcement would be prohibitive. Therefore, the program will mainly be one of developing concensus, and then providing *guidance* in implementation, rather than enforcement. . . . [t]he entire program should be designed to result in infrequent punitive enforcement.

The Massachusetts plan proposes to hire a lighting standards coordinator, who will spend half his or her time working with a lighting standards committee. The committee will include representatives of commerce; commercial real estate; state, city, and county governments; schools; hospitals, and other institutions; and members of the state energy standards committee. The committee is to develop standards for submission to the State Building Code Commission. The coordinator is directed to develop standards for new buildings that are no less stringent than Section 9 of ASHRAE Standard 90-75.

Other states have simply adopted the ASHRAE standard or have blandly stated that they intend to adopt standards no less strict than the standard. North Carolina has deviated from this pattern in its plan (on file with the Department of Energy), stating that it is not developing a separate lighting standard but is including lighting in its overall thermal efficiency standard. According to the North Carolina state plan,

> Chapter 9 of ASHRAE Standard 90-75 established a maximum power budget for lighting, while North Carolina's proposed standard establishes

a maximum allotment for all energy consuming items in the building, including lighting. While the lighting energy is included in the overall budget, the thermal efficiency standard sets a maximum energy budget for lighting at 3.0 watts per square foot. The main difficulty in establishing a separate power budget for lighting is that it is very difficult to enforce. It would require separate metering of the lighting circuits which is a complex and expensive measure. North Carolina's approach would not require any special metering to verify a building's compliance with the code. On an average basis, it is felt that the proposed standard for North Carolina would be more stringent than the requirements set forth in Chapter 9 of ASHRAE Standard 90-75.

Ohio has also proposed a system that is keyed to a maximum number of watts per square foot, ranging from three watts per square foot for classrooms and drafting rooms down to one-quarter watt per square foot for indoor parking. Outdoor parking is limited to one-tenth watt per square foot. The state collects fees based partially on the number of square feet of area to be inspected. At a public hearing held in late 1978, many criticisms of the expense of the proposed standard were voiced, and the general expectation at the time of writing is that the Ohio legislature would amend the act so as to make the standards applicable only to buildings owned and operated by the state.[9] The proposed Ohio standards are simply a copy of the Massachusetts standard.[10]

CONCLUSION

The savings that many commercial enterprises have made in their lighting budget is tantalizing. Those savings have occurred when the attention of the person paying the bill has been drawn to the issue. Regulation of lighting energy consumption is designed, at least in part, to draw attention to those issues, but in practice, mandatory standards have proven hard to draft. Perhaps an approach that calculates the savings possible and presents this information to the owner at the building design stage can be effective in encouraging energy conservation. More detailed strategies may prove too difficult to devise and to enforce.

NOTES

1. H. Melville, *Moby Dick* (1851), p. 202. I am grateful to William A. Thomas of the American Bar Foundation for drawing my attention to this quotation.

2. See, Ross and Baruzzini, Inc., "Energy Conservation Applied to Office Lighting" (prepared for Federal Energy Administration, April 15, 1975), p. II-1.

(available from the National Technical Information Service, PB-244 154). See generally, General Services Administration, Public Buildings Service, "Lighting Systems Study" (Washington, D.C.: U.S. Government Printing Office, March 1974). See also Federal Energy Administration, "Lighting and Thermal Operations: Energy Management Action Program for Commercial, Public, Industrial Buildings, Guidelines" (Washington, D.C.: U.S. Government Printing Office, n.d.).

3. Assumptions: electricity cost 4.2 cents per kilowatt hour, lamps used for seven and one-half hours per day.

4. Information on Crowly and on ARCO is from Walter McQuade, "There's A Saving Grace in the New Office Lighting," *Fortune*, December 1977, pp. 151 *et seq.*

5. Arthur H. Rosenfeld and Stephen E. Selkowitz, "Beam Daylighting: An Alternative Illumination Technique," 1 *Energy and Building* 43-50 (1977).

6. See *IES Lighting Handbook*, 5th ed. (New York: Illuminating Engineering Society, 1972), p. 16-2.

7. P. L. 94-163.

8. Federal Energy Administration, "Energy Conservation in New Building Design: An Impact Assessment of ASHRAE Standard 90-75" Conservation Paper Number 43B (Washington, D.C.: Government Printing Office).

9. Ohio House Bill 491. Standards under discussion are Chapter 4101:2-87, Lighting Efficiency Standards for Existing Public Buildings, draft scheduled for public hearings, December 7, 1978. See *The Columbus Dispatch*, December 8, 1978.

10. Section 2207 of the Massachusetts State Building Code.

Chapter 5

Ventilation and
Air Infiltration

Excessive air infiltration is the silent thief of energy. During the winter, moist humid air seeps out through cracks around windows, doors, electric sockets, and light fixtures and through the walls themselves, to be replaced with cold, dry air that must be heated and humidified. In the summer, costly air-conditioned air is displaced by hot, moist air. Ventilation of some sort is a basic human need, and the addition of some new air is necessary for maintaining odor control and a feeling of freshness. However, combating the effects of large amounts of either overdry or overwet air seeping into a building at temperatures outside the normal comfort range wastes tremendous amounts of energy in American buildings.

The forces that cause air flows within a building, ways to eliminate unwanted flows, and laws that may encourage building owners and operators to take action are the subjects of this chapter. Professionals customarily divide the subject of air flows within a building into two parts—ventilation, which is the deliberate introduction of air into a building by either natural or mechanical means, and infiltration, which is the unplanned flow of air into a building through any route. The divisions of this chapter reflect this distinction. In addition, the ventilation and infiltration problems associated with existing buildings are generally segregated from those associated with new buildings.

How much energy does unwanted air flow waste? One study conducted in Minnesota showed that in a representative well-insulated single story home, 15 percent of the heat was lost through the walls, 13 percent through the roof, 5 percent through the floor, and 27 percent through doors and windows (by conduction); fully 40 percent was lost through air infiltration. Another study, conducted by the Princeton University Center for Environmental Studies, examined the heat loss in a group of townhouses used by typical families in Twin Rivers, New Jersey. The center's conclusions, based on careful records kept over a number of heating seasons, suggest that in modern townhouses built under the federal Minimum Property Standards, about one-third of the heat loss may be traced to air infiltration. The center noted that even the very process of heating a home brings in additional air to operate the furnace and that heating this additional air can require as much as 4×10^5 kilocalories of energy at a cost of about $5 per year (for natural gas). Ordinary homes waste enormous amounts of energy through such practices as leaving fireplace dampers open.

Comparable statistics on potential energy savings are more difficult to obtain for commercial buildings because building designs and construction methods are so varied that the "typical" commercial building probably doesn't exist. However, one study based on computer calculations suggested that reducing ventilation and infiltration could save 8 percent of the fuel used in a large building and save $8 per 1,000 square feet of space per year.[1] The federal General Services Administration, in its manual *Energy Conservation Design Guidelines for New Office Buildings*, notes that local building codes sometimes require unnecessarily large ventilation capacities in new structures and suggests that when the minimum rates are not in "conformance with present day engineering practice," the architects and engineers should appeal to GSA for authorization to disregard the codes, a privilege that only the federal government can exercise for itself.[2]

Fortunately, the losses of energy entailed by air seepage and excessive ventilation rates are usually easy and cheap to avoid. Unfortunately, using legal means to compel buildings to embrace existing technical solutions is difficult. Excessive air infiltration ("leakage") occurs because current good buildings practices are violated or ignored. Excessive ventilation occurs because rates actually used in practice exceed established legal minimums or because those minimums are set unrealistically high in the first place. Legislation that directs workmen to be more careful or that requires inspectors to inspect more thoroughly is unlikely to solve the problem. Employing design solutions, inventing materials and construction techniques that automatically eliminate careless construction practices, and educating workmen and inspectors to the importance of careful construction are far more likely to affect this major source of energy use in buildings.

VENTILATION

Ventilation, the purposeful flow of air within a building, may be caused by natural forces. The breeze through open windows and doors is a form of ventilation. Ventilation may also be caused by fans operating in ducts installed for the purpose.

Ventilation designed with energy conservation in mind should look for the solution that minimizes the use of mechanical equipment and maximizes the use of naturally heated or cooled air. This can be accomplished by encouraging use of outside air for ventilation when the outside weather is within suitable temperature and humidity ranges and discouraging outside air movement within a building when outside temperatures hit extremes. Of course, some situations stand as exceptions to this general rule. For example, mechanical ventilation systems conserve energy when they carry hot, steamy air from a shower room to the outdoors, instead of sending it through the central air-conditioning system to be cooled and dehumidified. But even in this case, the control setup must be arranged so that the mechanical exhaust fans shut off as soon as the heat and humidity in the shower room dissipates if the attempt to conserve energy is to succeed.

Energy-conserving ventilation methods can also accomplish another goal, that of circulating air within a building so that temperature extremes are moderated and so that heat unwanted in one part of the building can be carried to another part where it will be used. This ventilation can be accomplished through flows of air that can be adjusted according to the differing needs of the building at different times.

Building codes have been an influence in increasing the amount of ventilation required in Ameircan buildings. Special purpose rooms, such as kitchens and bathrooms, are subject to minimum ventilation requirements. Homes are required to have specified sizes and/or numbers of windows that open, requirements often expressed as a percentage of the floor area. Building codes grew out of justifiable fears of dark and dank tenements where sun and fresh air never reached. But they have typically called for the provision of too much artificial ventilation, far beyond the amount of air needed for health or comfort in modern buildings.

Ventilation requirements may be found in each of the four major building codes; the following examples, drawn from the 1976 edition of the Uniform Building Code, are illustrative. Section 605, which applies to buildings used for assembly, educational purposes, nurseries, hospitals, sanitariums, jails, storage, stores, and office buildings, restaurants, and other nonresidential occupancies, states that

The mechanically operated ventilating system shall supply a minimum of 5 cubic feet per minute of outside air with a total circulated of not less than 15 cubic feet per minute per occupant in all portions of the building and such system shall be kept continuously in operation during such time as the building is occupied. . . .

For hotels, apartment houses, convents, and the like, the standard contained in Section 1305 requires a mechanical ventilating system "capable of providing two air changes per hour. . . .One-fifth of the air supply shall be taken from the outside." In bathrooms and laundry rooms, five changes per hour directly from outside air are required.

For dwellings, the Uniform Building Code uses a different standard. Section 1405 permits natural ventilation, but says that

In lieu of required exterior openings for natural ventilation, a mechanical ventilating system may be provided. Such a system shall be capable of providing two air changes per hour in all guest rooms, dormitories, habitable rooms, and in public corridors. One-fifth of the air supply shall be taken from the outside. In bathrooms, water closet compartments, laundry rooms, and similar rooms a mechanical ventilation system connected directly to the outside, capable of providing five air changes per hour, shall be provided.

(Note that the standard for residential uses is not directly translatable to the cubic feet per minute standards used for nonresidential occupancies, since air changes per hour depend on the volume of the room.)

These standards provide a margin of safety and comfort that exacts a high price in energy consumption. Even though the nonresidential standards permit building ventilation systems to be shut down when no one is occupying the space, unnecessarily large volumes of air are circulated in all but the most extreme circumstances of use.

Another major influence in increasing the required amount of ventilation has been the standards promulgated by the American Society of Heating, Refrigerating and Air-conditioning Engineers, Inc. Standard 62-73, "Standards for Natural and Mechanical Ventilation," currently contains excessively high requirements that fail to take energy costs into account.

The goals of regulation should be to permit circulation of only that amount of air that health and comfort require, to permit the use of outside, unconditioned air to the maximum extent possible during the cooling season, and to encourage innovative design solutions to the ventilation problem.

Several legal strategies, including laws and regulations, can be adopted to control inappropriate ventilation. One such set of controls is designed to encourage builders to design new structures to use natural ventilation rather than mechanical, energy-consuming ventilation whenever design reviews show that natural ventilation will save energy on a year round basis. Another strategy is to examine carefully each provision of every building code, looking for and rooting out inappropriately strict ventilation requirements. Finally, incentives can be provided to encourage the use of controls and devices that automatically substitute outside air for mechanically heated or cooled air under appropriate climate conditions.

This list is in no sense complete; many more existing devices or controls could be suggested to reduce unnecessary ventilation. The three highlighted items merely suggest approaches that can be adapted to analogous situations.

Use of Natural Ventilation Instead of Mechanical Ventilation

Natural ventilation requires no energy to operate; therefore, its use should be widely encouraged. Unfortunately, however, during very cold or very hot months, those openings in buildings that permit natural ventilation in moderate seasons must be sealed and insulated to prevent air leakage. Unwanted or excessive "natural ventilation" is often a major source of energy loss. The General Services Administration manual cautions:

> in many cases, systems designed for natural ventilation or for solar benefits may enjoy only brief periods of energy conservation during the year. The facilities which are designed to allow the use of natural elements may create energy burdens for the remainder of the year. For instance, using windows and louvres for natural ventilation may increase unwanted infiltration rates for long periods in the winter, increasing the energy requirements for heating. Thus, an energy study with an annual weather profile is necessary to determine if designing for extensive natural ventilation would be energy saving.[3]

Many design features can encourage natural ventilation in commercial buildings. Central shaft atriums combined with louvres and screened windows that open far enough to ventilate but not so far as to present a safety hazard are only two design possibilities. Natural ventilation is significantly harder to achieve in large highrise buildings than it is in smaller buildings. In residences, the possibilities for enhancing natural ventilation include windows, screened porches, skylights that open, special ventilation grills installed on opposite sides of the house, and doors that permit the breeze to flow. If architects and other professionals were educated to understand the value of natural ventilation, these design features, and others, would become commonplace. That education appears to be taking place to some extent already, and the law can be used to encourage the trend. Either direct controls can be put into effect or building codes can place on the designer the burden of demonstrating why natural ventilation is not used.

As noted in Chapter 7, architectural design controls, especially for interior design features or for arrangements that do not visibly alter the outside of the structure, are relatively untried in this country, with the exception of a few tightly controlled historic areas. American law does not dictate how windows must be placed nor whether screened porches must be a feature of new buildings. However, in an ordinance passed in Davis, California (reprinted in full as an appendix to Chapter 7), an indirect encouragement for placing windows on more than one side of residences is provided. The ordinance states:

> F. *Ventilation for Summer Night Time Cooling.* Where design of the dwelling unit is such that openable windows may only be provided along one elevation, mechanical cross ventilation must be installed to provide 15 air changes per hour ducted to the exterior.

Rather than requiring that certain external changes be made in the design of a building, a costly and thus potentially an objectionable practice, this ordinance gives the designer an option. The architect can either include ventilation in the original design or, if that is impractical, provide mechanical assistance. (Other valid design considerations, such as a pleasant view, a nearby noise source, or architectural integrity, might dictate such a substitution.) Of course, if the designer chooses the mechanical ventilation solution rather than the design solution, required ventilation will be mandated, thus putting energy-consuming equipment where it might not have been otherwise. The Davis ordinance is particularly suited to areas where there is a substantial cooling at night; much of the country falls in this pattern during large parts of the summer.

Other architectural design controls aimed at encouraging the maximum use of natural ventilation can also be enacted. For example, the building code might require that all new buildings have vestibules (double door arrangements that prevent large volumes of outside air from entering or leaving the conditioned space). Or it could require that openable windows be installed in commercial buildings. Yet major design changes, changes that truly affect the construction and use of buildings, might be difficult to pass and, once passed, would certainly be subject to challenge in court because of their alleged economic effect. If a judge were persuaded that the short term effect on the stream of income of the building owner were diminished by the required design changes, then a highly persuasive case for energy savings (and private benefit to the building owner) would have to be made. Suppose, for example, that an ordinance were passed requiring that all commercial buildings have atriums. Virtually all older commercial buildings featured air shafts for light and ventilation, so the requirement would have historical precedent. But social and aesthetic objections to homogeneity might be raised at the legislative level. Economics would also come into play: persuasive evidence might be marshaled that the loss of revenue from the rentable commercial space used by the atrium or air shaft exceeded the value to the building owner of the energy that he would save. Unless a clear case could be made to the contrary, such relatively drastic regulation would face a difficult challenge in the courts.

Reduction of Mechanical Ventilation Rates
During the Heating and Cooling Seasons

In commercial buildings, air must be transported mechanically during the heating and cooling seasons. But the volumes of air that are customarily used in this process often exceed any reasonable necessity. If less air were used, energy would be conserved both because less air would have to be heated or cooled from the outside and because fan motors would run more slowly.

Most building codes have minimum ventilation requirements. Many of these minimum requirements are based on ASHRAE Standard 62-73, "Standards for Natural and Mechanical Ventilation." The later ASHRAE Standard 90-75, "Energy Conservation in New Building Design," requires that in using Standard 62-73, the *"minimum* column value for each type of occupancy *shall* be used for design." In other words, the energy conservation standard directs designers to use the least amount of ventilation that the older standard thought suitable. To the extent that the Standard 90-75 is adopted by states or local building code jurisdictions, this provision could reduce the level of energy used by ventilation systems.

The Arthur D. Little study of the economic, energy, and other impacts of ASHRAE Standard 90-75 examined five prototypical buildings. Based on computer models and on a strict application

Table 5-1.   Effect of ASHRAE Standard 90-75 on Building Ventilation.

	Ventilation (cubic feet per minute per cubic foot of volume)		
	Conventional Building	ASHRAE Standard 90-75 Modified Building	Percent Change
Single family residence	0.00	0.000	0
Multifamily low rise	0.05	0.025	−50
Office	0.25	0.148	−41
Retail store	0.30	0.216	−28
School	0.50	0.250	−50

Source: Federal Energy Administration, *Energy Conservation in New Building Design: An Impact Assessment of ASHRAE Standard 90-75* (Washington, D.C.: U.S. Government Printing Office, n.d.), p. 227.

of Standard 90-75, the study suggests that the reductions shown in Table 5-1 will come about in ventilation if Section 5.3.2.3 of Standard 90-75 is adhered to. Thus, except for the special case of the single family residence, the ASHRAE Standard 90-75 calls for substantial modification in the amount of air permitted for artificial ventilation. In addition to the reductions in air movement brought about by lower ventilation rates, ASHRAE Standard 90-75 also requires that crack and door leakage be reduced (to less than 0.5 and 1.25 cubic feet per minute per foot of crack in a twenty-five mile per hour wind) and that exterior openings be caulked or otherwise sealed. Arthur D. Little calculated that these modifications would reduce air changes per hour about 7 percent for a single family residence and by about 40 percent in other categories of buildings.

Taking both the reduction of ventilation and the elimination of drafts into account, the Arthur D. Little study rated the reduction of ventilation and air infiltration under Standard 90-75 as one of the major impacts of the new standard as a whole on the building occupants. Because of the smoking habits of some, this impact may not always be a happy one for others. The report concludes:

The principal impact of ASHRAE 90 on health, safety, and welfare of building occupants will result from reduced ventilation and infiltration. . . . The reduced ventilation and infiltration values assumed for energy calculation purposes are expected to result in excessively increased exposures of nonsmokers to cigarette smoke particulates, an increase in odor complaints, and demands for separate smoking and nonsmoking areas. To minimize these problems, smoking spaces in public buildings should be ventilated at ASHRAE 62-73 recommended rates rather than the minimum rates, and improved odor control techniques should be developed.[5]

Unfortunately, the Arthur D. Little report does not consider the use of other means to minimize energy consumption while dealing with the odor of smoke. Such means include banning smoking altogether, using electronic purification equipment, or making relatively small well-ventilated areas available for smoking.

Recent studies have suggested that tightening homes and offices may have another unwanted effect. Cooking and burning of gases (such as in gas heaters and kitchen ranges) produce oxides of carbon, sulfur, and nitrogen, as well as carcinogenic nitrosamines. Therefore, attention must be paid to insuring adequate ventilation in kitchens. The formation of such compounds is another good reason for elimination of pilot lights.[6]

Other strategies for lowering the amount of mechanical ventilation could be devised, but they are fundamentally similar to the approach taken in the ASHRAE standard. Localities should consider altering their building codes to reflect lowered required mechanical ventilation rates.

Increased Use of Outside Air

A final strategy for saving energy is to require, to the maximum extent possible, that systems be built to use unconditioned outside air instead of conditioned air. Such systems, called "economizer cycles," have controls that test the temperature and humidity of the outside air. When the temperature-humidity combination is within preset limits, dampers open that permit outside air to be drawn by fans through the building. As the outside temperature and relative humidity move outside the limits set on the controls, the dampers also shift. At all times, a well-designed economizer system minimizes the use of mechanical air conditioning equipment by maximizing the use of outside air.

As a practical matter, economizer cycles with controls and dampers are best used in commercial buildings, rather than in residences. (Less sophisticated systems depending on attic fans and open windows and on human control rather than automatic are the residential version of the economizer cycle.) For the commercial building, ASHRAE Standard 90-75 deals with economizer cycles in Section 5.6, in which the use of such a control and ducting setup is specified for larger systems, "whenever its use will result in lower usage of new energy." Section 5.6 also permits a number of exceptions, generally when economizer cycles would not save energy on a systemwide basis.

The economizer cycle requirement contained in Standard 90-75 is singled out in this chapter, not because it is the only or the best system for conserving energy in ventilation, but rather because it serves as a proxy for a host of other technical and technological energy-conserving possibilities for saving energy. Although these methods and systems vary enormously, for legal purposes, there is virtually no difference between requiring an economizer cycle and requiring a heat recapture wheel. Any such system can be required as a part of a heating or cooling system by means of direct regulation.

It is tempting to sit down with a building engineer and draw up a list of "good ideas" for saving energy, then enact that list into law. But before legislatures begin presenting building designers with an entire shopping list of present-day technical solutions, caution should be exercised. Laws that "freeze" certain building designs into the building code have their drawbacks. They tend to stifle innovation and to keep new equipment from being introduced. They are hard to revise when a new, better product is invented and needs to become certified before it can be used. Although laws may cover most cases, the generally preferable solution may have drawbacks in a particular case; mandatory laws prevent such exceptions.

There are ways to avoid this bad effect of mandatory requirements. One method is to use a building energy budget (discussed in Chapter 7) that does not prescribe methods for achieving a required energy consumption level and thus does not mandate the use of particular design solutions. But even in this case, other sections of the building code must be carefully examined to make certain that ostensibly nonenergy provisions do not inadvertently force energy waste. For example, if the old minimum mechanical ventilation rates apply in the code, the fact that an energy budget approach is adopted would not necessarily lower those ventilation rates to the acceptable levels proposed by ASHRAE Standard 90-75; separate action would be required to bring the rates in line with conservation goals. Thus, since energy budgets alone may not solve the energy problem, a full review of all regulations governing construction must be undertaken.

A second method for forcing builders and designers to consider various technical solutions to saving energy in ventilation (or in other energy conservation measures, for that matter) is to prepare a list of possible solutions, assigning to each solution a point value based on the average contribution that the particular technical solution is estimated to make to energy conservation in a large building. Architects and engineers would be required to show that they had included building features having a certain minimum point value in order to obtain a building permit. To insure that the point values and list of equipment did not freeze innovation, the state building code agency (if one existed) could be required each year to hold hearings to reassess the point values assigned to current items on the list and to consider additions or deletions. Public hearings for the purpose would provide an opportunity for manufacturers or designers of ventilation equipment to demonstrate the energy-saving potentials of new products that they recommend for inclusion on the list. The building code agency would handle the certification of the new equipment, with an administrative appeals procedure for a backup.

States considering such an administrative arrangement will have to weigh carefully the relative value of various ventilation schemes within the climate zone of the state. Areas with hot, humid weather may benefit relatively less, since the dehumdification action of mechanical air conditioning is important there; conversely, in hot dry climates, night air cooling might be awarded a relatively higher value.

Conclusion

Reducing the rates of ventilation and depending more upon the use of outside air in ventilation processes can save considerable sums of money and energy. To the extent that excessive ventilation is mandated by law through building codes, legal action is relatively simple. In those areas that the law has difficulty controlling, educating professionals on energy-efficient ventilation may be the only effective way to influence the design of buildings.

AIR INFILTRATION

Unlike ventilation, which is deliberate, air infiltration itself is accidental and largely unwanted at any time. Two forces cause infiltration of air into a structure. The most obvious one is the pressure of wind against the building, as anyone who has stood by a window or a poorly sealed door during a wind storm can attest. The second source of infiltration, the draft or chimney effect caused within a building by differences in temperature, is less obvious. One easy way to visualize this effect is to consider how a fire in a fireplace behaves. At first, the smoke may roll over the fireplace lip into the room because there is no draft. But once the flames heat the air, that hot air rises up the chimney (taking the smoke with it) and is replaced by cooler air from the room, at least as long as the heat from the fire continues. In a much less dramatic way, exactly the same thing occurs within any heated building. Lighter than cool air, hot air tends to rise toward the top of a building. In a house, the usual pathway is the staircase. In a large building, the warmer air flows up internal staircases, ventilation shafts, elevator shafts, utility cores, and other vertical airways. As the hot air rises, it creates a partial vacuum at the lower floors, and outside air is pulled in through any opening or flaw in the construction of the building.

Some of the causes of air infiltration are hard to control. Very little can be done about the speed at which the wind blows on a building. Windbreaks and careful selection of a site can help to reduce the impact of the wind on buildings, but these precautions are not always easy to arrange. A row of dense evergreens of about the same height as the structure being protected can reduce the wind's impact; because of the turbulence of the wind as it hits the windbreak, the windbreak should stand no further from the wall it protects than a distance equal to five times its height.[7]

The effect of wind can also be minimized by adapting the shape or openings of the house to the prevailing wind. One design solution is to put doorless and windowless walls facing the direction from which cold winds usually blows. But blank walls also prevent the wind from cooling the building during the more temperate months when this would be helpful; even this solution is not without its energy costs.

In the same way, the law can't do very much in the face of the physical fact that heat rises, and therefore the chimney effect will be found in all buildings. Because the physical effect cannot be controlled does not mean that it cannot be minimized by tightening the construction of the building itself, leaving fewer gaps through which air can pass and up which air can rise. The construction techniques that can be used to prevent air infiltration are quite simple. Installing barriers that are impermeable to air (such as plastic or coated vapor barriers) and caulking all openings and joints carefully are two practical construction techniques for sealing buildings. Yet legislating the use of such techniques is a bit like legislating courtesy, since good construction practice already calls for use of vapor barriers and caulking. However, the advantage of putting them in the law is that some legal mandate would then exist. ASHRAE Standard 90-75 demands caulking or weatherstripping around windows and door frames, between wall cavities and window or door frames, between wall and foundation, between wall and roof, between wall panels, at penetrations or utility services through walls, floors and roofs, and all other openings in the exterior envelope. Sound building practice generally requires caulking at places where materials join; such caulking retards air infiltration as well as protecting the structure from water seepage and damage. The fact that existing buildings are so "subject to the draft" suggests either that more stringent laws are needed or that existing laws must be followed more strictly. It is not reasonable to expect that building inspectors will or can take the time to test each caulk and joint in the large number of buildings that they must inspect each year, so other incentives must be discovered for better construction practices. Failing that, some attention needs to be paid to improving building materials so that airtight joins result automatically from the construction technique or the materials used. An example of such a product is a well-made, factory-produced window unit that can be installed on site without adding weatherstripping or fitting movable parts into the frame. But even this unit will permit air leakage if the installer does not frame it carefully and caulk around the frame where the factory unit and the exterior facing meet.

Keeping the members of the construction trade up to date on the building codes and their implicit rationales, as well as on the best building techniques, is one way in which the state can insure that contractors and workers understand the purpose of regulations that require caulking and weatherstripping. But education cannot protect against laziness or cost cutting. Random inspection of construction sites specifically for the purpose of looking for energy conservation construction features might be another method of insuring quality workmanship. In the construction of large buildings, the architect customarily serves as the watchdog of the owner's interests, certifying that building specifications are being carried out. (In fact, architects often contract out part or all of this duty to commercial building inspection firms.)

Financial incentives to motivate contractors to enforce quality control might also serve the goal of quality craftsmanship. Performance guarantees, demanded by the lending institutions that back construction projects, could be made a part of standard financing arrangements, either voluntarily or by statute. (Lending institutions ought to have an interest in energy conservation, since the money that is spent on fuel in an energy-inefficient building could, instead, be used to make a higher monthly payment on an energy-efficient building and thus be available to earn more interest income for the lender.) A performance guarantee might require that the contractor and the designer of the building promise to the eventual owner of the building that the building would not exceed a certain infiltration rate (tested according to methods used at the National Bureau of Standards and elsewhere). The owner of the building would be entitled to sue on the bond given under the performance guarantee if independent testing (paid for by the losing party) demonstrated that infiltration rates exceeded the amount named in the bond. (Unlike the more general guarantee of energy performance criticized in Chapter 3, a bond on infiltration would be more directly related to quality of construction than to habits of the occupants. Thus, it might not be as subject to theoretical and practical problems.) Contractors and building designers who consistently miscalculated the infiltration rates of their buildings would find it increasingly difficult to obtain bonding for those performance guarantees and would either have to pay more for them or would have to tighten up their quality control practices.

A performance bond for this purpose is a practice that could grow up without any state legal intervention at all. The performance bond system would enhance energy conservation because it would goad the builder to be careful. On the other hand, small home builders in particular and builders generally would not willingly issue such performance guarantees unless construction financing depended on them or unless state law required them to do so. Additionally, setting the limits of the bond so that it would be reasonable for the purchaser and for the builder alike would be difficult. For all of these reasons, a state might want to use tightly constructed buildings as test laboratories in order to establish a range of reasonable but tough standards for inclusion in the guarantee.

Existing Buildings

The strategies for reducing air infiltration into existing buildings are so straightforward and inexpensive that they are ideal for educationally based programs rather than mandatory regulations. The perfect educational program will be one that conveys the simplicity of the task required and gives a local calculation of the amount of money that may be saved if the suggested improvements are made. The major goal of such an educational program is to motivate building owners to take constructive action before remedial action becomes necessary. A number of educational programs sponsored by federal, state, and local governments and by insulation, weatherstripping, or utility companies have already been mentioned in Chapter 3 in the context of insulation.

Programs for decreasing air infiltration in existing commercial buildings should also begin with education and information. Energy audits provide the most direct method for pointing out to the owner or operating engineer the opportunities for saving energy by reducing infiltration. Manuals containing direct suggestions also educate and motivate the building trade to embrace conservation goals. The federal guide for operators of federal buildings exemplifies the kind of checklist that points out opportunities for energy saving.

CONCLUSION

Reducing unwanted air infiltration is a simple and direct method for cutting the energy that a building consumes. No new technologies are required, and the building trades are familiar with the methods for carrying out the job. Reducing ventilation rates can be accomplished easily both at law and in practice, although the comfort of nonsmokers and the special health and aesthetic considerations that apply to kitchens, laboratories, and bathrooms must be kept in mind.

If ventilation and infiltration rates are both cut down, potentially enormous amounts of energy could be saved. Therefore, it is worth spending time training inspectors, enforcing both existing and new building standards, and developing new products that lessen the opportunities for worker error in installation.

NOTES

1. See generally, Howard Ross and Dr. David Grimsrud, *Air Infiltration in Buildings: Literature Survey and Proposed Research Agency*, #LBL-W7822 (U.S. Department of Energy, May 1978). See also, R. H. Socolow, "Energy Utilization in Townhouses in a Planned Community in the United States," Center for Environmental Studies (Princeton University) Report No. 26 (Paper prepared for delivery at "Energy Conservation in the Built Environment," Garston, England, April 6-8, 1976).

2. *Energy Conservation Design Guidelines for New Office Buildings*, 2nd ed. (General Services Administration, Public Buildings Service, Washington, D.C.: Government Printing Office, 1975).

3. *Id.*

4. Resolution No. 1833, Series 1975, City of Davis, CA. § 4 (f).

5. "Energy Conservation in New Building Design: An Impact Assessment of ASHRAE Standard 90-75," Conservation Paper Number 43B (Washington, D.C.: U.S. Government Printing Office, n.d.); p. 231.

6. See Samuel Silberstein, "Exposure to Indoor Pollution," Informal Report BNL 23891, Biomedical and Environmental Assessment Division, Brookhaven National Laboratory, October 10, 1977. See also, Samuel Silberstein, "Outdoor

Sources of Indoor Air Pollution," Biomedical and Environmental Assessment Division, Brookhaven National Laboratory, June 1978.

7. See Jerome Kerner, "Site Planning and Use of On-Site Resources," in Eccli, ed., *Low-Cost, Energy Efficient Shelter for the Owner and Builder* (Emmaus, Pennsylvania: Rodale Press, 1976), p. 57.

Chapter 6

Improving Building Equipment

Improving the efficiency of the mechanical equipment that heats and cools the air, ventilates, and warms the water in a building is often the cheapest and easiest method for saving energy, particularly when the building is old or hard to insulate. Although adding bulky basic equipment items, such as heating-cooling ducts or independently controlled heating zones, is often difficult or impossible, substituting efficient equipment for older equipment is comparatively easy. Moreover, unlike the basic architectural design of the building itself, which is fixed, the mechanical equipment can be upgraded or altered several times during the life of a building. Such improved equipment, if familiar and readily available to the consumer, makes continuing techno- logical advances possible. Finally, many equipment changes cost much less than architectural changes in the building; indeed, they often cost less than adding insulation. Therefore, as fuel prices rise, economic pressures alone will encourage changes in the building equipment much sooner than they will call for the abandonment or major restructuring of the building itself.

This chapter deals with the techniques that state governments can use to encourage or mandate the use of energy-efficient equip- ment in buildings. Because the problems and the opportunities associated with commercial buildings differ from those of private residences, the law, and thus this chapter, treats them differently. Federal law now is in place to label and control the efficiency of household appliances that use large amounts of energy. No such regulatory system is currently on the horizon for commercial equipment.

Although it would be possible to institute state regulation or control of the efficiency of all the energy-consuming equipment in a building, no matter how hard to find or how insignificant its energy consumption, in fact it only makes sense to concentrate on devices that are large users of energy or on uses that are easy to control through the application of public policy. Thus, no regulation worth enacting proposes to control electric hairdryers, at least in part because they use but scant energy when compared to the nation's total consumption. On the other hand, outdoor decorative lighting on public buildings probably should be controlled simply because of its visibility, its symbolic value (particularly on public buildings or buildings of energy-producing utilities), and the ease with which its misuse can be detected. But readers should think of the major energy-consuming devices (such as furnaces and air conditioners) when the term "building equipment" is used in this chapter.

HOW MUCH ENERGY DOES EQUIPMENT USE?

As one might imagine, predicting the amount of energy that a given family or business uses for each purpose is difficult. A working couple living in a well-insulated apartment building has fundamentally different energy use patterns than a large family living in a rambling old home, with house and refrigerator doors in constant motion. Nor would statistically identical families living in different parts of the country have the same energy use profile. But as a national average, Table 6-1 shows how American residences used energy in 1972.

For commercial structures (including apartments with more than three living units) the figures vary considerably, and experts cannot agree upon the exact distribution of energy consumption among commercial uses and for each use among end-users. The figures in Table 6-2, however, at least suggest the range and the variations that exist.

Table 6-2 shows, for example, that hotels used a total of 0.673 Quads of energy (1 Quad equal 10^{15} BTUs). Of that total amount, 0.107 Quads, or 15.9 percent of the energy used by hotels, was used for air conditioning. This table and Table 6-1 clearly show that heating, hot water, and (commercial) lighting are important areas to examine for potential savings.

The total figures for the buildings sector are also impressive. These figures suggest that residences used about 16.4 percent of

Table 6-1. Household Energy Use by Function.

	Percent usage
Space heating	55.1
Water heating	15.0
Cooking	4.8
Clothes drying	2.2
Refrigeration	6.7
Air conditioning	5.4
Other (including lighting)	10.8
	100.0

Source: National Petroleum Council, *Potential for Energy Conservation in the United States: 1974-1978: Residential/Commercial* (Washington, D.C.: National Petroleum council 1974), p. 6, citing Stanford Research Institute data, adjusted.

the nation's energy to sustain building operations; commercial establishments, including multiunit apartments, used an additional 16.5 percent.[1] Since heating accounts for over half the energy cost of operating a building, one can estimate that about 16 percent of the nation's energy is spent on heating. (By comparison, automobiles use about 12 percent of the nation's energy for fuel.)

The potential for improving the efficiency of building equipment by fairly conventional means is great. But a recent study conducted under the auspices of the American Physical Society suggests that even the efficiency improvements now under consideration are small compared to those theoretically possible. Ordinarily, we calculate the efficiency of a furnace or some other device by comparing the amount of heat energy extracted from the device with the amount of energy put in. In an electrical resistance furnace, for example, we put in one kilowatt hour of electricity and extract one kilowatt hour of heat. In this case, it is tempting to judge the furnace as 100 percent efficient and, therefore, unimprovable. From a gas or oil furnace we might extract 60 percent of the heat that the flame generates as usable for heating a building. The rest of the energy would be dissipated through the stack, duct leakage, and other points.[2] It might seem that the performance of the gas or oil furnace could be improved, but that we could not hope to so much as double its efficiency.

The American Physical Society's study suggests that expressing efficiency in this conventional manner is misleading, since such comparisons don't take into account the possibility of changing the method by which we extract useful energy. Instead, the pre-

Table 6-2. Energy Use by Function and Building Category.

Building Category	Space Heating		Air Conditioning		Water Heating		Lighting		Other		Total
	Quadrillion BTUs	Percent	Quadrillion BTUs	Percent	Quadrillion BTUs	Percent	Quadrillion BTUs	Percent	Quadrillion BTUs	Percent	Quadrillion BTUs
Stores	0.996	45.3	0.536	24.4	0.108	4.9	0.455	20.7	0.106	4.8	2.201
Schools	1.139	61.7	0.137	7.4	0.174	9.4	0.335	18.1	0.061	3.3	1.846
Supermarkets	0.495	50.4	0.073	7.4	0.050	5.1	0.149	15.2	0.215	21.9	0.982
Hospitals	0.460	51.7	0.144	16.2	0.127	14.3	0.051	5.7	0.108	12.1	0.890
Offices	0.433	49.4	0.179	20.4	0.041	4.7	0.149	17.0	0.075	8.6	0.877
Hotels	0.359	53.3	0.107	15.9	0.066	9.8	0.105	15.6	0.036	5.3	0.673
Colleges	0.345	60.1	0.078	13.6	0.062	10.8	0.072	12.5	0.017	3.0	0.574
Other	0.708	62.2	0.059	5.2	0.142	12.5	0.146	12.8	0.084	7.4	1.139
Subtotal (nonresidential)	4.935	53.7	1.313	14.3	0.770	8.4	1.462	15.9	0.702	7.6	9.182
Apartments	1.649	57.5	0.105	3.7	0.429	15.0	0.141	4.9	0.545	19.0	2.869
Total	6.584	54.6	1.418	11.8	1.199	9.9	1.603	13.3	1.247	10.3	12.051

Source: National Petroleum Council, *Potential For Energy Consumption in the United States: 1974–1978: Residential/Commercial*, table 21, p. 61, recalculated to show percentages and to total certain figures disaggregated in original source.

sumption is that the general methods we now use to warm our houses and to cook our food are the best or the only ways to use energy. The study suggested an alternative method for calculating efficiencies: one could compare the amount of heat or work usefully transferred by a given device or system with the maximum possible amount that could usefully be transferred by any device or system using the same energy input as the given device or system to accomplish the same task. As the report of the study group notes, this method "provides immediate insight into the quality of performance of any device relative to what it could ideally be. It shows how much room there is for improvement in principle. . . . It is a technical goal to be placed alongside economic, environmental, and conservation goals."[3]

Comparing electrical home-heating methods is one way of exploring the change in perspective that this alternative way of computing efficiency affords. As noted above, almost all of the electrical energy in a conventional resistance heat electrical furnace is transformed into heat energy. If we assume that the furnace efficiency is 100 percent, we do nothing more. But if we take that same amount of energy and use it not for heating a wire, but for running a compression refrigeration system in a heat pump, in theory we can extract six or more units of heat out of the outside atmosphere (at moderate temperatures) for every unit of electricity we use. (In practice, present models of heat pumps will extract two or more units of heat per unit of electricity consumed.) Compared to the resistance furnace, the present heat pump is two or more times as efficient, so that the 100 percent efficiency we believed we had achieved means little. When we compare a heat pump with the theoretically perfect device for heating a home, we see that even a heat pump is far from totally efficient at doing the job. The American Physical Society study suggests that space heating in this country has an overall efficiency of only 6 percent, water heating only 3 percent, and refrigeration only 4 percent when compared to the theoretically perfect methods for heating and cooling air and water.

In this chapter and book, efficiencies are stated in conventional terms. But readers should hold in mind that these are misleading and that real gains in efficiency may be many times larger.

THE IMPORTANCE OF MAKING CHANGES

National attention to the buildings sector has been focused mainly on questions of improving building insulation and building design.

As important as these issues are, a study by Eric Hirst of the Oak Ridge National Laboratory suggests that the highest, fastest returns on a national conservation effort would come from upgrading appliance efficiencies.[4] Hirst's figures are developed for residential structures, but we can go beyond the data and surmise that improved machinery in any structure will provide comparable energy conservation gains.

Hirst postulated that for the thirteen categories of household energy-consuming products covered by the federal Energy Policy and Conservation Act[5] (which is discussed later in this chapter), improvements in operating efficiency would meet the statutory improvement targets set up in the act, and that all types of building equipment would continue to improve, although at a slower pace, from 1980 to 2000. Hirst assumed that overall equipment efficiencies, compared to 1970-75 figures, would improve 25 percent by 1980 and 40 percent by 2000.

Using twelve different sets of parameters, Hirst worked out their effect on energy consumption using the computer model of residential energy use developed at Oak Ridge National Laboratory. The model Hirst used simulates national household energy use, using four different fuels, six different end uses, and three different kinds of houses. It is, according to Hirst, "sensitive to the major demographic, economic, and technological determinants of household fuel use."[6] The first run assumed that virtually no changes took place in public policy; the twelfth run assumed that a number of important policy changes occurred, including higher fuel prices, better insulation, and improved equipment efficiencies. Within the residential sector, the difference between the first run (based on high use assumptions) and the twelfth (based on low use assumptions) showed a possible savings of 41 percent or 13.4×10^{18} Joules. The biggest percentage change in use during that twenty-five year period came from improved equipment efficiencies (34 percent).[7] Hirst concludes:

> Implementation of a program to increase efficiency of residential equipment by 1980, as specified in the Energy Policy and Conservation Act, can cut energy use in the year 2000 by at least 10%. However, additional improvements after 1980 yield considerably greater savings. Run 9 assumes that equipment efficiencies continue to improve after 1980, but at a slower rate; the energy savings in the year 2000 in run 9 are 60% greater than those from run 8. These results suggest the need for additional research to further improve energy efficiencies of household equipment, and the need for programs to ensure that manufacturers produce and consumers purchase increasingly efficient household equipment.[8]

The considerable savings that will accrue within the residential sector suggest the importance of pressing forward with a strong program for improving equipment efficiencies. If states (or the federal government) press equally hard on the manufacturers of commercial equipment to make improvements in efficiency, the total savings to building owners and the nation can be relatively rapid and highly significant.

HOME APPLIANCES CONTROLLED BY THE 1975 ENERGY POLICY AND CONSERVATION ACT

Sections 321 through 339[9] of the federal Energy Policy and Conservation Act establish an "Energy Conservation Program for Consumer Products Other than Automobiles." EPCA has been slightly amended by Section 161 of the federal Energy Conservation and Production Act[10] to permit a longer time than originally allowed for the development of efficiency improvement targets; ECPA made no other changes in the appliance efficiency sections of EPCA. The voluntary targets have, however, now been eliminated. The National Energy Act of 1978[11] further amended the basic program. As will be explained in greater detail later, the NEA permits establishing mandatory appliance efficiency standards more quickly and sets a priority for establishing standards. In addition, NEA grants to the Department of Energy the authority to establish energy standards for appliances beyond those thirteen listed in the original act, under certain conditions.

Basically, the federal program has three parts: one covers standardized testing procedures; another, standardized energy efficiency labels; and the third, the procedures for establishing mandatory energy efficiency standards. The federal program is designed to provide useful consumer information at the point of sale and to provide an incentive to manufacturers to improve the efficiency of their products.

Under the act, a consumer product is defined as any article (other than an automobile) that consumes energy in operation, is sold for personal use or consumption by individuals, and is covered by the provisions of the act.[12] Initially, the act covers thirteen categories of products: (1) refrigerators and refrigerator-freezers, (2) freezers, (3) dishwashers, (4) clothes dryers, (5) water heaters, (6) room air conditioners, (7) home-heating equipment other than furnaces, (8) television sets, (9) kitchen ranges and ovens, (10) clothes washers, (11) humidifiers and dehumidifiers, (12) central air conditioners, and (13) furnaces.[13] In addition, the secretary of energy may add any other type of consumer product to this list (and thus bring it under the control of the act) if the addition is necessary or appropriate to carrying out the purposes of the act and if the "average annual perhousehold energy use by products of such type is likely to exceed 100 kilowatt-hours (or its BTU equivalent) per year."[14]

Testing Program

EPCA directs the National Bureau of Standards to assist in developing test procedures for each of the products covered to determine both the estimated annual operating costs of such appliances and at least one other useful measure of energy consumption of each product that is likely to assist appliance buyers. The test procedures should be designed to produce meaningful results and must not be "unduly burdensome to conduct."[15]

Once a standardized test covering a category of products is promulgated, no maker or seller of that product may make any statement about the energy consumption or energy costs of its product unless the product has been tested according to the standardized testing procedure and unless the manufacturer's statements disclose fairly the results of the test.[16]

Labeling Program

Just as the testing program requires the cooperation of the Department of Energy and the National Bureau of Standards, the labeling program is a joint effort between the Department of Energy and the Federal Trade Commission. Once the DOE adopts a standard testing procedure, the Federal Trade Commission must produce a standard label for the product.[17] Appliance labels must present two useful kinds of information:[18] first, they must disclose the energy consumption of the particular product, expressed in terms of the estimated annual operating cost of that model; second, the label must state the range of estimated annual operating costs for products of a similar type. Thus, the consumer can judge not only the costs of running a particular model, but also the available alternatives.

In the *Federal Register* of July 21, 1978, the Federal Trade Commission gave notice of its proposed rulemaking to carry out the mandates of EPCA. The labels proposed by the Federal Trade Commission were designed with the assistance of a design consulting firm; a research firm tested the labels for comprehension by consumers. The labels attempt to be quite comprehensive in the information they present. They show annual operating costs, assuming average usage and average energy prices. In addition, where appropriate, they have a chart that shows how different energy prices or different usage patterns will affect the annual operating costs. Faithful to the act, the labels also have a scale that shows the range of energy costs for similar products and where the particular model falls on that scale. The energy labels are to be of a relatively uniform design (yellow with black writing and white lines) and will be affixed with instructions that they are to be removed only by the ultimate consumer.

The labels are all comparatively small for the amount of information they contain, with the exception of those appliances that depend on other energy-consuming devices to supply them with hot water or heat. For example, the source of hot water is crucial to the expense of operation of dishwashers and clothes washers; for furnace humidifiers, the furnace provides heat that makes the water evaporate. Labels for these products are substantially larger than other labels. Finally, the FTC proposes that for hot water heaters, a rating based on amount of hot water available in an hour's time is a more informative way of presenting information than the usual rating of capacity of the hot water storage tank. The proposed label will help customers estimate their own peak demand for hot water in any given hour, so that similar models can be compared.

Under the law and the regulations, the information contained in the final labels must appear in catalogs, on the appliance itself, and in point of sale materials. (The energy information need not appear in broadcast or printed advertisements, although such advertisements must not be misleading as to energy consumption of the products.)

The labels as proposed are not without difficulties. Some public interest groups have complained that the cost data are misleading because they rely on past energy prices rather than future energy costs. For example, the Environmental Defense Fund, in a formal comment to the Federal Trade Commission, filed October 2, 1978, stated,

(1) The proposed labeling program uses past energy price data rather than using relevant energy prices—that is, prices which will prevail in the years in which the labeled appliances will actually be used. Because of dramatically increasing price trends, this grossly understates the annual operating costs of appliances; and
(2) Due to the failure of the proposed program to adequately take account of the enormous regional variations in energy prices, the proposed

program fails to provide consumers with a workable way of determining the *actual operating costs* consumers will incur and instead provides only a grossly misleading national average.

EDF suggests that the federal government set up a toll free telephone number for consumers to find out their own local rates and a multiplier to apply to the energy prices for their locale. However, it is doubtful whether such a system would solve the information problem in a satisfactory manner; at least the present labels give a comparative rating among models, although they tend to strongly understate the cost advantages of buying a more efficient model in a time of rising energy prices.

Consumer Reports for January 1979 points to a potentially misleading effect of the proposed labels. The magazine wonders whether some consumers may be misled into thinking that the federal government has tested the appliance for "performance, convenience, safety, durability, or some other factor not involved with energy." Consumers Union, the publishers of *Consumer Reports*, proposed to the FTC that it require a disclaimer that the products have not been tested for those nonenergy features.

Manufacturers of appliances covered by the regulation have also lodged objections, based largely on what they fear will be misinterpretation of the test results by consumers. Small differences may be, they fear, seized upon by consumers instead of more important variations among models in performance on nonenergy grounds. This objection flies in the face of classic free market theory that calls upon consumers to be completely informed about potential purchases and to exercise consumer sovereignty in comparing energy consumption against number of vegetable crispers. It seems strange to hear appliance manufacturers claim that more information will hinder consumer choices.

On February 12, 1979, the Federal Trade Commission staff recommended to the commission major changes in the rule as published earlier in the *Federal Register*. Major changes recommended by the staff included dropping requirements for labeling for television sets, humidifiers and dehumidifiers, clothes dryers, ranges and ovens, and heating equipment other than furnaces. The staff also suggested that EER numbers (energy efficiency ratings) be given for furnaces and for room and central air conditioners, in place of the annual operating cost figures originally proposed. In the staff report,[19] the labeling requirements for some of the categories were called either economically unjustified or unhelpful to consumers. Defending the use of EERs rather than annual costs, the FTC staff cited the wide variation in climate and heating-cooling requirements as making the information difficult to present fairly, understandably, and accurately.

The commission will consider the report and other information available to it, issuing a final rule during 1979.

Effect of the Testing and Labeling Programs on State Law

Both the testing program and the labeling program are "preemptive"—that is, they cannot be changed by a state wishing to adopt a different testing procedure or label.[20] However, two roles are left open for the states to play. First, although the federal act provides that the Department of Energy and the Federal Trade Commission shall engage in a program of consumer education concerning the meaning and importance of the new labels,[21] states can assist the education process. Public utility commissions can require stuffers with utility bills that explain how to use the federally mandated labels. (New York State has already undertaken a bill stuffer program directed at publicizing the costs of running electrical appliances; such a program could easily be adopted and expanded elsewhere.) Consumer education offices at the state level can produce, distribute, and translate educational materials, and schools can include information about energy efficiency labeling in consumer education courses.

States can play another role as well. Under the terms of the federal act, establishing the test procedures and designing the information and format of the efficiency label itself are rulemaking procedures.[22] According to the federal Administrative Procedure Act, which governs all actions taken by the federal bureaucracy in the absence of specific statutory language, when the government undertakes rulemaking, it must provide interested parties the opportunity to be heard.[23] Although the current set of rulemaking proceedings for testing and labeling now is nearly completed, state governments can intervene in new rulemaking under EPCA if additional products are added to the coverage of that act. In principle, states can also petition for a new ruling to reopen the old testing or labeling procedures at any time.

Energy Efficiency Standards Program

As noted in the preceding paragraphs, the labeling and the testing programs are almost exclusively federal programs. Since picking the relevant matters to test and weighing the importance to both manufacturers and consumers of nationwide and industrywide uniform tests defies a consensus, the federal preemption is probably justified. Moreover, as long as the tests reflect at least the approximate efficiency of the piece of equipment in actual use, details of test procedures are crucial only if they are not uniformly implemented. Nationally standardized procedures insure this uniformity.

The mandatory standards program is more of a mixed collection of federal preemption and state potentials. As the act was originally written, there were no mandatory standards for appliances. Instead, the law called upon the administrator of the Federal Energy Administration to set an energy efficiency improvement target for each of the types of products mentioned in the act. The minimum standard acceptable was to be, for all appliances taken together, an energy consumption level 20 percent below 1972 use levels. The maximum standard was to be set at the highest efficiency that would be "economically and technologically feasible,"[24] though "economically and technologically feasible" was nowhere defined in the provision. Once a goal was set, manufacturers would have been required to make information available to the Federal Energy Administration in order to allow it to monitor the industry's progress toward compliance with the goals. Under the original law, if the manufacturers failed to meet the goals established as voluntary targets, the federal government was given the power to convert the voluntary targets into mandatory standards if it could show that the improvement would be economically justified and technologically feasible and that the labeling program alone would not be likely to induce production and sale of appliances meeting the target. Under the procedures mandated under the original act, it would have taken a year to impose a mandatory standard, even if all the findings had been made and remained unchallenged.

The 1978 National Energy Act substantially revised this rather cumbersome procedure and permits the federal government to proceed directly to imposition of mandatory appliance efficiency standards. Under the NEA,[25] the secretary of energy is directed to develop standards for the thirteen categories of appliances covered by the original Energy Policy and Conservation Act. NEA directs the secretary to give priority in setting standards to (1) refrigerators and refrigerator-freezers, (2) freezers, (3) clothes dryers, (4) water heaters, (5) room air conditioners, (7) home-heating equipment other than furnaces, (8) kitchen ranges and ovens, (9) central air conditioners, and (10) furnaces. In other words, from the original list of thirteen product categories, dishwashers, television sets, clothes washers, and humidifiers and dehumidifiers are to be given lower priority. The standards set by the secretary must meet the following statutory test:

Energy efficiency standards for each type (or class) of covered products prescribed under this section shall be designed to achieve the maximum improvement in energy efficiency which the Secretary determines is technologically feasible and economically justified. Such standards may be phased in, over a period not in excess of 5 years, through the establishment of intermediate standards, as determined by the Secretary.[26]

Since the setting of the standard depends heavily on what the secretary determines is "economically justified," the act requires the secretary to consider several factors:

Before determining whether a standard is economically justified under [this section] the Secretary . . . shall determine that the benefits of the standard exceed its burdens based, to the greatest extent practicable, on a weighing of the following factors:
(1) the economic impact of the standard on the manufacturers and on the consumers of the products subject to such standard,
(2) the savings in operating costs throughout the estimated average life of the covered products in the type (or class), compared to any increase in the price of, or in the initial charges for, or maintenance expenses of, the covered products which are likely to result from the imposition of the standard,
(3) the total projected amount of energy savings likely to result directly from the imposition of the standard,
(4) any lessening of the utility or the performance of the covered products likely to result from the imposition of the standard,
(5) the impact of any lessening of competition determined in writing by the Attorney General that is likely to result from the imposition of the standard,
(6) the need of the Nation to conserve energy, and
(7) any other factors the Secretary considers relevant.[27]

Unfortunately, these "guidelines" to the secretary are so broad as to encompass virtually every factor that could be relevant! But the major theme is that the secretary is directed to compare the total life cycle cost of the appliance with the standards to the cost without. A fair reading of the congressional intent of this section is that the secretary must take life cycle cost minimization as the lodestar of setting the goal, unless other public policies (such as antitrust or ruin of an industry) are violated because of the standard.

The NEA also permits the secretary of energy to set efficiency standards for products other than the original thirteen categories if there is a finding that:

(1) the average per household energy use within the United States by a product exceeded 150 kilowatt-hours (or its BTU equivalent) for any twelve-calendar-month period ending before such determination;

(2) The aggregate household energy use within the United States by a product exceeded 4,200,000,000 kilowatt-hours (or its BTU equivalent) for any such twelve-calendar-month period;

(3) Substantial improvement in energy efficiency is technologically feasible; *and*

(4) A labeling requirement alone will not be sufficient to induce manufacturers to make and consumers to buy products that achieve maximum energy efficiency.[28]

Within two years after the passage of the act (that is, by November 9, 1980), the secretary must list those appliances that will be subject to mandatory standards; he may add to the list from time to time.

In a concession to the smaller manufacturer of appliances, small businesses (defined as ones whose total gross revenues from all operations for the preceding twelve month period do not exceed $8 million) can be exempted from control for up to two years following the prescription of an energy efficiency standard. For the purposes of deciding whether a business is covered, the total operations of its parent company must be considered.

Under the older law, there was considerable room for states to supplement the federal program. However, the NEA limits the scope of state action. Although state standards that were in force on or before January 1, 1978 covering any of the thirteen product categories are not immediately preempted, states may not impose new appliance standards for any of the thirteen categories after that date; federal law prohibits imposition of state standards until July 1, 1980, if the federal standards for any of the thirteen categories are not ready by that time. Any state standards promulgated after July 1, 1980 are temporary and cease to be effective when the federal government finally promulgates a standard. The conference committee report on the NEA reminds the secretary that the fact that a federal standard is due soon should weigh heavily in his decision to permit a state standard to prevail. The burden on a state seeking to impose a temporary standard is in fact quite heavy.

Carrying over from the older law, states and manufacturers continue to have the right to petition the secretary of energy either to be exempted from the preemtion (in the case of a state) or to preempt a state standard (in the case of a manufacturer). The secretary must issue a finding that the state standard would unduly burden interstate commerce.

The effect of the preemption is quite complete. The conference committee report notes that:

Under subsection 424(b), preemption would apply to both a State standard and any "other" requirement respecting the energy efficiency of any product. Thus establishment of a Federal standard, for example, with respect to the energy efficiency of gas ranges would automatically preempt both State efficiency standards affecting such ranges and any other State requirements affecting gas range energy efficiency such as a State prohibition on gas pilot lights.

Since NEA, states will therefore find it far more difficult to enter directly into the arena of standard setting.

This change in the law is unfortunate, since many states—most notably California—were leaders in pushing appliance manufacturers and the federal government toward tougher appliance standards. The California standards for refrigerators, freezers, and room air conditioners that become effective in November 1979 influenced Arizona, Wisconsin, and Minnesota to adopt similar standards and caused refrigerator manufacturers nationally to design to the tough standards. The advantage of a tough state stance is thus weakened in the name of national uniformity. The next section of this chapter explores some of the non-standard-setting options that may still be open for a state to explore.

THE STATE ROLE IN HOME APPLIANCE ENERGY EFFICIENCY

Though labeling, testing, and standard setting are all now almost completely under federal control, states still have an important part to play in improving the efficiency of home energy-consuming equipment. To understand the role is to understand why energy efficiency has not already sold itself and why some supplementary state action might be helpful.

For at least four reasons, people do not act in their own economic self-interest when they buy goods. First, they may not have sufficient information to calculate the operating costs of a piece of equipment. They may not even realize that there are differences in efficiency. This information gap can be filled by carefully designed, uniform federal labels. Second, consumers may have inadequate or incorrect information on the trends of fuel costs. They may believe, for example, that the rise in energy costs is commensurate to the rate of inflation; they may think that cost escalations are spurred by some business or government conspiracy that can be stopped by vigorous action; or they may misunderstand the relationship between resource scarcity and prices. These misunderstandings will cause consumers to undervalue the importance of energy efficiency. State (and federal) governments must be frank with their citizens about the inevitably higher fuel costs that can be expected; they must cease trying to freeze energy prices at artificially low prices by means of subsidies, tax rebates, and special provisions that confuse welfare objectives (such as lifeline rates) with general subsidies (such as lifeline rates extended to all residential customers). State governments must be convinced that shrunken supplies of hard to obtain energy will inevitably mean higher prices; the laws of economics cannot be circumvented. Once persuaded, state governments must attempt to convince their citizens of these matters. Unfortunately, however, political courage is not a commodity that can be generated by legal or regulatory means.

The third—and perhaps the most important—reason is that consumers may find that a more energy-efficient appliance will have a higher first cost than its less energy-efficient cousin. (Of course, energy efficiency does not necessarily cost more. But if increased efficiency is cheaper, no governmental action beyond accurate labeling is necessary, assuming that consumers believe the savings are worth the trouble it takes to compare models.) From the government's point of view, offering a purchaser financial incentives to help himself economically raises important philosophical questions. Should government interfere with the marketplace in order to encourage socially desirable behavior? If subsidies are given to homeowners, isn't that simply a means of subsidizing the relatively well off with tax revenues collected from all income classes? If tax deductions or rebates are given, doesn't that further favor those with higher incomes to whom deductions or rebates are most important?

All these issues are legitimate political questions and deserve to be aired and acted upon by legislatures. State and federal policies often consider other social goals sufficiently important to warrant intervention in the marketplace, even when the benefits and burdens of the intervention do not fall equally on all income classes. Tariffs to protect domestic industries that might be vital in time of war artificially raise the price of those domestically produced products during peacetime. Lifeline utility rates lower the cost of electricity to some consumers by raising the rates paid by others. Income tax deductions for mortgage interest payments encourage homeownership by raising the tax rates for all taxpayers, homeowners or not. Federal insurance on bank deposits costs all depositers money, but is used only by those who deposit their savings in mismanaged banks. These are only a few of the instances in which states and the federal government have decided that payments to a small (often comparatively wealthy) class of citizens in the name of a larger social goal are worth the cost to all citizens. Energy conservation could well join this list, because incentives to owners of buildings to save energy can be viewed as an investment in a longer, slower, and more humane transition to an era of renewable energy sources. Moreover, unlike many of the well-accepted subsidies that interfere with the market, energy conservation is not regressive. Put another way, conservation in appliance energy use can help poor people as well as rich ones. In fact, if rich people waste energy through use of wasteful appliances, poor people lose twice—first, when everyone's energy costs rise because more expensive supplies are brought on line, and second, when the appliances are put on the used appliance market for poor people to buy.[29]

If a legislative decision is made to encourage citizens to invest initially larger sums in purchasing energy-conserving household equipment, a variety of programs may be considered. The following checklist of legislative strategies is only illustrative:

Loan Guarantees

A state can guarantee loans to consumers for household machines that meet energy conservation standards set above the minimum federal base. In principle, the state guarantee should grant either lower interest rates or loans during times when such loans would not otherwise be given. The loan guarantee is a relatively inexpensive device for states to adopt; the guarantee alone costs no taxes, and it requires picking up only a small percentage of all the loans actually guaranteed. Apparently no state has such legislation, and some states have constitutional provisions that forbid the lending of the state's credit or guarantee to private parties.

Direct State Loans

A state can directly loan consumers money to buy energy-conserving equipment. A bill was introduced into the 1975–1976 regular session of the General Assembly of Ohio to add the following provisions to the Public Utilities Code of the state:

> The Public Utilities Commission, may . . . make loans to finance the installation of insulation, storm windows, weather stripping, heat pumps, or other energy conservation materials or equipment in dwellings. Such loans shall be made for terms not to exceed three years. All loans for improvements to dwellings equipped with all-electric furnaces, air conditioners, waterheaters, ranges, refrigerators, dishwashers, clotheswashers, and clothesdryers shall bear interest at an annual rate of five percent. For other dwellings, a loan shall bear no interest if the borrower is sixty-five years old or older or is a low income person as defined by rule of the Commission, or in the case of other borrowers shall bear interest at an annual rate of five percent.

> The Commission shall adopt and may amend or repeal rules . . . setting forth: loan application procedures; eligibility requirements including but not limited to mortgages or other security interests to secure a loan; limits on the amount of individual loans; loan priorities; inspection procedures; borrower reporting requirements that will enable performance evaluation of each project; and energy conservation standards for rental dwelling units.
>
> All loan funds under this section shall be made from the Energy Conservation Revolving Fund.
>
> There is hereby established in the State Treasury a separate fund to be known as the "Energy Conservation Revolving Fund," to consist of funds appropriated and grants or contributions received for and repayments on loans for home improvements for energy conservation purposes.[30]

The bill called for appropriation of $55 million per year for two years to set up the loan fund. The bill failed to be enacted into law.

The costs of such a proposal include administrative costs, the loans that are defaulted upon, and the difference between the interest the state receives on the money from borrowers (5 percent in the Ohio example) and what it could earn using the money in some other way. This latter cost, which businesses call opportunity cost, is difficult to calculate for a state government, since governments do not exist for income-maximizing purposes. But calculating the opportunity cost gives the state a rough measure of the cost of carrying out one activity rather than some other activity.

Direct state loan programs given the state the ability to direct the money into high priority programs. Unfortunately, they may call for the creation of new administrative machinery to process the loans and follow repayments. A state might, accordingly, wish to empower commercial lending institutions to administer the program for them in return for a fee.

Loans from the Public Utility

To the extent permitted by the National Energy Act, utility companies may be the vehicles for loaning money to consumers for energy-conserving capital equipment. This possibility is discussed in Chapter 3 of this book, and a Montana law is mentioned as an example of such a program. As noted in the earlier discussion, the NEA restricts such lending activities unless they existed before the NEA's passage. Although there is a provision for a utility to petition to be exempted from the federal prohibition on lending (or other energy conservation) activities, it is uncertain how stringently that waiver will be construed in practice.

Forgiving All or Part of Certain State Taxes

Although state taxes are usually smaller than their federal equivalents, the state can affect energy usage patterns significantly by offering consumers a variety of tax credits, forgivenesses, or rebates on purchases and use of energy-conserving building equipment. For example, the state of Maine proposed to add the following materials to a list of items exempt from sales and use tax:

Sales of tangible personal property including storm windows, storm doors, insulation, furnace dampers, heat recovery heat exchangers and such other items as The Director of the Maine State Housing Authority certifies as building materials used primarily for the conservation of energy consumption in buildings.[31]

This provision does not exclude energy-efficient building equipment, although a specific mention of such equipment would improve the drafting.

Many states have adopted provisions exempting solar collectors and other solar heating equipment from property tax assessments. A number of states have also granted tax credits for the purchase of solar equipment (up to 55 percent in California). Similar statutes can provide property tax relief or income tax credits for purchase of energy-efficient capital equipment for the home.

Direct Grants for Purchase of Capital Equipment

Direct grants through income transfers (welfare) can be made to older persons or to low income families. The state could record on the title of the property the amount of a loan, including a depreciation table, made to a lower income or older person to buy equipment that was attached permanently to the home. At the time of sale or death, the depreciated value of the equipment provided to the older or low income person could be recouped by the state.

Lower Utility Rates

Somewhat lower, "promotional" utility rates might be granted to customers who purchase energy-conserving major equipment. The lower rates would be made up by higher rates for other customers, thus sparing the state direct cash outlays. The rates, similar to those that used to be common for all-electric homes, should hold for a limited time only, so that persons buying energy-conserving equipment do not reap a permanent bonanza. This system may well be unlawful in some states if it is construed to amount to rate discrimination. Moreover, to give lower utility rates may simply encourage higher uses of energy for other purposes, exactly the opposite effect from that desired.

No one of these programs would convince large number of persons to make a substantially higher initial outlay for energy-efficient equipment, but a combination of them might alter buying habits. If a vigorous public education effort topped off the subsidies and loans, a workable — although expensive — state program might emerge.

Recall that there were four problems that must be dealt with in overcoming consumer resistance to higher prices for energy-conserving equipment. Lack of information, misunderstanding of fuel price trends, and higher first costs have already been discussed. The fourth problem is that of balancing money spent for energy conservation against money spent for other features of an appliance. Although the state or federal government may believe that citizens should pay extra for energy conservation or do without some other feature in order to be able to afford energy conservation, citizens may see their own interests differently, preferring to use their money in an entirely different fashion (buying a larger family room, for example) or buying for some other nonenergy feature (obtaining a particular trusted brand or a larger vegetable crisper). When a purchaser is deciding which home furnace or air-conditioning unit to buy, he is interested in a variety of features, and running cost is only one of them. Should society try to interfere with his choice? How should government go about attracting his attention to the important national issue of energy conservation?

Raising the price of energy-inefficient items helps. Lowering the cost of energy-efficient equipment helps. Labels help. But a more drastic method is to pull energy-inefficient equipment off the market. Government can simply outlaw the sale of equipment that does not meet a certain standard set by law or regulation. Federal law has taken this step. By establishing minimum efficiency standards for household machines, the federal government has removed a purchasing option from the consumer's control. No longer will the consumer be able to buy an appliance at a given price that gives him, say, more capacity or more decorative features instead of more efficiency; the energy efficiency is mandated, and other features may not be played off against it.

Consumers acting alone might not always choose to spend money for performance features, but mandating certain performance characteristics is not a radical notion in the American economy. Seat belts in cars, protective shields on electrically driven saws, and cleanliness standards in food preparation and packaging are all accepted examples of intervention in the name of some social good.

If the market fails to nurture socially desirable behavior, such intervention may be justified. Standards regulating the purity of food became necessary at least in part because there was little economic incentive for producers to be more careful than the most careless manufacturer in the industry; since food adulterations were difficult for consumers to detect, government intervention was necessary. In a similar way, energy efficiency may be difficult for one manufacturer to promote when other manufacturers are pushing cosmetic features. On such grounds, social intervention in the marketplace might be warranted, although this argument must be used with care, since, if accepted too broadly, it contains no clear end.

Conclusion

We have seen that even in the presence of federal regulation, states have some legal room to act in the area of energy conservation programs for household appliances. Educational programs, interventions in federal proceedings, and granting of special incentives for purchase of energy efficient equipment can still form a part of a state's program. Because of the importance of appliances to the nation's energy use in the future, such intervention is probably a good idea. One limited way to begin is to help poorer consumers understand the nature of the choices that are available in purchasing equipment and then, to the extent necessary, to provide financial assistance so that they can make energy investments that will help them and cut energy consumption for all of us.

ENERY CONSERVATION IN COMMERCIAL AND INDUSTRIAL NONPROCESSING EQUIPMENT

Although home-heating, cooling, and appliance type equipment overlaps to some extent with that used for commercial and industrial applications, many building-related pieces of equipment are intended solely for the nonresidential market. Sometimes the differences are strictly those of size; in other cases, entirely different systems (such as terminal reheat systems, economizer cycles, and the like) are used. Under the terms of the federal Energy Policy and Conservation Act, articles intended solely for commercial use are not covered by the testing, labeling, or possible mandatory efficiency standards, since they are not "distributed in commerce for personal use or consumption by an individual."[32] With dual market items, performance benefits that come from disclosure and regulation for the benefit of individual consumers under the provisions of the federal act covering home equipment will presumably be available to commercial and industrial customers as well.

Those items of equipment that are clearly outside the control of the federal statute and the role of the states in improving information about and performance of those items, are the subject of this section. Treatment of large industrial machinery and other productive factory equipment is beyond the scope of this book. This chapter will consider four different strategies that a state might adopt: (1) educational and technical transfer programs, (2) labeling programs combined with standard setting, (3) taxing policies, and (4) pricing strategies.

Educational Strategies and Technical Transfer Programs

Although businessmen are assumed to know their own costs better than consumers do, they may have a grip on their present costs only. The expenses associated with changes in production methods or switches to yet unproven machinery frequently meet with as much resistance from businessmen as from other consumers, while savings linked to such changes may be unknown or but poorly understood. Smaller businessmen who do not have the resources to test the performance of different systems tend to be especially wary of sweeping change. For all these reasons, government can play an important role in assisting in the dissemination of energy conservation information and in training businessmen to calculate the savings that attention to the life cycle costs of business equipment can afford. Fortunately, successful examples of states engaged in business training for energy conservation abound. These programs are discussed in greater detail in *Energy Efficiency in Industry* by Normal L. Dean,[33] and this discussion draws heavily on research conducted by Dean.

The model for all governmental outreach programs is the Cooperative Extension Service, operated jointly by the United States Department of Agriculture and state outreach programs funded in the state land grant universities. This service, founded in 1914, has been a major force in spreading highly technical agricultural information to America's farmers. Although national in scope, the Cooperative Extension Service is local in flavor because of its network of agents at the county level and because research funded in state universities provides information of local use to the farmers served by the Extension Service. In the last two decades, a somewhat similar program was created under the now defunct federal Technical Services Act. These local technical transfer services are, of course,

Table 6-3. University Extension Services.

University	Telephone	Contact	Program Title
Georgia Technical	404/894-2000	Jame Lowry	
Iowa State University	515/294-3420	Waldo Wagner	Center for Industrial Research and Services
Kansas State University	913/532-6011	William Honstad	
Michigan State University	517/355-0118	Ira Olstrum	
University of Missouri (Rolla)	314/341-4111	Edwin Lorey	University of Missouri (Rolla) Extension
University of New Mexico	505/277-0111	Carey O'Bryan	Technology Application Center
North Carolina State University	919/737-3262	John Hart	Industrial Extension Service
Pennsylvania State University	814/865-0427	H. Leroy Marlow	Pennsylvania Technical Assistance Program
University of Tennessee	615/242-2456	Ruben Harris	Center for Industrial Services
	615/974-4251	John Gibbons	Environment Center
Texas A & M University	713/845-3211	Steve Riter	
University of Wisconsin	608/262-3980	Bruce Murray	University of Wisconsin Extension

Source: Norman L. Dean, *Energy Efficiency in Industry* (Cambridge, Mass.: Ballinger Publishing Company, forthcoming).

designed to assist businessmen in more than energy matters; but within the last few years, energy research has been of increasing interest to those served by technical transfer programs. Table 6-3, reproduced from Dean's book, lists the names, addresses, titles, and telephone numbers of a few of these technical extension services.

A typical statute establishing technical training facilities is the one creating the Center for Industrial Services in Tennessee:

Be it enacted by the General Assembly of the State of Tennessee, That there is hereby established a Center for Government, Industry, and Law which shall operate as a Division of the University of Tennessee to provide

continuing research and technical assistance to State and Local Government and Industry and to meet more adequately the need for information and research in business and government.

. . .

. . . [A]s a part of this Center there is created an Industrial Research
Advisory Service to render service to the industries of this State by providing information, data and materials relating to the needs and problems
of industry which might be supplied and solved through research; . . .

The Pennsylvania Technical Assistance Program (PENNTAP),
which provides research and technical advice without charge to any
organization within the state, is another sound program. As one of
its functions, PENNTAP disseminates promising new technologies to
potential users within the state. Conferences, seminars, short courses,
workshops, and a daily radio program are but a few of the methods
it uses to spread new ideas to its users. During 1975, PENNTAP
responded to 1,642 inquiries, an average of one request a day for
each of the seven full-time field agents assigned to PENNTAP.

Utility Company Advisory Services. In addition to state technology programs operated by the university-based extension services,
technical advisory services for business and industry run by public
utility companies are also common. Although these services are
financed from the rates paid by all customers, typically they are
available (or at least publicized) only to the utility's biggest energy
customers. To the extent that such programs are not already operated by local utilities, they should be encouraged. Their services can
range from consultation with smaller commercial users for the purpose of improving operating and maintenance procedures (such as
thermostat settings and relamping) to full-scale building energy
audits.

If public utility commissions have not authorized the provision of
such consulting services to customers, the public utility commissions
could, by rule, authorize them. The cost would be a legitimate business expense.

Other Educational Devices. A variety of other educational devices can be used by existing or newly created educational groups.
PENNTAP has a telephone hotline to back up its daily radio program. The University of Wisconsin Extension has a 120 point radio
system, transmitting through telephone lines, for person-to-person
education. The Iowa State University Center for Industrial Research
and Service attempts to send its field representatives out at least once
a year to every business organization in the state that might benefit
from the technological assistance the service offers.

Although educational services are valuable, legislation alone clearly cannot guarantee that they will meet their objectives. Confidence in the agent's advice, an active and imaginative program staffed by competent personnel, and high visibility will all help translate the many existing good ideas into action on a building-by-building basis.

State-enforced Testing and Labeling for Nonhousehold Building Equipment

Testing and labeling of commercial building equipment is not regulated by the federal Energy Policy and Conservation Act. To a great extent, testing and performance rating is covered by the actions of private groups such as the American National Standards Institute and the American Society for the Testing of Materials. These groups promulgate standardized testing procedures for covered classes of equipment. Although the tests do not have the force of law, most manufacturers will use them because they understand that informed architects, engineers, or purchasing agents will demand the information. In the absence of uniform agreed upon testing procedures, efficiency labels will be meaningless. Therefore, a state wishing to require efficiency labels must develop or refer to a comprehensive testing procedure as a basis for efficiency labeling. A number of methods can be used to develop such testing procedures. First, for appliances that have analogs in home equipment covered by the federal Energy Policy and Conservation Act, a state might simply adopt the DOE-approved test for a particular class of equipment. Second, for some categories of building equipment, a state could pick a relatively simple measure of efficiency—one that required no testing procedure at all, but rather basic arithmetic. The Energy Efficiency Ratio used in California to judge the efficiency of air-conditioning units is one such simple efficiency test. Although a test itself may be easily enough described in a state regulation, the pitfall of this approach is knowing whether the chosen efficiency rating is appropriately difficult to attain or whether it simply represents the present status quo. This problem can be solved by choosing a variation of this second kind of testing procedure: equipment can be rated and the minimum performance standard based upon the energy requirements of the most efficient equipment marketed.

A third method is to permit a state administrative agency to select a representative testing and labeling procedure after conducting full hearings aimed at taking the interests of the public, the owners, and the producers into account. This approach, although it fails to provide the specificity within the legislation that the others do, would probably result in the most workable final set of testing regulations.

In the case of state regulations on both testing and labeling, the legal problem of potential burdens on interstate commerce may arise. This problem may be especially troubling in the case of industrial and commercial equipment, and therefore, the legal controversy is outlined here. The nub of the problem is that the United States Constitution has given to Congress the exclusive right to regulate trade and commerce among the states. This provision grew out of the experience of the Confederation, before our present Constitution was drafted and ratified. This experience taught that local protectionism could destroy free internal trade; free internal trade was seen as a major incentive to form a nation.

Yet it is immediately clear that the Congress cannot regulate all aspects of every commercial transaction. The Constitution makes it clear that when Congress has exercised the power granted to it under the Commerce Clause, all contrary or frustrating state regulations or taxes must give way, but the troubling question remains: Which state regulations are valid in the absence of any congressional declarations? This question has been at the root of literally hundreds of cases, and has not always been possible to structure it into a simple or internally consistent doctrine. Starting with the case of *Cooley v. Board of Wardens of the Port of Philadelphia*, decided in 1851,[34] this conflict has been expressed in a number of ways. In *Cooley*, a Pennsylvania law required that all ships hire local pilots to guide them into and out of the Philadelphia harbor. Cooley was fined for violating this statute and argued that the Pennsylvania law constituted a burden on interstate commerce. The court disagreed, saying in part, that

> Whatever subjects of this power [i.e., the congressional power to regulate interstate commerce] are in their nature national, or admit only of one uniform system, or plan of regulation, may justly be said to be of such a nature as to require exclusive legislation by Congress. [However, the nature of local pilotage] is such, that until Congress should find it necessary to exert its power, it should be left to the legislation of the States; that it is local and not national; that it is likely to be the best provided for, not by one system, or plan of regulations, but by as many as the legislative discretion of the several States should deem applicable to the local peculiarities of the ports within their limits.

Inconsistent regulations, uncompensated for by substantial state interests in safety or health, may be struck down. The leading case in this regard is *Bibb v. Navajo Freight Lines*.[35] In *Bibb*, the state of Illinois required all trucks, whether intrastate or interstate, to be equipped with a particular kind of rear fender mudguard. The mudguard, the evidence showed, would have been illegal in Arkansas and would have been different from those permitted in at least forty-five other states. The Supreme Court, Mr. Justice Douglas writing the opinion, held that the Illinois statute, though nondiscriminatory against interstate commerce, was unconstitutional:

> A State which insists on a design out of line with the requirements of almost all the other States may sometimes place a great burden of delay and inconvenience on those interstate motor carriers entering or crossing its territory. Such a new safety device—out of line with the requirements of the other States—may be so compelling that the innovating State need not be the one to give way. But the present showing—balanced against the clear burden on commerce—is far too inconclusive to make this mudguard meet that test.
>
> We deal not with absolutes but with questions of degree.[36]

As suggested in the analysis above, local regulations that protect health and safety are more likely than other regulations to sustain an attack against a charge that a state regulation burdens interstate commerce. Does energy conservation and protection of natural resources have this special protection? Unfortunately, no cases have yet been decided on this point. The closest appellate case concerns the constitutionality of a regulation by the state of Oregon requiring a deposit on bottles used for soft drinks and beer. The Oregon appellate court upheld the Oregon regulation; the Supreme Court of Oregon denied review, and the case was not further reviewed by the United States Supreme Court.[37] The Oregon case may be relevant to the regulation of nonhousehold building equipment efficiency, since the plaintiffs—brewers, soft drink companies, and makers of non-returnable bottles and cans—argued that Oregon's unique system of regulation—which prescribed a lower deposit rate for standardized bottles that could be used by any manufacturer—impeded the national and regional market structure for the beverages. A note in the *Harvard Law Review*, "State Environmental Protection Legislation and the Commerce Clause,"[38] concludes that, even though the Oregon bottle case was correctly decided, the opinion failed to follow the direction of the case law, which is toward balancing the local good that was being sought against the ensuing disruption of interstate commerce. "Even though interstate commerce regulation by a state survives a test which balances its effect," the note reads, "the likelihood of conflicting commands by different states in the future may demand recognition at the outset that only uniform regulation is permissible."

What appears to be the current test for balancing the burden on interstate commerce against the state's interest in its own regulation was recently set out by the Supreme Court in *Pike v. Bruce Church, Inc.*[39] In *Pike*, which struck down an Arizona requirement barring the shipment of local cantaloupes out of the state unless they were crated, the Court said:

> Where the statute regulates evenhandedly to effectuate a legitimate local public interest, and its effects on interstate commerce are only incidental, it will be upheld unless the burden imposed on such commerce is clearly excessive in relation to the putative local benefits.

This brief discussion of the cases—confusing to both lawyers and nonlawyers alike—suggests a few practical rules that a state legislature should consider in enacting specific regulatory legislation. But these general rules should be placed against the background that no general rules will guarantee success. Professor Philip Soper has written:

> It bears repeating that the resolution of pre-emption and Commerce Clause issues very much depends on the facts of each particular case. While this makes it difficult to devise general theories applicable to all cases, one theme that dominates many of the judicial decisions in this area deserves emphasis. That theme concerns the presumption of validity in favor of state and local regulations, requiring those who challenge such legislation to present a convincing case in order to succeed.
>
> . . .
>
> . . . [A]ttempts to cope with environmental problems have led to increasing recognition of the complexity of the solutions and of the often inadequate knowledge base for providing such solutions. These facts strongly support an approach to interpretation of the Commerce Clause that preserves maximum flexibility for state experimentation in the absence of explicit contrary directions from Congress. As already noted, one court has, in fact, gleaned just such a general policy direction from a variety of federal legislation in the environmental area. [Citing the Oregon bottle case], [t]his trend should be continued and reenforced as courts continue to face questions of preemption and claims of undue interference with federal interest in the environmental area.[40]

Against this legal background, how should states act to maximize the possibility that their energy conservation regulations will withstand a challenge? There is no guarantee in advance, but taking the following steps will help.

1. To the extent possible, legislation should emphasize the connection between the regulation and the health and safety of the citizens of the state. Stressing the importance of energy conservation as a national goal for the preservation of security and of a functioning economy may foster such a connection.

2. Legislation should emphasize the state's particular need for regulation and the manner in which the chosen regulation solves that problem deftly and with a minimum of interference with interstate commerce.

3. States should not put burdens on commerce that invite retaliation from other states. Thus, local products, businesses, or services should not be exempted from regulation.

4. To the extent possible, states should attempt to pattern regulations on standards or tests that are used in other states or that at least do not conflict with other states' requirements or seem particularly onerous. If multistate development of standards is possible through a grant from a regional commission or some other regional body, regulations so developed are apt to be viewed as more reasonable than those devised by a single state.

Use of State Taxing Power to Enhance Energy Efficiency

Direct regulation may be augmented or entirely replaced by state taxation or other disincentives in order to promote the sale of energy-efficient equipment. This strategy is discussed at length in another book in this series, *Economic Disincentives for Energy Conservation*, by Joe W. Russell, Jr.[41] Use of such taxes to improve the efficiency of air-conditioning units will illustrate the general approach. While it is technologically possible to build air conditioners with greatly improved efficiencies, the more efficient units sometimes cost more to purchase. Manufacturers fear that buyers, failing to take into account lifetime savings, will choose the less expensive first cost option. A tax could be used to encourage consumers to purchase, and manufacturers to make, more efficient units.

One possible approach to levying such a tax is illustrated here using large commercial air-conditioning equipment as an example. We begin by measuring the efficiency of each unit and expressing this as an energy efficiency ratio (EER). The EER of every model of air conditioning sold within the state can be listed to rank all similar pieces of equipment in order of efficiency. The median EER (the EER at which equal numbers of units rank above and below) is selected as the zero point, and units with efficiencies at the median (that is, at the zero point) would be entirely free from taxation. Units with lower efficiencies can be taxed on a sliding scale that charges so much per unit for each one-tenth of a point of EER that the unit falls below the zero point. Similarly, units with efficiencies above the median can get tax credits based on their positions, calculated in tenths of a point, above the zero point. Use of such prorated taxes and tax breaks will drive the price of the low efficiency models up while lowering the price of the more effective models. Such a system has the virtue of administrative simplicity, since no difficult calculations are required and since the tax can be collected at the time that other sales taxes on building equipment are collected. Furthermore, the zero point can be recalculated every few years so that the energy efficiency zero point remains a "moving target."

Of course, this taxing plan does not guarantee that the revenue earned from the tax will match the revenue expended in the credit, since the zero point does not take market shares for each model into account. A highly efficient model could, at least temporarily, command a large share of the sales and thus require state spending in support of the rebate. There is probably no easy method to deal with this revenue problem in advance, since sales information on a model-by-model basis is customarily treated as confidential business data and companies are thus unwilling to reveal such facts to government.

The taxing plan also has one other defect; it is difficult to implement accurately for equipment that is difficult to place accurately on an energy efficiency scale. As the calculations become more complex or controversial, the administrative simplicity of this taxing plan diminishes.

Taxation of goods arriving through interstate commerce presents another thicket of constitutional problems. Taxation that is not directed toward raising revenue but is aimed at accomplishing certain goals, such as energy conservation, may also face difficult constitutional challenges. These challenges are discussed at greater length in Russell's volume on economic disincentives; readers are referred to that book for a discussion of the issues.

Pricing Strategies

Educational strategies for improving energy conservation in commercial building equipment are always safe for a state to pursue. But the preceeding two sections discussing the legal and regulatory problems surrounding state labeling, efficiency standards, and tax disincentive programs give some notion that such programs may be hard to implement at the state level. The necessity of expensive standard setting (along with an adequate testing procedure), the high risk of a challenge from equipment sellers and manufacturers, and the possibility of inadvertently setting the standards or the taxes either too high or too low are all reasons to be cautious about adopting regulatory strategies for commercial building equipment.

Does the need for caution counsel inaction on the part of states until the federal government acts? Not necessarily. Some regulation may be acceptable and workable. But the general difficulties of intervening in the marketplace should make state governments cautious.

Let us turn to another strategy that has the benefit of elegance, simplicity, and economic rationality and the drawback of political unpopularity. This is, of course, permitting the energy prices paid by consumers to rise. Simply stated, the price of energy to consumers within the state can be permitted to rise to the replacement cost of that energy. As will be set out more fully below, such a course would encourage price-sensitive businessmen to make the conservation investments that are economically justified at the new, higher prices.

The case in favor of adopting so-called marginal cost pricing for all forms of energy rests upon a few basic principles of economics. Economics begins with the acceptance of the notion that all resources are limited, at least when compared to human desires for them. Choices have to be made. In this country, those choices are ordinarily expressed through the operation of the free market economy. The free market economy holds a special place as the historical ideal; all economic activities that take place outside the free market system have to be defended either as special cases for which no free market can or should exist or as deviations designed to fill some gap missed by the orderly, automatically functioning market. In a country that champions the free market system, the energy commodity is strangely ringed with regulations. Virtually every form of energy produced in sizable quantities is regulated either directly or indirectly. This regulation is most easily perceived at the state level in the case of natural gas and electricity sold to business and residential consumers. Public utility commissions in every state (with the exception of Texas, which has now adopted a limited form of statewide regulation) grant public utility companies monopolies in exchange for certain promises by those companies. The most important promise exacted from the utilities is that conditions of service and rates will be subject to regulation by the public utility commission.

Much of the system of regulation and pricing has been explicitly or implicitly designed to hold the price of energy low. (In contrast, energy prices in Europe have deliberately been kept high, at least historically.) The American policy undoubtedly provides benefits: affordable energy for poorer citizens is one. Unfortunately, the policy has its costs: more energy is used than might be if the price were higher; environmental damages have not been calculated into dollar prices; and the enormous, postwar industrial capital structure depends on a continued supply of energy that is no longer as cheap as it once was. Some economists criticized the decision to keep the price of energy low, arguing that public regulation's proper function is to mimic, as nearly as possible, what a free market would do if one existed; their criticisms have met little general acceptance in the political arena. Let us discuss what a free market in energy supplies would look like and what consequences it would have for businessmen deciding to purchase energy-consuming building equipment.

Standard economic theory holds that an efficient firm operating in a free market economy should price all of its products at the cost it takes to make the last unit it produces. (The cost of the final unit produced includes, of course, a profit, representing the reward investors demand for the use of their money on a risky venture.) The last increment of production is at the edge, or margin, of production, so economists call this method of pricing "marginal cost pricing." Long-run marginal or incremental cost pricing applies this principle to the future, to a firm's planning horizon. It does not deal with what the next unit of production will cost (that is, what is the short-run marginal cost), but seeks to answer the question: If we expand to increase production, what will the final unit from the expanded facilities cost? Put another way, long-run marginal cost pricing includes not only the additional costs of producing units with existing capacity, but also the capital charges for building new capacity required to meet the foreseeable increasing demand for a product. If each firm in a given market adopts marginal cost pricing, then for a given pattern of income distribution at a given time, no person or firm can make any trade that will increase his satisfaction without decreasing the satisfaction of one or another of his trading partners. Labor, natural resources, energy, and capital will all be called for at exactly the correct rate—no more and no less.

The key to this perfectly balanced condition in which each person is as happy as he or she can be, given a certain income level, is accurately pricing goods and services at the marginal cost. If the price of energy (or any other good or service) is set below the marginal cost, consumers will want to use more of that product than they would otherwise: it will appear to be a real bargain. In a normal, competitive situation, a firm selling energy below the marginal cost would find that it was not generating sufficient revenue to cover its marginal costs and would either raise its price (thus dampening demand) or decrease production. A firm selling energy (or some other good) above its competitors' marginal cost would find that its competitors could undercut its price and continue to make a profit.

Monopolies, oligopolies, and industries regulated by the government (industries whose products' prices are administered rather than set by market forces) raise problems that one cannot depend on automatic forces to solve. When consumers have no effective choice among suppliers, the price can either be generally too high or, for some customers who are subsidized by other customers paying too much, too low. Thus, monopolies, especially those supplying real necessities of life like salt, water, electricity, or food, have the power to exact more money from their consumers. Public regulation has tried to address this problem. In the case of ordinary commercial products, the antitrust laws have been used to make certain that firms or combinations of firms do not acquire or use monopoly power. But there are some businesses that are so-called "natural monopolies." They are "natural" in the sense that there would be wasteful duplication if competition were permitted to exist. Suppose, for example, there were five telephone companies in one city. Each would dig up the streets, each would have its own telephone directory, and a subscriber to one system would find it difficult to call his friends who used the other companies. These natural monopolies have been permitted to exist with strong public regulation intended to keep them from acting in a predatory manner.

One of the most regulated features of natural monopolies is the price charged to customers for the services provided. It has, unfortunately, been regulation that has departed from the goal of mimicking the free market system and instead has sought to keep costs to consumers lower than marginal costs (at least in recent years). The way that electricity is priced illustrates how far public regulation departs from the market ideal. The prevailing method for pricing electricity in this country is to begin with the total revenue requirements of the utility, including the cost of operating its plants, paying off its debt, running its billing and repair services, and paying salaries, among other things. In practice, the average costs of providing services to each class of customers—residential, commercial, industrial, and so on—are calculated, so that the customers in a class must produce a set portion of the utility's revenue. Only after the total dollars are calculated does the regulatory commission decide how to price the electricity in order to raise that sum. The ordinary method is to take, for each customer class, the average cost of producing electricity and to charge that class's customers that average amount per kilowatt hour.

Numbers may help illustrate this point. Suppose that an electric utility company has a system composed of ten generating plants, with an average capital cost of about $300 per kilowatt. But new capacity—that capacity needed to meet increasing demands—costs $800 to $1,200 per kilowatt. Electricity generated from the new plant will cost the utility from 4 to 5.5 cents per kilowatt hour; but electricity generated from the system as a whole will only be 2 cents per kilowatt hour.

The effect of this pricing scheme is clear. A building owner is faced with a decision: Should I add a little more heating capacity to this building or, instead, should I spend money on some extra shading and insulation? In calculating the total cost of both decisions, the owner will of course consider the cost of operating the additional heating capacity. He will see that the energy to operate the heater is charged to him at 2 cents per kilowatt hour. But the cost to the utility to provide the kilowatt hour is really 5 cents because it is a new load. The use of an average pricing scheme, where old and new prices are averaged together, will translate into artificially low rates at the time our hypothetical building owner is making his decision. Looking at the average rates, he may well decide to add more heating capacity rather than to use a more efficient building design and more efficient building equipment. Yet the same levels of comfort and service to the building's occupants are provided in each case: they differ only in that the decision to use more energy will cost more in the end and use more resources.

Two effects will issue from the decision of our hypothetical building owner. First, his decision will add to the demand on the utility, virtually guaranteeing that the utility will have to add new capacity sooner than it would have had to otherwise. Put another way, average prices help guarantee that growth projections by utility companies become self-fulfilling prophecies. Second, from the building owner's point of view, as time passes and new, more expensive generating equipment is added to the system to meet the demands imposed by our new building and others, the average price will begin to rise rapidly. Our owner's original calculation will swiftly become obsolete as prices rise toward a new average price that is heavily influenced by the higher priced new capacity, and he will find that he would have been better advised to choose a more efficient design of building or equipment. The further irony is that so long as the utility system continues to use the average price method of calculating costs and so long as installing new capacity costs much more than operating at old capacity, each new building owner making the decision will be victimized by this expensive con game. Even more serious, society will find itself running a continuous race to catch a mechanical rabbit; the decision to move toward an energy-conserving society will forever be postponed.

Another effect of this mispricing is harder to see and more insidious: the market for energy-conserving equipment and designs will be smaller than it would be if more people demanded better, more efficient equipment and buildings. Without a market in which to sell goods and services, entrepreneurs will not be attracted into the energy conservation supply business. Thus, the nation will not get as many innovative solutions to energy use problems as it would if energy prices were right. The result is a triple threat—we use more, so we have to build more, so we don't invent our way out of the problem!

This brief description of the advantages of adopting marginal cost pricing for energy sold by a state's public utilities does not begin to exhaust the social advantages of this system of pricing as a whole; nor, unfortunately, does it begin to exhaust the system's complexities. But it should begin to suggest why, particularly for the commercial and industrial consumer making energy-related decisions, no other method of encouraging conservation will be so effective. Unless the prices for energy are such that businessmen making purchasing decisions have the correct information about future costs, all other regulatory and education efforts to making building equipment more efficient will buck the tide of price.

One final word is in order about marginal cost pricing as an alternative to average cost pricing. Persons suggesting a change from one system to the other frequently hear it said that marginal cost pricing is untested and that there are many different economic theories of marginal cost pricing, each of which leads to a different method of calculating marginal rates. But the same statement can be made about average cost pricing. The current average cost pricing system's look of solidity and settled truth is merely that of age. The difficult questions of application and interpretation have long since been resolved, so that it has a suspicious look of being obvious. The so-called complexities and uncertainties of the new system can, in the same way, be worked out, and decisions can be made so that the newer system would soon come to be as certain and to operate as automatically as the old.

One major public utility commission, the Public Service Commission of the State of New York, has recently decided that marginal cost pricing principles should be an important factor in setting New York's gas and electricity rates. Although marginal costs are not the only basis for setting utility rates, their adoption places the burden of arguing for some other basis upon the New York utility wishing to use the alternative basis.

Summary

The task of improving the wide variety of nonresidential building equipment is far more complex than the more limited task the federal government has undertaken in regulating household appliances. Instead of the thirteen neatly defined categories contained in the Energy Policy and Conservation Act, a state considering regulation, taxation, or some other means of controlling building equipment must examine a much broader range of building systems. Moreover, these building system are typically and specifically engineered for a particular building, and they use components from many different manufacturers combined into a unique system. With these factors in mind, a state entering into this field must move cautiously. A rational procedure would be first to regulate the items most similar to household equipment and most frequently sold as a unit package. Small commercial air-conditioning and refrigeration equipment and small building package heaters are representative of items in this category. In all cases, the state should consult with a variety of interests, using advisory committees with knowledgeable representatives from different interest groups as an integral part of the planning process for equipment improvement.

CONCLUSION

Equipment improvement is the most frequently overlooked opportunity for energy conservation in the building field. The more easily understood goal of improved insulation and the more glamorous alternative of solar energy both obscure the greater and more quickly available savings to be gleaned from improvements in equipment efficiencies. The federal NEA—pushed by vigorous action by the states—will go a long way toward influencing the residential market. The nonresidential market continues to present enormous opportunities for state action, although the legal and practical pitfalls to individual state action cannot be taken lightly. Although the long-range goal for improving efficiency in this area, as in many others, is to work toward economically rational pricing policies for all forms of energy, numerous educational, regulatory, and taxation strategies can counter the specific failures of our present system to call forth efficient equipment design. These opportunities are too momentous to be ignored.

NOTES

1. National Petroleum Council, *Potential For Energy Consumption in the United States: 1964-1978: Residential/Commercial*, p. 31, table 7.

2. K.W. Ford, G.I. Rochlin, and R.H. Socolow, eds. *Efficient Use of Energy* (New York: American Institute of Physics, AIP Conference Proceedings No. 25, 1975); Marc H. Ross and Robert H. Williams, "Assessing the Potential for Energy Conservation" (Albany, New York: The Institute for Policy Alternatives, July 1, 1975). On thermodynamics generally, see, H.C. Van Ness, *Understanding Thermodynamics* (New York: McGraw-Hill, 1969).

3. Ford et al., *supra* note 2 at 4–5.

4. Eric Hirst, *Residential Energy Conservation Strategies*, ORNL/CON-2 (Oak Ridge, Tenn.: Oak Ridge National Laboratory, September 1976). See also Eric Hirst and Janet Carney, *Residential Energy Use to the Year 2000: Conservation and Economics*, ORNL/CON-13 (Oak Ridge, Tenn.: Oak Ridge National Laboratory, September 1977); and Eric Hirst, *Energy and Economic Benefits of Residential Energy Conservation RD&D*, ORNL/CON-22 (Oak Ridge, Tenn.: Oak Ridge National Laboratory, February 1978).

5. P.L. 94-163, December 22, 1975, 89 Stat. 871.

6. Hirst, *Residential Energy*, *supra* note 4 at 6, n. 8. For a description of the model, see Eric Hirst, Jane Cope, Steve Cohn, William Lin, and Robert Hoskings, *An Improved Engineering-Economic Model of Residential Energy Use*, ORNL/CON-8 (Oak Ridge Tenn.: Oak Ridge National Laboratory, April 1977).

7. Hirst, et al., *supra* note 6 at 28, table 9.

8. *Id.* at 33–34, Conclusion 4.

9. 42 U.S.C. 6291 to 6309.

10. P.L. 94-384, August 14, 1976, 90 Stat. 1125.

11. P.L. 95-619, November 9, 1978, "National Energy Conservation Policy Act, §§ 421–427.

12. EPCA, § 321(a)(1), 42 U.S.C. § 6291(a)(1).

13. EPCA, § 322(a)(1)–(13), 42 U.S.C. §§ 6292(a)(1)–(13).

14. EPCA, § 322(a)(14), 42 U.S.C. § 6292(a)(14). See § 422 *et seq.* of P.L. 95-619 for modification of this provision.

15. EPCA, § 323(b)(1); 42 U.S.C. § 6293(b)(1).

16. EPCA, § 323(c), 42 U.S.C. § 6293(c). The secretary of energy is authorized to determine that a testing procedure cannot be developed that will serve the purposes of the act. See EPCA § 324(a)(1)(A), 42 U.S.C. § 6294(a)(1)(A), referring to EPCA § 323(b), 42 U.S.C. § 6293(b).

17. The Federal Trade Commission may decide not to require a label if the commission finds that such labeling is not economically or technically feasible, or if it finds that "labeling in accordance with [this program] is not likely to assist consumers in purchasing decisions." EPCA § 324(b)(5)(B), 42 U.S.C. § 6294(b)(5)(B).

18. EPCA § 324, 42 U.S.C. § 6294.

19. Federal Trade Commission, *Labeling and Advertising of Consumer Appliances: Final Staff Report to the Federal Trade Commission and Recommended Rule*, *16 CFR Part 305* (Washington D.C.: U.S. Government Printing Office, February 1979).

20. EPCA §§ 327(a)(1) and 327(a)(2)(B), 42 U.S.C. §§ 6297(a)(1) and 6297(a)(2)(B).

21. EPCA § 337, 42 U.S.C. § 6307.

22. EPCA § 324, 42 U.S.C. § 6294; EPCA § 323, 42 U.S.C. § 6293.

23. This general rule is specifically augmented by the provisions of EPCA, which require the secretary to "afford interested persons an opportunity to present oral and written data, views, and arguments." EPCA § 323(a)(3), 42 U.S.C. § 6293(a)(3) (testing), and EPCA § 324(b)(2), 42 U.S.C. § 6294(b) (2) (labeling).

24. EPCA § 325, 42 U.S.C. § 6295. The act actually differentiated between humidifiers, dehumidifiers, central air conditioners, and furnaces and all other covered categories of appliances. The 20 percent minimum improvement in efficiency referred to in the text applied to all appliances except those four just mentioned. For humidifiers, dehumidifers, central air conditioners, and furnaces, the target was to be "designed to achieve the maximum improvement in energy efficiency which the Secretary determines is economically and technologically feasible to attain for each such type manufactured in calendar year 1980." EPCA § 325(a)(2), 42 U.S.C. § 6295(a)(2). Moreover, for those four appliances, the secretary had longer to promulgate voluntary standards. The time was further lengthened in both cases by Section 161 of the Energy Conservation and Production Act, P.L. 94-385, 90 Stat. 1125. However, as noted in the text, the National Energy Act has directed the secretary to prepare mandatory standards; therefore, the voluntary targets are now beside the point.

25. National Energy Conservation Policy Act, P.L. 95-619, § 422 *et seq.*

26. *Id.*

27. *Id.*

28. *Id.*

29. I am grateful to David Goldstein of Lawrence Berkeley Laboratory for pointing out the progressive features of efficiency standards.

30. S.B. 196, 111th General Assembly, Regular Session, 1975-1976.

31. Proposed addition to § 1760 of Title 36 of the Maine Revised Statutes.

32. EPCA, § 321(a)(1).

33. Norman L. Dean, *Energy Efficiency in Industry* (Cambridge, Massachusetts: Ballinger Publishing Company, 1979), ch. 3.

34. Cooley v. Board of Wardens of the Port of Philadelphia, 12 How. 299, 13 L. Ed. 966 (1851).

35. Bibb v. Navajo Freight Lines, 359 U.S. 520.

36. *Id.* at 529-30.

37. American Can Company v. Oregon Liquor Control Commission, 517 P.2d 691, (Or. App., 1973).

38. Note, "State Environmental Protection Legislation and the Common Cause," 87 *Harvard Law Review* 1762 (1974).

39. Pike v. Bruce Church, Inc., 397 U.S. 137 (1970).

40. Philip Soper, "The Constitutional Framework of Environmental Law," in Dolgin and Guilbert, eds., *Federal Environmental Law* (St. Paul, Minnesota: West Publishing Company, 1974) pp. 99-100.

41. Joe W. Russell, Jr., *Economic Disincentives for Energy Conservation* (Cambridge, Massachusetts: Ballinger Publishing Company, 1979).

Chapter 7

Design Features, Shading, and Orientation for Energy Conservation

One of the great architectural visions of the 1920s in Europe was Mies van der Rohe's dream of soaring crystalline towers, transparent and glittering, monuments to the new technology of steel and glass. The vision has come to be realized many times over . . . in the office blocks of all modern cities. Both the financial logic and the aesthetic conception which dictate their form are in direct contradiction to a logic of energy conservation, which they acknowledge neither in their shape nor in their orientation. . . . Brave efforts have been made to encounter these problems with the use of specially treated glass, with blinds and shades; but the problems are ones which should perhaps not have been allowed to arise in the first place. Mies' gnomic dictum 'Less is more', though it might convey the formal asceticism of his works, is little better than a bad joke in the context of the energy performance of his buildings, for which 'Less with more' might be apter.[1]

State governments can use specific legal techniques to encourage or require builders and owners to save energy. Most of the techniques can be applied to any building in a region. For example, although the thickness of insulation that is cost-effective depends on the local climate, the basic legal tools for forcing the insulation of homes are fairly constant; only a few figures need be shifted to adapt such a regulatory strategy to regional differences. Such legal and regulatory schemes formed the heart of Chapter 3 of this volume.

Other chapters in this book deal with energy conservation problems so individual that no general rules can be distilled. A state can offer or require energy audits of large commercial buildings, for example, but there are few general rules that apply across the board. Chapter 5 on air infiltration and Chapter 4 on lighting are examples of areas where individual differences overwhelm the law's ability to make general rules.

This chapter deals with a third type of challenge: how to encourage energy conservation by mandating building design changes. Our search here is for laws that force the builder to examine his site carefully, to consider ways to increase the shading of his building in the summer, and to work with, rather than against, the natural forces of prevailing winds, sun, and reflections from bodies of water. One theme is that the minimization of energy use is best accomplished without prescribing the exact solutions or mix of features that will do a job. The goal should be variation of execution with uniformity of result. Many of the themes that are discussed earlier in this book reappear in this chapter in order to hold the discussion together in one place. This repetition illustrates the fact that design concepts are increasingly being included in more traditional regulatory strategies. Although the format of the regulation differs, the final building may look similar.

In most states, cities, or counties, regulations that influence building design and orientation will take the form of building or zoning codes. If these regulations are to stand up in court, they must meet two tests. First, they must have been devised and accepted by an agency or other body that has been properly delegated the power to do so. Second, they must be written so that the powers they grant to the enforcing agency are specific enough that the agency must "play by the rules"; the agency's discretion must be clearly defined and limited. This issue is discussed later in this chapter, but is basic to successful use of any regulatory strategy this book describes.

EXAMPLES OF DESIGN SOLUTIONS TO CLIMATE CONTROL

Thousands of design, siting, and shading options exist that conserve energy. To illustrate some of them, let us consider some examples of energy-saving structures; in addition, a number of references in footnotes lead readers to more thorough discussions.

Manchester Energy Conservation Office Building

The General Services Administration, "housekeeping agency" for the federal government, has designed and is monitoring a building in Manchester, New Hampshire, to test a variety of mechanical and shading options to reduce energy consumption in federal office buildings. The building equipment is innovative and highly instrumented, but this discussion will look principally at features that maximize beneficial uses of solar energy and minimize unwanted solar radiation. When the building was first conceived, it was to be just another federal office building; by the time design work was ready to begin, the General Services Administration had recognized the importance of building design, and the building was designated an "energy conservation demonstration project." The Manchester federal office building was a good choice: it is of average size (126,000 square feet of net office space with 42,000 additional square feet of underground parking) and is located where buildings require more energy than average for heating and lighting because of severe winters.

The planning and execution of this building was not typical. The energy conservation consulting firm, Dubin-Mindell-Bloome Associates, was made a full member of the design team and suggested alternate methods of design, construction, and equipment choices.

According to Isaak and Isaak, Architects, P. A., the designers who worked on the building, there were five major design considerations:

- *Site Selection.* By the time the decision to build a demonstration building was made, the site (in an urban renewal area) was already selected. Unfortunately, the orientation of the building could not be ideal, given the site; the long sides of the rectangular site faced east and west, the directions of maximum exposure to morning and afternoon sun.

- *Building Shape.* The building site would ordinarily have dictated a long, rectangular building. In addition to the uneven solar loading noted above, such a shape also increases the wall area of a building. Increased wall area leaks more heat, out during the winter and in during the summer. The ideal building shape to prevent heat transfer is a sphere—the shape with the minimum surface for a given volume. As domes are usually impractical, compromises must be made. Perhaps the best compromise for a medium-sized building is a cube. Construction companies are used to dealing with its ninety degree angles, and it exposes a small surface in any given direction.

  The Manchester office building was originally designed as a six story building with a two-to-one length to width ratio (long axis running north to south). When redesigned, it was made almost cubical. An exception is the first floor, which extends beyond the confines of a cube to allow space for agencies to have convenient contact with many visitors.

- *Window Area.* In an area like Manchester, where solar heat is welcome in the winter, the small southern facade of the cube exacted a penalty. The solar gains through windows had to be balanced against the heat losses through those same windows, since they can never be as well insulated as a wall. It was finally decided to severely limit the amount of glass. Ordinary office buildings have 30 to 50 percent of their gross wall area glazed, but in Manchester, the energy conservation consultant first suggested that glass be limited to 5 percent. After further discussion, taking into account the views available, this figure was raised to 12 percent of the east, west, and south walls. It was reduced to zero on the north side, where there would be very little direct sun. The inside north wall of the building is used for elevators, utility rooms, and storage areas.

- *Natural Shading.* Trees and plants can shade walls and windows and prevent the summer sun from overheating a building.[2] In the Manchester office building, covering the north and west walls with ivy was considered, but the maintenance problems associated with ivy on masonry forced the abandonment of this plan. Large plants were not possible as an underground parking garage left an insufficient depth for roots.

- *Artificial Shading.* An ideal shading system permits all the sun's energy to enter through windows during the heating season, but none during the cooling season. The Manchester building is designed so that during the summer 80 percent of the sun's energy is excluded on the east and west sides and 100 percent of its energy is excluded on the south. During the winter, on the other hand, about 90 percent of the sunshine is admitted on the south and about 80 percent on the east and west sides. These figures are achieved by ingenious baffles and deep overhangs, designed for the specific latitude and seasonal paths of the sun at Manchester.

The Manchester solutions would not, of course, apply in all parts of the country or even necessarily in other building sites in Manchester. But they give a notion of a few design and siting considerations relevant to any carefully constructed office building.

Energy-conserving Residential Designs

A similar checklist may be used by the builder of a home. One excellent book, *Low-Cost, Energy-Efficient Shelter for the Owner and Builder*, suggests the following important factors:[3]

1. The sun's path over the site, paying attention to nearby ridges, tree lines, structures, and seasonal variations;

2. Prevailing wind directions of winter storms, summer breezes, and so forth;

3. Most pleasing views; and

4. Areas around the site that require screening at or away from the house.

As a homeowner does not have the resources or the engineering skill available to a developer of an office complex, he must use simpler techniques to admit or exclude the sun. Possibilities include trees, awnings, overhangs, window placement, and plantings. Developers of entire tracts of houses can hire expert advice and spread the cost among many units. The law should find ways to encourage individual home builders to consider energy consequences in their designs, but require still more from larger developers.

POTENTIAL ENERGY SAVINGS THROUGH DESIGN CHANGES

Intelligent design and siting can save a lot of energy. Energy savings of 40 to 60 percent were predicted for the Manchester office building, but that building might have saved even more if the emphasis were strictly on proven conservation measures rather than on experimentation. Instead, Manchester was designed to test various approaches to find which are best. The former head of the General Services Administration established a much more modest goal for new federal buildings: they should be designed so they could operate with 20 to 30 percent less energy than comparable existing modern buildings. Even this modest interim goal has now been strengthened.[4]

The American Institute of Architects, in its study *Energy and the Built Environment: A Gap in Current Strategies*, estimated that "[n]ew buildings initially designed to be energy efficient could save as much as 80 percent of the fuel they would consume at present levels." The gross fuel savings possible from even smaller improvements are enormous: the AIA itself found that with 30 percent energy savings for existing buildings and 60 percent savings for new structures, the United States would save twelve and a half million barrels of oil a day by 1990.[5] (By comparison, consumption of all forms of energy in 1975 amounted to an equivalent of thirty-four and a half million barrels of oil a day.)

Whatever the exact figures may turn out to be, it is clear that design that complies with the dictates of nature rather than the artificial desires of man can pay off handsomely in the small arena of the accountants as well as in the grand arena of living softly on the earth. The cost effectiveness of minor design changes is high, the changes in lifestyle few, and the barriers more psychological than real. The following sections deal with public policies to assist builders and buyers over the psychological hurdles.

LEGAL STRATEGIES TO ENCOURAGE CONSIDERATION OF DESIGN FEATURES

There are two ways to force energy conservation through design features. On the one hand, the law can select a target or make a requirement limiting energy consumption. Such a target or requirement can be expressed in, say, BTUs per square foot per year, and it might vary with the climate or type of building. If the target figure were sufficiently low, then merely relying on technical solutions to cut consumption (such as more efficient furnaces or better insulation) will be insufficient. The designer would be forced to consider the solar heating load, wind chill, shading, and other factors. Because this type of regulation limits consumption but does not dictate any particular solution to meet the limit, it is analogous to the situation of a family with limited income that must budget to stretch their funds over all necessities. Not surprisingly, this regulatory system is called an "energy budget." The success of an energy budget hinges on the selection of a maximum figure—one low enough to force innovative solutions, but still realistically high enough to permit construction to continue.

The second general method of forcing consideration of design factors is to require that certain design features be incorporated in every building of a similar type in a particular area. A variation of this technique is to condition the granting of a building permit or zoning approval upon a showing that as many design features as possible have been incorporated into the plans. This variation shifts the burden of proof to the builder or designer to show why he has not used suggested techniques. It is flexible enough to eliminate some hardships and architectural aberrations that mandatory design regulations might force.

Energy Budgets for Design Considerations
The development of the Building Energy Performance Standards has been briefly detailed in an earlier chapter and will be discussed again later here. But some history and variations on the budget

theme may help set this latest effort in a historical context that explains the development of alternative concepts for budget design. The federal government provided the original leadership in this area by proposing the use of energy budgets for its own buildings. The National Bureau of Standards was the source of the complex information needed to establish early energy budgets. In addition to the federal efforts, some actions have been taken or proposed by states. The following sections consider the pure energy budget originally proposed by the federal government for its own use, variations on it used by states, and the new BEPS now under development.

Federal Energy Budget. In 1974, the General Services Administration, a federal agency whose Public Building Service constructs and manages a vast number of buildings for federal civilian agencies, published a guidebook for its new office buildings, *Energy Conservation Design Guidelines for Office Buildings*. A second edition, *Energy Conservation Design Guidelines for New Office Buildings*,[6] was issued a year later, incorporating changes and improvements in the state of the art. In both editions, the guidelines established a design energy use goal of 55,000 BTUs per equivalent gross square foot per year.[7] This figure was established by AIA Research Corporation and Dubin-Mindell-Bloome Associates on the basis of studies in preparation for the Manchester project.[8] In addition to the 55,000 BTU guideline, the General Services Administration also requires figures on the raw source energy consumption of proposed buildings. This second figure includes energy losses in the production and transportation of electricity and district chilled water or steam. Raw source energy is limited to 100,000 BTUs per equivalent gross square feet per year. The raw source budget thus serves somewhat the function of the resource utilization factors (RUFs) used in BEPS.

The *Design Guidelines* books suggest methods to meet the goals, but do not prescribe any method or combination of methods. Among the methods suggested are careful site selection, building configuration, orientation, and shading.

Florida's Energy Budget. In 1974, the Florida Legislature passed the "Florida Energy Conservation in Buildings Act."[9] The law, which applies only to state-owned or leased buildings, provides for a life cycle costing approach. It also instructs (in Section 6) the Department of General Services, Division of Building Construction and Maintenance, to "develop an energy performance index . . . to audit and evaluate competing design proposals [for buildings] submitted to the state." An energy performance index is defined in Section 3:

"Energy Performance index" (EPI) is . . . a number describing the energy requirements of a facility per square foot of floor space or per cubic foot of occupied volume as appropriate under defined internal and external ambient conditions over an entire seasonal cycle. As experience develops on the energy performance achieved with state buildings, the index (EPI) will serve as a measure of building performance with respect to energy consumption.

Working with energy consultants, the Florida officials produced a *Florida Energy Conservation Manual* for implementing the requirements of Section 6.[10] The manual states its purpose as follows:

[This manual] has been developed to provide a method of compliance to the recently enacted statute on energy conservation. Thus, this manual provides both the Department of General Services and the Architect/ Engineer general guidelines for the evaluations of building designs that will conserve energy in new Florida state-owned and leased buildings. Briefly, to comply with the law, the Architect and Engineer will be able to develop their design in any form they choose with the exception that any design building energy consumption must meet the *Energy Performance Index* or budget as shown in Chapter 2.

The *Energy Performance Index* (EPI) should be considered as a maximum limitation. The Architect will use criteria set forth in Chapter 3 to effectively meet the EPI for any type of building. The purpose of the design standards is not to limit architectural freedom but is intended to create an awareness that all designs must effectively minimize the use of energy. Compliance to these standards will require either computer analysis of the designs or a hand calculated analysis.

The state is divided into eight regions; buildings are grouped according to their general type. Chapter 2 of the manual consists of charts for each category of building. Thus, there are different EPIs for one story dormitories, for two and three story dormitories and for multifloor dormitories; likewise for penal institutions, hospitals, office buildings, and so forth. The numbers circled in Table 7-1, for example, show that for two or three story mental health buildings located in or near Tampa, heating may consume no more than 9.6 kilowatt hours or 32,800 BTUs per gross interior square foot of floor area.

According to Florida officials, the program applies to all state buildings over 50,000 square feet for which a request for construction funds was made after March 1975. If a department plans to build, it makes a capital request to the legislature. Once funding is approved, the Bureau of Construction (within the Department of General Services) contracts with an architect-engineering consulting

Table 7-1. Energy Performance Index.

TWO OR THREE STORY MENTAL HEALTH BUILDINGS

Weather Stations by Region

1. Panama City and Pensacola
2. Tallahassee
3. Jacksonville
4. Tampa

5. Orlando
6. Patrick AFB and Daytona Beach
7. Keywest
8. Miami and West Palm Beach

Region	Energy	Lighting	Heating		Cooling		Total		Other Uses	
1	Point of Use	10.1	11.3	38.6	18.0	61.4	39.4	134.5	25.0	85.3
2	Point of Use	10.1	10.7	36.5	17.6	60.1	38.4	131.1	25.0	85.3
3	Point of Use	10.1	12.1	41.3	18.5	63.1	40.7	138.9	25.0	85.3
4	Point of Use	10.1	(9.6)	(32.8)	18.5	63.1	38.2	130.4	25.0	85.3
5	Point of Use	10.1	8.5	29.0	18.5	63.1	37.1	126.6	25.0	85.3
6	Point of Use	10.1	9.0	30.7	18.5	63.1	37.6	128.3	25.0	85.3
7	Point of Use	10.1	4.2	14.3	18.5	63.1	32.8	111.9	25.0	85.3
8	Point of Use	10.1	7.4	25.3	18.6	63.5	36.1	123.2	25.0	85.3
		KWH	KWH	MBTU	KWH	MBTU	KWH	MBTU	KWH	MBTU

ENERGY USE PER GROSS INTERIOR SQUARE FOOT/YEAR

Source: Florida Department of General Services, *Florida Energy Conservation Manual,* (March 1975), p. 30, fig. 2-9.

team. That team familiarizes itself with Chapter 3 of the manual, which contains suggestions for design features and mechanical systems that will help structures comply with the energy performance index. The team need not follow the manual's suggestions, but Florida officials feel it would be difficult to meet the energy performance index if the manual were ignored.

The team first develops a preliminary schematic design. This rough draft is subjected to computer analysis (the so-called Florida Lifecycle Energy Evaluation Techniques program, FLEET), and if it appears likely to meet the energy performance index, a preliminary design is made. The preliminary design is also subjected to FLEET analysis. The architectural shell is run a final time through the computer program together with different schemes for the heating–ventilating–air-conditioning system, the lighting, and the operating and maintenance systems. Lower first cost systems are preferred unless a higher first cost system has a lower life cycle cost. Unfortunately, the dollar budget limitation set by the legislature at the beginning of this process can eliminate systems with high first costs, even if they have low life cycle costs. There are plans to monitor the costs and energy use of buildings produced under this plan.

According to Florida officials, the program promises large energy savings. One new building of 200,000 square feet is expected to consume about 40,000 BTUs per gross square foot per year; existing state office buildings of similar size consume about 125,000 BTUs even after some energy conservation retrofitting. The program also forces communication about energy operating costs at the time major decisions affecting those costs are made—during design and construction. Apparently the architects working for the state like the system's flexibility.

The major limitation of the program is that it affects only state buildings. The state has also developed a noncomputerized and less expensive system for figuring energy consumption, but it is not as accurate.

Ohio Modified Energy Budget. The GSA and the Florida systems are pure energy budgets. Unfortunately, a pure energy budget is difficult to use because it is hard to predict the proper BTU per square foot standard. Although exceedingly valuable data on predicted energy use have been collected in the course of developing the BEPS, as will be pointed out later, there is substantial concern whether the predicted energy use is an accurate surrogate for actual use in the field and whether the data that were collected under the BEPS program are sufficiently detailed and accurate to base regulations on them. Finally, a pure budget system almost always requires the use of a computer calculation that may prove too expensive for a small builder.

In October 1973 the Ohio Board of Building Standards held a task force meeting to consider how they could use the Ohio state building code to encourage energy conservation in new construction. After considering various methods, the task force recommended a modified energy budget approach. As already noted, a pure energy budget limits the total amount of energy that may be consumed over a year by all a building's systems. The Ohio board felt this was theoretically sound but too difficult to apply. Therefore, Ohio chose an approach that looks at the capacity of the major systems in a building, then sets an upper limit on the total connected capacity. Factors that influence capacity limits include (1) the class of a building (its occupancy classification under the building code); (2) its area; (3) the number of stories; and (4) the height of each story. Under the Ohio standard, a total connected energy load is:

> [T]he total building lighting load plus the total output capacity of all terminal heating units or the total building lighting load plus the total output capacity of all terminal air-conditioning units, whichever is greater. When the terminal unit uses electrical energy as the energy source, the

input capacity to the terminal unit shall be used in lieu of the output capacity.[11]

Capacity of terminal units includes the output capacity of coils, the energy input to supply and return air fans, and the energy input to pumping equipment necessary for coil control. Total connected energy load does not include energy from renewable sources, energy used in exhaust fans in kitchens, industrial and laboratory uses, or the energy used for heating, ventilating, or air-conditioning systems "used exclusively for the purpose of overcoming process loads." It also omits all energy used for purposes other than lighting, heating, ventilating, or air conditioning.

To summarize, the Ohio standard looks at only the ordinary heating and cooling and lighting inputs of a building; energy used to remove offensive or dangerous gases, for cooling unusually hot processes, and for running computers, elevators, copiers, and other equipment is not included.

The total connected energy load is converted to a basic energy allotment by dividing the load by the gross floor area of a building. Values for the basic energy allotment vary from a low of 8 BTUs per square foot for garages to a high of 120 BTUs per square foot for aircraft hangers.

As noted, the basic energy allotment is adjusted for the peculiarities of individual buildings. The adjustment for the area of the building tends to give smaller buildings a higher allotment per square foot (as floor area decreases, the ratio of volume to total surface area decreases). The adjustment for the number of stories gives shorter buildings a higher allotment than taller buildings of similar square footage. The adjustment for the height of each story allows buildings with lower ceilings a slightly smaller allotment than buildings with higher ceilings.

The original regulations required builder to file an energy analysis report along with an application for a building permit.[12] Those reports were to provide the Ohio Board of Building Standards with data during the year between enactment of the energy building code and the time it took effect. It was originally hoped that this data would help the state determine whether the basic energy allotments were realistic. In February 1975 the board made those reports voluntary, because of a question raised by the state attorney general's office about the legality of the action by the board. Senate Bill 299 was introduced, amending the basic legislative authority of the Board of Building Standards by making the conservation of energy one of the purposes of state regulation.

In addition to the capacity rating of the equipment covered, the minimum efficiencies of the heating and cooling equipment (at various load factors) are also controlled under the Ohio standard. One purpose of controlling these efficiencies is to permit the uniform calculation of heating and cooling loads, so that similar buildings will have comparable ratings.

The major problem with the method used by Ohio is that the total connected load is, at best, only an approximation of the energy consumption of a building. It is, therefore, subject to all of the objections to the energy budget method (that we are trying to control energy use without very definite figures on what actual practice would allow) plus the additional objection that in some cases the relationship between connected load and consumption may vary enormously. This point can be clarified by comparing two types of buildings—churches and sanitariums. Both of these building types are assigned an identical basic energy allotment (50 BTUs). A church is used for only a few hours on Sundays. On the other hand, the sanitarium is used twenty-four hours per day, 365 days per year, and is kept warmer than normal to benefit the patients. Comparing the actual energy consumption of these two buildings would reveal that the sanitarium uses far more than the church. In this extreme case, therefore, the basic energy allotment figures are meaningless. In a less extreme example, the total annual consumption of school classroom buildings may vary enormously from that of nontransient dormitories, yet they are given the same basic energy allotment. This defect, which arises from the fact that the energy allotment is insensitive to the actual usage patterns of a building, is a recurrent problem in developing energy budgets. To make a budget, assumptions must be made about the way people will use it; yet those assumptions frequently are too simplistic.

The second major difficulty with the Ohio approach is that it ignores a number of important energy uses within a building. It excludes items that Florida's method includes as "other uses" (such as exhaust fans, water heating, cooking and other processing, and elevators). Improving the efficiency of such machinery can save a lot of electricity. Moreover, by excluding the heating, cooling, and ventilating necessitated by processes such as air conditioning to eliminate a process heating load, the standard may actually encourage waste of process heat that could be used elsewhere in the building. Measures such as insulation, which would reduce the heat escaping from the process itself, are not forced under the Ohio approach.

The virtue of the Ohio system is its ease of administration. Building departments do not need to rely on expensive, complicated computer programs to determine whether a building complies with the standard. The calculations required by Ohio can be done with inexpensive pocket calculators. The building owner or designer also benefits, as he can tell from the beginning whether the building will comply with the standard, and he does not have to produce preliminary, draft, and final designs. However, whether the Ohio system succeeds depends, of course, on the skill with which the budget figures are chosen, and how well the voluntary reports of projected and actual consumption compare.

Use of an Early Draft of ASHRAE 90-75: Minnesota. The energy budget methodologies covered so far are pure or modified budgets. Minnesota, however, adopted an alternative approach drawn from an early version of the ASHRAE Standard 90-75. This approach permits a builder either to comply with the energy budget method or with the usual ASHRAE component specification method. The code furthers the goal of energy-efficient buildings by requiring each component of a building (roof, walls, windows, and foundation) to comply with definite heat transmission standards. When these component performance specification standards are followed, the building as a whole is expected to have improved thermal characteristics.

Architects have been the principal opponents of component performance specification on the ground that it inhibits innovative building designs and may, in some instances, increase the total energy consumption of a building. For example, limiting the size of windows increases thermal efficiency but adds to the lighting load.

The alternative calculation methodology adopted by Minnesota is an attempt to deal with the complaints of the architectural profession. Under Minnesota's amendment to its statewide building code,[13] the commissioner of the Buildings Department was required to promulgate amendments to the state building code to establish "maximum standards for permissible heat loss on all new construction or remodeling involving heating or heating changes, specifically including minimum insulation requirements for heating units on exterior walls." Pursuant to this amendment, the commissioner issued draft "Design and Evaluation Criteria for Energy Conservation in Buildings" in December 1974. In an accompanying notice, the state said: "[T] hese proposed energy conservation requirements are performance oriented and are not intended to be specifications for construction." After the sections that set out certain performance standards for building components, two methods for calculating an energy budget are described.

Section 4.6.1 permits alternative designs as long as "the total building heat loss and heat gain in winter and summer design conditions, respectively, is equal to or less than designs developed to satisfy" the component performance specifications in the previous sections. This alternative permits, for example, a skylight that raises heat loss above the standard if a better insulated wall compensates by reducing the heat loss. If the heat losses and gains at least balance, a variation is permitted.

Section 4.6.2, referring to Section 10, permits alternative building and system designs "that can be shown to equal or reduce the total energy supplied to a similar building which would have followed each of the detailed requirements of Sections 4 through 9." This alternative is a variation of an energy budget, with the budget figure expressed as an alternate building style rather than as BTUs per square foot per year.

ASHRAE Standard 90-75. As noted above, the Minnesota approach is based on an early draft of the ASHRAE standard. Both plans encounter the same difficulties in the application of alternatives. Designers are asked to design and make energy calculations on two different buildings. Although the Minnesota law requires that the buildings compared be similar in size, use category, and hours of use, an innovative building design will be difficult to compare with the "standard" ASHRAE building that the code requires. Instead of comparing the energy use of two buildings of similar design, a designer would have to design two different buildings, compare their energy consumption, and then make changes in his innovative building design. Those changes, if they reduce the size or change the use of the building, would require yet another standard building design for comparison. The difficulties of trying to strike a moving target probably insure that the permitted alternatives will seldom be used.

Federal Building Energy Performance Standards. The development of the federal Building Energy Performance Standards (BEPS) has been detailed in Chapter 3. It probably is fair to characterize the BEPS as the triumph of the architectural profession over the ASHRAE standard. The American Institute of Architects (AIA) has long objected to the ASHRAE approach on the grounds that it may stifle innovation. Soon after the ASHRAE component performance Standard 90-75 was issued, AIA began to develop a methodology for determining energy budgets. The methodology attempted to deal with the lack of data needed to set up reasonable energy budgets by looking to existing buildings and using their historical energy performance to provide a target for architects and building designers to shoot for. In brief, the AIA proposed that within a relevant jurisdiction (a state or smaller area that has both legal control over buildings and a uniform climate) a random sample of buildings of a particular type should be selected for study. That set of buildings would represent statistically all the buildings of the type within the area under study. For each of the sample buildings, the annual energy consumption data would be obtained from the building owner. The data from the sample buildings would then be ranged from highest to lowest consumption, and the median (that is, the point at which the number of buildings with greater consumption is equal to the number of buildings with less consumption) calculated. That median point, which would be recalculated each year, would then serve as the energy budget. In the words of the AIA report, "The value of this median line becomes the energy budget and represents a goal for designing a building that can be successfully operated within the 'least energy consumed' half of the total group."[14] The AIA energy budget, it was asserted, would provide design professionals with a goal that also might serve as a baseline for governmental incentives and for code approval of building energy performance. The AIA stated its position clearly: "With respect to state and local building codes, the energy budget approach is a true alternative to a prescriptive approach. It provides great freedom for the architect and engineer to design an innovative building which meets the total needs of the client."[15]

The BEPS were developed by the American Institute of Architects Research Corporation (AIA/RC) and bear a striking resemblance to the original concept developed by the AIA in its report. However, there are some differences. First, the AIA proposed that actual buildings be used to gather baseline data. Instead, the BEPS (as set forth in the Advance Notice of Proposed Rulemaking[16]) apply only at the design phase of the building, and therefore, the energy consumption has to be predicted by means of a proprietary computer program, AXCESS. Unfortunately, the computer program has not been cross-checked against actual buildings to test whether the program's assumptions are borne out in building use. Further, the BEPS severely limit the items they consider within the energy budget of the building. Without an actual building to look at, the proposed standards deal with only heating, cooling, and lighting, and not with other important energy uses. For example, it is estimated that in a hospital, electricity use is so large for nonheating and cooling applications that heating and cooling amount to only 40 to 50 percent of electricity use.[17]

The other major difference between the early AIA suggestion and the BEPS as developed by AIA/RC is that the AIA model explicitly required that the standard be made tougher each year. Although the AIA standard was lower (it demanded only the median or fiftieth percentile as compared to the BEPS, which may be set at the top twentieth percentile), this lack of a continually improving standard is a serious limitation in the proposed BEPS.

As noted in Chapter 3, it is difficult to comment knowledgeably about the BEPS, since their final form is still unknown. But they are important because they stand a strong chance of becoming the national energy conservation in buildings code if they survive the heavy criticisms that have been levied against the early versions released to the public and if Congress agrees that they should be made mandatory for the states to adopt and enforce.

Shortcomings of the Energy Budget Approach for Design Changes

As noted earlier, the energy budget methodology depends on setting an energy budget lower than mechanical efficiency and insulation improvements alone can meet, to force siting, shading, and other solutions to lower energy consumption in a building. But there may be sound technical and political reasons for not choosing this flexible method for enforcing creativity on architects and builders. First, as mentioned repeatedly in this chapter and as shown by the effort made to develop the BEPS, picking credible figures for an energy budget is very difficult. Energy budgets must be sufficiently localized to be realistic. For example, houses built in an area with frequent strong winds may have much greater heating needs than homes built where there are the same number of heating degree days, but where the air is calm.

Second, energy budgets must also reflect the variation in energy requirements for different use categories. For example, a hospital may genuinely need more energy than an office building. But the functions may not be able to be expressed in a common unit, such as BTUs per square foot. An office building is relatively homogeneous in its use patterns: except for the lobby areas, most people in most of the building are performing tasks that require generally about the same amount of energy. But in a hospital, the amount of energy used in an operating room is vastly different from that used in a solarium or a kitchen. To try to develop a budget that deals uniformly with different building types is hard, and the data base may not yet support it.

Finally, and most important, energy budgets must allow for the tremendous uncertainty about how much energy is really needed for the annual operation of buildings. This uncertainty comes from three factors. First, the way individuals actually use a building may be so different from the assumptions made in planning a budget that the budget is meaningless. Second, buildings vary in their construction quality; pieces of insulation may be missing that permit vast quantities of heat to escape without anyone understanding why the bills are so high. Finally, the heating and cooling of buildings is complicated. We are very low on the learning curve of understanding what within and without a building affects its energy consumption. When our knowledge is so limited that we may not realize that perfectly standard design features cost thousands of BTUs per year, relying on computer programs that must simplify and assume is a weak basis for regulation.

The uncertainties that exist are compounded because we have so little data on actual buildings. The professionals working on standards know that data are limited and sometimes of poor quality. For that reason, those who set energy budget figures may tend to err on the lenient side to insure that buildings are not intolerably cold in the winter or hot in the summer. This defect will, of course, tend to diminish over time as research orgnizations (such as the National Bureau of Standards, the Princeton Center for Environment, and others), state and federal government, and owners themselves accumulate experience. But at the moment, it will take political courage to use energy budgets as a means for forcing widescale use of innovative building designs for energy conservation. On the other hand, there is no question that they are the direction in which regulation should aim, particularly as our experience and knowledge increase.

MANDATORY DESIGN FEATURES

The previous discussion has suggested that energy budgets may currently be a flawed method for causing improvements in buildings. Let us now consider other legal techniques that are addressed specifically at forcing design changes suitable for a particular climate. Readers should be cautioned that specific legislation of this type may be counterproductive, because trade-offs that make sense in one part of a state may not be rational from an energy point of view elsewhere in the state. For instance, designs appropriate to the cold winter, mild summer climate of California's Trinity Alps would only increase energy consumption in the Mojave Desert, and vice versa. Therefore, the suggestions in this section should not be adopted by localities or states without revisions that account for local climatolgical conditions, latitude, heating and cooling degree days, terrain, humidity, and wind.

Strategies to Force Shading of Buildings

Solar heat gain through unprotected windows adds to a cooling load during the summer, but is a useful supplement to a mechanical heating system in the winter. Ways to provide shading range from the obvious one of planting deciduous trees, which drop their leaves when no shading is required and grow new ones just as the cooling season begins, to installing carefully designed shading devices that allow for seasonal changes in the position of the sun. This second shading method was briefly described in connection with the Manchester federal office building.

One of the ways that specific mandates for shading can be enforced is through the power of a locality to zone. But zoning powers are not unconstrained in law: it is always a question whether a locality has been given the power to zone for a particular purpose such as energy conservation and, if that power exists, whether the locality has so much authority that its actions are unfettered. The following two sections deal with the delegation issue and the discretion issue.

The Delegation Issue.   A zoning ordinance may require builders to install adequate shading, but before adopting such an ordinance, the municipality must be certain that the power to zone has been properly delegated to it. For the vast majority of communities, this is no problem, but some American cities (Houston is an example) do not have zoning powers. The municipality must also consider whether the power to consider energy conservation is expressly granted or implied by the enabling legislation. Therefore, the legal question is whether the enumeration of powers contained in the typical zoning enabling legislation can be construed to include energy conservation as a purpose of zoning.

There is little question that the general "police powers" of a state are sufficiently broad to cover energy conservation regulations. The concept of police power is malleable and constantly changing. It is a lawyer's term meaning regulations undertaken for the common good, for which no individual compensation is given even though the rights of individuals may be affected. It was once debated whether zoning itself was a proper police power of the state, but it is now agreed that it is. As the Supreme Court of the United States noted in the leading case, *Village of Euclid v. Ambler Realty Company*, "the line which in this field separates the legitimate from the illegitimate assumption of power is not capable of precise delineation. It varies with circumstances and conditions."[18]

The broad reach of the police power to encompass energy conservation goals does not, however, completely answer the question of whether the language of the typical zoning enabling legislation ("to protect health, public safety, and the general welfare") is limited by later, specific language in the enabling legislation. Most zoning enabling legislation follows the general police power statement with language giving additional purposes for zoning—namely, to protect and enhance property values and to ensure harmonious land uses. In law, such specific examples may limit the broad language rather than enlarge it. Therefore, a locality considering a mandatory shading ordinance or other similar changes should obtain a local legal opinions on its own zoning enabling legislation. If it will not support an energy conservation purpose, legislative action may be needed.

A number of states have taken the precaution of adding specific enabling legislation to their building code to permit energy conservation to be considered. A similar precaution for zoning and subdivision and other land use controls might be wise.

The Discretion Issue. Having passed the hurdle of whether zoning or building codes will support energy conservation goals, the next question is whether an ordinance's standards are specific enough for a court to sustain. A court will find a statute invalid if it gives too much discretion to the board of zoning commissioners or the building code department.

A close legal analogy is the judicial controversy over the validity of "look alike" or "look different" zoning ordinances. These ordinances, in Norman William's words, "prohibit either (a) buildings which look too much like others on the same block, or (b) buildings which look too dissimilar to other buildings nearby—or, incredibly enough, sometimes both at once."[19] Architectural controls, of which look alike and look different zoning ordinances are an example, have been used in many communities to exclude modern or externally innovative homes. Although the ordinances are not so worded, their purpose often seems to be to prevent any homes that would not suit Henry VIII; on the other hand, they have also been used to prevent cookie cutter developments in which trivial variations in trim or a simple reversal of the facade elements are the builder's sole concession to the human desire to differentiate one's castle from a neighbor's humble abode.

As might be expected, these ordinances have been vigorously attacked. They are usually, but not always, upheld. One leading case, *State ex. rel. Saveland Park Holding Corporation v. Wieland,*[20] upheld an ordinance granting building permits only to structures in which:

> the exterior architectural appeal and functional plan of the proposed structure will, when erected, not be so at variance with either the exterior architectural appeal and functional plan of the structures already constructed or in the course of construction in the immediate neighborhood or the character of the [general area] . . . as to cause a substantial depreciation in the property values of said neighborhood . . . .

After focusing on the words "neighborhood" and "substantial," the court held that the ordinance's provisions were "not so indefinite or ambiguous as to subject applicants for building permits to the uncontrolled arbitrary discretion or caprice of the Building Board."

The standards in *Saveland Park* were much more vague than would be necessary in a mandatory shading ordinance. Thus, a carefully drafted statute is likely to be upheld as a proper use of discretion. Moreover, because it is possible to show that a "shade" actually either performs or doesn't perform the function for which it was designed (that is, to shade), the discretion issue may be much easier to overcome.

Example of a Shading Ordinance: Davis, California. A leading example of a well-designed mandatory shading ordinance is the comprehensive Ordinance Number 784 from the City of Davis, California, reprinted in an appendix to this chapter.[21] It covers building orientation, window placement, ways to take advantage of natural breezes, and other factors that make buildings less dependent for comfort on energy supplied through wires or pipes.

In a recent report on the Davis ordinance, the authors (who were active in the drafting and passage of the ordinance) state:

> Energy conservation was approached in Davis as a fundamental element to be included in planning, building design, transportation, household management, and most economic decisions. Acceptability of the new ideas came gradually as the consultants were able to show the community that energy conservation involves doing the same things more efficiently and economically rather than changing comfort, convenience, or lifestyle.[22]

The process of adopting the ordinance was not without difficulty. Although based on well-documented studies (the University of

California campus in Davis provided a pool of talent and an educated citizenry), builders initially opposed it. Developers and architects argued that the code would raise the cost of housing and limit design possiblities. The opposition was successful in modifying some of the original concepts in the code: somewhat darker than proposed colors were allowed on the roof; somewhat larger windows and somewhat less shading on them was also permitted. The code was evaluated after a year's experience. Initially, five of the nine builders in Davis had opposed it. After working with it for a year, six supported it, two supported it in concept but not excactly as written, and one of nine opposed it. The additional costs imposed by following the code were estimated by the builders themselves as averaging only $284 per house; that pays back in between three and four years.[23]

The Davis ordinance begins with broad documented findings on the general nature of the energy shortage and the particular effects of weather patterns in the Davis area on energy consumption. These findings are important, because they define the scientific basis for the rest of the ordinance and help sustain it against a legal attack charging that its regulations go beyond the scope of the police power.

The regulations issued pursuant to the ordinance (also reprinted in the appendix to this chapter) deal with shading in several ways. First, window placement is controlled to discourage north-facing windows. Second, all glazing not oriented to the north must be shaded from direct solar radiation between 8:00 A.M. and 4:00 P.M. (Checks are made at 8:00 A.M. 12:00 noon, and 4:00 P.M. to insure that this standard is met.) For windows facing southeast or southwest, additional shading checks are required (at 10:00 A.M. for southeast windows and 2:00 P.M. for southwest windows) because the sun may strike those exposures at that time. In addition, the total unshaded glazing may not exceed 1.5 percent of the dwelling unit's floor area. Tinted, metalized, or frosted glass is not considered sufficiently shaded.

Several types of exterior shading system are permitted.[24] If they are permanent structural additions, the builder must guarantee their durability for five years. For each hour in which checking is mandated, the device must intercept 100 percent of the sun's radiation or provide a minimum shading coefficient of 0.2 or less. Any excess must be added to the total of unshaded glazing (which, as mentioned, is limited). If the builder chooses not to use a permanent structural addition, obstructions (either on site or off site) that provide 80 percent attenuation of the sun's rays can be used. In one of the most innovative provisions of the ordinance, the use of plants as shading devices is permitted:

A shading system may be temporary, provided that it is designed and constructed to function to the standards above and built to last until its function is replaced by plantings. Plan and elevation drawings must show expected plant configuration and accurately state the number of years required for the projected plant growth. Final occupancy permits shall not be issued until the specified plants are in place.

In lieu of outside shading devices, the ordinance also permits special interior shutters. They must be a very light color on the sunward side (defined as a Munsell of 9.0 or greater), flat, weatherstripped to create a seal, and opaque. Interior shutters must be at least minimally insulated against heat transmission.

The strengths of the Davis ordinance are its specificity, its attention to exact working and scientifically measurable facts, and its strong buttress of supporting data. No town considering an energy conservation standard should omit a careful study of Davis from its debates on conservation.

Colorado

A bill was introduced in the Colorado legislature that would have allowed a very detailed regulation of energy conservation designs in new subdivisions. House Bill No. 1166, Section 3, proposed to require the subdivider to present:

Evidence to establish that provision has been made in the platting, in the layout of roads, and in other site changes for the orientation of structures to receive substantial benefits from the natural energies afforded by the sun, the wind, and other energy-related characteristics as determined by evaluation of the micro-climate details of the proposed subdivision site; Evidence to establish that long-term energy is available to support the subdivision without undue detrimental land use and environmental impacts and that energy-conserving measures have been incorporated in the preliminary plan or final plat subdivision submission.

Although this requirement is broadly written and would need detailed regulations to make it meaningful, it was never enacted. Its proponents intended it to be used mainly to encourage the use of solar collectors, but the broad language of the bill could have done much to force energy conservation planning into Colorado cities.

Building Orientation

Buildings that expose the least wall area to the sun or that take advantage of natural features (such as prevailing breezes off cool ocean waters) can limit the nonrenewable energy required for heating and cooling.

It is obviously not practical to require ideal building orientations in developed areas with space for only one or two more buildings in the middle of a block. The shape of the lot, the street grid, and the ways other nearby structures are oriented all limit the placement of a new building. However, in developing areas, like newly opened subdivisions or major urban renewals, builders should be required to consider the relationships between orientation and energy consumption.

Laws that affect building siting and orientation are discussed in detail in another book in this series, *Using Land to Save Energy*, by Corbin Crews Harwood.[25] The reader is referred to Harwood's excellent treatment of planning, regulation, and incentives. Another study from the Environmental Law Institute, by Gail Boyer Hayes, deals with the legal controls to protect access to sunlight for solar energy devices; that study also is a valuable, detailed treatment of the issues that are only touched on here.[26] However, readers of this book should be familiar with some of the highlights of the planning process that suggest opportunities for innovation.

Probably the most appropriate legal devices for influencing building orientation and placement are the controls that come before land may be developed. These are the site plan review (common for planned unit developments, for construction of less than a full subdivision, or other smaller scale planning), subdivision controls (for large-scale new developments), and urban renewal (for areas that have gone through one complete cycle of development and are being cleared for another cycle). These processes are quite similar, and site plan review can be used as a model because it has frequently included environmental concerns.

The American Institute of Architects has studied environmental design review boards extensively; their study includes a model ordinance and a legal analysis by the highly regarded land planning professor George Lefcoe. The discussion here is indebted to Professors Wiliams'[27] and Lefcoe's[28] excellent treatments.

As in the case of architectural ordinances, review boards need fairly specific standards so that both the governed and the governors can predict whether a proposed design will pass review. For example, an energy conservation site review may include the possiblity of working around existing shade trees, a building's orientation on the lot, and the orientation of the lot itself. A site plan review requirement might be drafted to make a developer take those items into account, and an ordinance might require:

Tree saving and replacement. If the development of the site necessitates removal of established trees, special attention shall be given to the planting of replacement trees or other landscape treatment, with an emphasis, to the extent feasible, on placement of deciduous trees that will shade the south, east, and west facades of the house during the summer.[29]

Building orientation. To conserve our limited natural resources of fuel and thus to extend the time such fuel will be available to citizens of this community for vital public health and safety services, the city of [name of city] hereby finds that building orientation in new subdivisions is an important contributor to energy conservation. Therefore, new developments shall, to the extent feasible, (1) place buildings so that their long axis runs east and west; (2) have a maximum floor area within a minimum surface area of exposed wall; and (3) consider the effects of solar radiation when determining window placement.[30]

Lot orientation. When laying out individual lots in proposed subdivisions, developers shall consider building orientations forced by lot size and configuration and any opportunities to use preexisting natural features to provide shading and shelter from the wind.[31]

These provisions are purposely vague; they merely suggest factors relevant to deciding whether to approve or disapprove a particular proposed development. The examples must be adjusted to suit different climates, since in some regions it may be desirable to expose structures to the wind rather than sheltering them.

CONCLUSION

Design considerations are currently the stepchild of legal regulation. The law's orientation toward mechanical solutions to heating, lighting, and cooling problems reflects the interests of the design professionals most actively involved in building development. In the past, the architect or the builder chose a configuration of rooms and spaces that pleased him and his client; the design was then handed to an engineer to develop the lighting, heating, cooling, and ventilating systems necessary for comfort. This division of responsibility between designer and heating-ventilating-air-conditioning professional led to the proliferation of universal architectural styles that are indifferent to climatic variations.

With the surge of interest in buildings' energy consumption, teamwork by designers and engineers is becoming more common. Perhaps landscape architects will also soon join such teams. The laws and ordinances contained in this chapter are partly a result of this renewed collaboration and partly a conscious attempt to hurry the marriage along.

NOTES

1. Philip Steadman, *Energy, Environment and Building* (New York: Cambridge University Press, 1975). Used with permission of the copyright holders, Philip Steadman and The Academy of Natural Sciences of Philadelphia.

2. Alabama Forestry Commission, Montgomery, Ala., *Value of Tree Shade to Homeowners*, A.F.C. Bulletin No. 2450, 2d ed. (1975.)

3. Eugene Eccli, ed., *Low-Cost, Energy-Efficient Shelter for the Owner and Builder* (Emmaus, Pennsylvania: Rodale Press, Inc., 1975), pp. 43-71.

4. General Services Administration, Public Building Service, *Energy Conservation Design Guidelines for New Office Buildings*, 2nd ed., preface by Arthur F. Sampson, administrator (Washington, D.C.: Government Printing Office, July 1975).

5. The American Institute of Architects, *Saving Energy in the Built Environment: The AIA Policy* (Washington, D.C., 1974).

6. General Services Administration, Public Buildings Service, *Energy Conservation Design Guidelines for New Office Buildings* (Washington, D.C.: Government Printing Office, July 1975). In February 1975, GSA issued *Energy Conservation Guidelines for Existing Office Buildings*.

7. General Services Administration, Public Buildings Service, *Energy Conservation Design Guidelines for Office Buildings* (Washington, D.C.: Government Printing Office, January 1974), p. 5-2. Equivalent gross square feet = gross area of floors made up of typical office space plus an office space equivalent (one-quarter of gross) for other areas of the building requiring energy for operation—that is, lighting, ventilation, elevators, and so forth—but not full comfort heating and cooling. For example: Building having two office floors of 100,000 gsf; a basement parking garage of 20,000 gsf; and a mechanical penthouse of 4,000 gsf. EGSF = 200,000 gsf + ¼(20,000 gsf + 4,000 gsf) = 206,000.

8. General Services Administration, *supra* note 6.

9. Fla. State Law 74-187.

10. Florida Department of General Services, Division of Building Construction and Maintenance, *Florida Energy Conservation Manual* (March 1975).

11. Ohio Department of Industrial Relations, Board of Building Standards, *Ohio Building Code* (1970 ed), § BB-48-05 (effective June 1, 1975).

12. *Id.* at § BB-02-01.

13. State of Minnesota Department of Administration, Building Code Division, *State Building Code*, §§ 6001-6013 (effective January 30, 1976).

14. See, American Institute of Architects, "A Guide for Architects for the Determination and Use of Annual Energy Budgets Related to the Design of Buildings," October 1976 (draft).

15. *Id.*

16. 43 *Federal Register* 54512, November 21, 1978.

17. Richard Stein, personal communication.

18. Village of Euclid v. Ambler Realty Company, 272 U.S. 365 (1926).

19. 3 N. Williams, Jr., *American Planning Law, Land Use and the Police Power*, § 71.16 (1975).

20. State *ex rel.* Saveland Park Holding Corporation v. Wieland, 269 Wis. 262, 69 N.W. 2d 217, *cert. denied,* 350 U.S. 841 (1955).

21. Adopted by the City Council of the City of Davis, California (October 15, 1975). The documenting evidence for the code as well as the draft proposal for it was contained in Jonathan V. Hammond, Marshall Hunt, Loren Neubauer, and Richard Cramer, *A Strategy for Energy Conservation: Proposed Energy Conservation and Solar Utilization Ordinance for the City of Davis, California* (Davis, California: The City, 1974).

22. Living Systems, *Davis Energy Conservation Report: Practical Use of the Sun* (available from city of Davis, California). See also, *The Elements, The Davis Experiment, One City's Plan to Save Energy* (available from Public Resource Center, 1747 Connecticut Avenue, Washington, D.C. 20009).

23. Living Systems, *supra* note 22 at p. 116.

24. Resolution No. 1833, Series 1975, Section 4E(3)(ii). This resolution adopted "procedures for compliance with the energy conservation performance standards for residential construction within the City of Davis."

25. Corbin Crews Harwood, *Using Land to Save Energy* (Cambridge, Massachusetts: Ballinger Publishing Company, 1977).

26. Information on this study is available by writing to Environmental Law Institute, 1346 Connecticut Avenue NW, Washington, D.C. 20036.

27. See generally, Williams, *supra* note 19.

28. American Institute of Architects, Committee on Design—Design Review Boards, *A Handbook for Communities* (Washington, D.C., 1974). Professor George Lefcoe was the legal consultant to the committee in the preparation of the report.

29. See 5 Williams, *supra* note 19.

30. Adapted from proposed ordinance of Princeton, New Jersey (1973) Section 6(a-d) quoted in 5 Williams, *supra* note 19.

31. *Id.*

Appendix
DAVIS, CALIFORNIA ORDINANCE

Ordinance No. 784
An Ordinance Establishing Energy
Conservation Performance Standards for
Residential Construction within
the City of Davis

The City Council of the City of Davis does hereby ordain as follows:

Section 1. Findings.

A. The people of the State of California face the likelihood of a major energy shortfall and the certainty of rapidly rising energy costs due to uncertainties about present and future supplies of natural gas, and the inability of powerplant construction to keep pace with the rising demand for electricity. Energy demand for the heating and cooling of residential structures has been rising faster than demand in other sectors and rising household energy bills are becoming an increasing economic burden for lower and middle income families.

B. The State of California has adopted an energy and noise insulation standard under the provisions of the California Administrative Code, Title 25, Chapter I, Subchapter 1, Article 5. This standard will make an important contribution to improving housing in the State, but due to the unique characteristics of the Davis climate, the State regulations are deemed to be inadequate for use in the City of Davis.

C. Many years of research[1] at the University of California at Davis have established the following facts:

1. An experimental room with large windows facing west regularly achieved temperatures in excess of $140°F$ during the

summer in Davis.[2] The problem of unshaded windows is inadequately dealt with in the State code. Consequently, dwellings which will overheat to such an extent that they are unfit for human habitation may be built under the State standard.

2. It has been found in experimental structures in Davis that solar heat gains from properly oriented windows can significantly reduce the need for heating in the winter.[3] This factor is not credited in the State code.

3. It has been found that the thermal capacity or heat storage ability of the building itself can help to ameliorate daily temperature extremes of both summer and winter.[4] This factor is not accounted for in the State code.

D. From 1973 to 1975 the City of Davis commissioned a study which corroborated the experimental results described above by extensively studying the performance of actual buildings in Davis. Both the thermal performance and actual energy use were examined.[5] It was found that:

1. Some dwellings became dangerously hot (100–110°F) in the summer due to direct solar heat gains through large east or west facing windows, while identical dwellings with north or south facing windows remained comfortably cool (75–80°F) and, therefore, used substantially less energy for cooling.

2. Dwelling units with south windows exposed to winter sun were significantly warmer during the winter (over 10°F warmer on cold, sunny days) and used significantly less energy for heating than dwelling units with windows facing other directions.

3. Some dwelling units with windows on only one side had no through ventilation and would not cool at night even on cool, windy, summer evenings, thereby requiring expensive cooling system operation.

E. As part of the above mentioned study, the Davis climate was examined in light of the needs for energy conservation and the following findings were made:

1. The daytime maximum temperature during July, the hottest month of the year, averages 95°F; however, the nighttime minimum averages 55.3°F. These nighttime lows are caused by thermally induced sea breezes originating over the Pacific

Ocean which flow into portions of the Central Valley through the Carquinez Straits.[6] These local climatic factors were found to all but eliminate need for summertime air conditioning in residential buildings if the following conditions are met:

a. The windows are protected from direct solar radiation;
b. The walls, floors and ceilings are adequately insulated;
c. Adequate thermal storage capacity is provided within the structure; and
d. Cross-ventilation for summer nighttime cooling is provided.

2. During January, the coldest winter month, the average 24-hour outside temperature is 45.3° F.[7] On the average, Davis receives sun for fifty-six percent (56%) of the time possible during the five winter months. The frequency and duration of winter sunshine is such that the need to heat residential buildings is substantially reduced if the following conditions are met:

a. The walls, floors and ceilings are adequately insulated;
b. Adequate south-facing glass exposed to the winter sun is provided; and
c. Adequate thermal storage capacity is provided within the insulated shell of the structure.

F. Due to the above stated factors, it has been found that:

1. Considerably better minimum performance levels can be required in Davis than provided by the State code without unduly restricting designs and raising costs, or requiring new technologies.
2. The present State code allows the construction of buildings that will be unfit for human habitation in the event of the interruption in gas or electrical service during one of the frequently occurring hot or cold weather events. Therefore, the present State code, by its failure to adequately address the heat loss and heat gain considerations of glazing and glazing orientation, does not adequately deal with the Davis climatic conditions.
3. Considerable reduction in the real cost of housing can be achieved in buildings with good thermal performance by lowering utility bills. In addition, the initial cost of improving the structure's thermal performance is usually offset by the resultant savings due to the smaller capacity heating and/or cooling equipment required for a thermally efficient structure.

Section 2. Definitions.

The following words and phrases shall have the meanings respectively ascribed to them by this section:

A. "Winter Design Day" shall refer to a day upon which it shall be assumed, for purposes of structural heat loss calculations, that all of the following climatological conditions exist:

1. The sun's path and resultant angles of direct sunlight shall be those which occur on December 21 of each year at latitude 38° 32' North. These angles can be approximated by using latitude 40° North data.

2. The sun's intensity through glazing shall be calculated for December 21 of each year at latitude 38° 32' North; this can be approximated by using latitude 40° North data.

3. The 24-hour average outside temperature is 45°F.

4. For the sake of determining the external air film coefficient, the wind speed shall be assumed to be 15.0 m.p.h. in accordance with ASHRAE procedures.

B. "Summer Design Day," as used in this ordinance, shall refer to a day upon which it shall be assumed, for purposes of structural heat gain calculations, that all of the following climatological conditions exist:

1. The sun's path and resultant angles of direct sunlight shall be those which occur on August 21 of each year at latitude 38° 32' North. These angles can be approximated by using latitude 40° North.

2. The sun's intensity through glazing shall be calculated for August 21 of each year at latitude 38° 32' North; this can be approximated by using latitude 40° North data.

3. The outside temperatures on August 21 shall be assumed to be, at each hour, Pacific Standard Time, as follows:

Time A.M.	Temp. °F	Time P.M.	Temp. °F
1:00	66	1:00	95
2:00	64	2:00	99
3:00	61	3:00	100
4:00	60	4:00	99
5:00	59	5:00	98
6:00	59	6:00	95
7:00	67	7:00	91
8:00	72	8:00	87
9:00	78	9:00	81
10:00	82	10:00	77
11:00	87	11:00	73
12:00	91	12:00	68

4. For the sake of determining the exterior air film coefficient, the wind speed shall be 15 m.p.h. in accordance with ASHRAE procedures.

C. "Floor Area" shall refer to the total habitable area of a dwelling unit (expressed in square feet) which is within the exterior face of the insulated shell of the structure and which is heated or cooled.

Section 3. Minimum Performance Standards Adopted.

The City of Davis hereby adopts minimum standards for the thermal performance of buildings to be constructed within the City Davis. In order to achieve maximum thermal performance, the performance standards have been carefully adjusted to the special problems and opportunities of the Davis climate. These standards shall apply to all residential structures designated Group H and Group I in the Uniform Building Code.

A. *Winter Performance Standard.* For a winter performance standard the Total Day's Heat Loss per square foot of floor area during the Winter Design Day shall be as follows: For single-family detached structures designated U.B.C. Group I, see Table 2; for multiple dwellings, U.B.C. Group H, the Total Day's Heat Loss shall not exceed one hundred twenty (120) BTUs per square foot of floor area. Commonwall Group I structures shall meet Group H standards. The resolution establishing methods of compliance with the performance standards will allow for numerically increasing the permissible standard on the basis of surface areas in common in order to equitably deal with the variability which occurs in this class of dwelling units.

B. *Summer Performance Standard.* For a summer performance standard, the Total Day's Heat Gain per square foot of floor area during the Summer Design Day shall be as follows: For single-family, detached structures, U.B.C. Group I, see Table 2; for multiple dwellings U.B.C. Group H, the Total Day's Heat Gain shall not exceed forty (40) BTUs per square foot of floor area. Commonwall Group I structures shall meet Group H Standards. The resolution establishing methods of compliance with the performance standards will allow for numerically increasing the permissible standard on the basis of surface areas in common in order to equitably deal with the variability which occurs in this class of dwelling units.

Section 4. Methods of Compliance with Performance Standards to be Established by Resolution.

Standard methods for calculating the performance of a proposed structure to determine compliance with the standards of this ordinance shall be adopted by resolution of the City Council.

Section 5. Administration and Enforcement.

A. The provisions of this ordinance and the resolution establishing the methods of compliance shall be administered by the Building Official of the City of Davis.

B. No building permit shall be issued by the Building Official for any new structure subject to this ordinance unless such structure is found to be in compliance with the winter and summer performance standards hereby established.

Section 6. Partial Exemption.

Structures designated U.B.C. Group I to be built on lots which are unimproved with structures and for which a tentative subdivision map has been approved prior to September 1, 1974, shall be exempt from glazing shading requirements adopted by resolution pursuant to Section 4 of this ordinance. To the extent that the exemption from glazing shading requirements causes a structure to exceed the performance standards established by Section 3 of this ordinance, such incremental excess shall be permitted.

Section 7. Partial Exemption.

Structures designated U.B.C. Group I to be built on lots which are unimproved with structures and for which a tentative subdivision map has been approved prior to January 1, 1976, but after September 1, 1974, and which lots front upon a portion of street having an axis between 292.5° and 067.5° true (N67.5°W and N67.5°E) and 247.5° and 112.5° true (S67.5°W and S67.5°E), shall be exempt from glazing shading requirements adopted by resolution pursuant to Section 4 of this ordinance. To the extent that the exemption from glazing shading requirements causes a structure to exceed the performance standards established by Section 3 of this ordinance, such incremental excess shall be permitted.

Section 8. Variances.

A. *Purpose.* The purpose of a variance is to allow variation from the strict application of the requirements of this ordinance and implementing resolutions where, by reason of the exceptional narrowness, shallowness or unusual shape of a specific piece of property, or other extraordinary situation or condition of such piece of property, or of the use or the development of property immediately adjoining the property in question, the literal enforcement of the requirements of this ordinance would involve practical difficulties or would cause undue hardship unnecessary to carry out the spirit and purpose of this ordinance. In most cases the variance shall only relate to the allowable area of unshaded glazing permissible under the resolutions implementing this ordinance.

B. *Application.* Application for a variance shall be made by the property owner or the Board of Building Appeals or the Community Development Director on a form prescribed by the City; and shall be accompanied by a fee as prescribed by resolution adopted pursuant to City Code Section 29-12.1, no part of which shall be refundable. No fee shall be charged if the variance is initiated by the Board of Building Appeals or the Community Development Director.

C. *Maps and Drawings.* Maps and drawings required to demonstrate that the conditions set forth in this ordinance apply to the subject property, together with precise and accurate legal descriptions and scale drawings of the property and existing buildings, and other data required, shall be submitted with the application for a variance.

D. *Grounds for Granting.* The Board of Building Appeals may grant a variance only when all of the following conditions are found:

1. That any variance granted shall be subject to such conditions as will assure that the adjustment thereby authorized shall not constitute a grant of special privilege inconsistent with the limitations upon other similarly situated properties which were developed under the limitations of this ordinance.
2. That because of special circumstances applicable to the subject property, the strict application of this ordinance is found to deprive subject property of privileges enjoyed by other similar properties which were developed under the limitations of this ordinance.
3. That the authorizing of such variance will not be of substantial detriment to adjacent property, and will not materially impair the purposes of this ordinance or the public interest.
4. That the condition or situation of the subject property or the intended use of the property for which the variance is sought is not so general or recurrent in nature as to make reasonable or practicable the formulation of a general regulation for such conditions or situations.
5. That there are not available reasonable alternative construction methods which will bring the proposed structure into compliance with the performance standards of this ordinance.

E. *Grounds for Granting—Examples.* The following types of physical or topographical factors are examples of conditions which may justify the grant of a variance from the glazing shading requirements to be established by resolution as provided by Section 4 of this ordinance:

1. Overriding off-site view considerations which are determined to add appreciable incremental value to the subject property.
2. Minimum size lots with fixed and adverse orientation problems.
3. Adverse lot orientation dictated by street or utility improvements or similar physical limitations where such limitations are in existence prior to the adoption of this ordinance.

F. *State Standards.* No variance shall be granted under this section which will result in a structure which exceeds the then existing State of California residential energy conservation standards.

G. *Notice of Variance Hearing.* Upon the filing of an appeal, the Building Official shall provide written notice of the filing of the appeal to all persons interested in the matter and shall cause notice of public hearing to be published in a newspaper of general circulation.

H. *Review of the Decision.* The decision of the Board of Building Appeals to grant or deny the application shall be subject to appeal in accordance with the resolution establishing the Board of Building Appeals.

Section 9. Appeals.

Any person aggrieved by a determination of the Building Official in the application of this ordinance may appeal such determination to the City of Davis Board of Building Appeals. Such appeal shall be in writing and shall be filed with the Building Official within fifteen (15) days of the determination appealed. All appeals shall be accompanied by payment of a fee in the amount set forth in the City's Community Development fee schedule.

Upon the filing of an appeal, the Building Official shall provide written notice of the filing of the appeal to all persons interested in the matter and shall cause notice of public hearing to be published in a newspaper of general circulation.

In consideration of an appeal, the Board of Building Appeals shall have authority to determine the suitability of alternate materials and methods of construction and to provide for reasonable interpretation of the provisions of this ordinance and implementing resolutions, provided, however, that no alternate material nor method of construction shall be approved which results in a reduction in the performance standards established by this ordinance for both summer and winter conditions.

The decision of the Board of Building Appeals shall be subject to appeal in accordance with the resolution establishing the Board of Building Appeals.

Section 10. Tables.

[Table 1, entitled *Solar Position and Intensity; Solar Heat Gain Factors for 40 Deg. North Latitude*, from *Handbook of Fundamentals, 1972*, American Society of Heating, Refrigeration and Air Conditioning Engineers, is omitted.—*Ed.*]

Table 2[8]. Detached Group I Dwelling Unit Thermal Standards

Floor Area (sq. ft.)	Winter Heat Loss (BTUs/[sq.ft.] [day])	Summer Heat Gain (BTUs/[sq.ft.] [day])
500	363	118
1000	239	103
1500	208	98
2000	192	95
2500	182	93
3000	176	91

Note: Direct interpolation shall be used for floor areas not shown.

Section 11. Conflicting Ordinances Repealed.

All ordinances or portions of ordinances which conflict with the provisions of this ordinance are, to the extent of such conflict, hereby repealed.

Section 12. Effective Date.

This ordinance shall become effective on and after the ninetieth (90th) day following its adoption.

Passed and Adopted by the City Council of the City of Davis on this 15th day of October, 1975.

Bibliography of Past Research on the Thermal Aspects of Building Design in the Davis Climate

Cramer, R.D., R.B. Deering, Virginia Gould Kay and L.W. Neubauer, "Temperature Control for Houses," *Journal of Home Economics*, Vol. 50, No. 3 (March, 1958).

Cramer, R.D. and Loren W. Neubauer, "Diurnal Radiant Exchange With The Sky Dome," *Solar Energy*, Vol. IX, No. 2 (April–June, 1965), pp. 95-103.

Cramer, R.D. and Loren W. Neubauer, "Thermal Effects of Floor Construction, *ASHRAE Journal* (January, 1961), six pages.

Cramer, R.D. and L.W. Neubauer, "Solar Radiant Gains Through Directional Glass Exposure," American Society of Heating, Refrigeration and Air Conditioning Engineers, 1958; presented at Lake Placid, New York (June 22-29, 1959); *ASHRAE Transactions*, Vol. 65 (1959), p. 499.

Cramer, R.D. and L.W. Neubauer, "Summer Heat Control for Small Homes," *Transactions of American Society of Agricultural Engineers*, Vol. 2, No. 1 (1959), pp. 102, 103, & 105.

Cramer, R.D. and L.W. Neubauer, "Thermal Effectiveness of Shape-I," *Solar Energy*, Vol. X, No. 3 (July, 1966), pp. 191-199.

Deering, R.B., "Effective Use of Living Shade," *California Agriculture* (September, 1955), pp, 10, 11, & 15.

Deering, R.B., "The Importance of Microclimatic Problems in Garden Design," *The National Horticultural Magazine* (October, 1953), pp. 226-230.

Deering, R.B. and F.A. Brooks, "The Effect of Plant Material Upon The Microclimatic of House and Garden," *The National Horticultural Magazine* (July, 1954), pp. 162-167.

Everson, G.F., L.W. Neubauer and R.B. Deering, "Environmental Influence on Orientation and House Design to Improve Living Comfort," *Journal of Home Economics*, Vol. 48, No. 3 (March, 1956), pp. 161-167.

Hammond, Jonathan, Marshall Hunt, Richard Cramer, Loren Neubauer, *A Strategy for Energy Conservation* (1974).

Neubauer, L.W., "Optimum Alleviation of Solar Stress on Model Buildings," *Transactions of the American Society of Agricultural Engineers*, Vol. 15, No. 1 (1972), pp. 129, 130, 131, 132.

Neubauer, L.W., "Orientation and Insulation: Model versus Prototype" *Transactions of the American Society of Agricultural Engineers*, Vol. 15, No. 9 (1972), pp. 707, 708, 709.

Neubauer, L.W., "Shapes and Orientations of Houses for Natural Cooling," *Transactions of the American Society of Agricultural Engineers*, Vol. 15, No. 1 (1973), pp. 126, 127, 128.

Neubauer, L.W. and R.D. Cramer, "Effect of Shape of Building on Interior Air Temperature," *Transactions of the American Society of Agricultural Engineers*, Vol. 11, No. 4 (1968), pp. 537, 538, 539.

Neubauer, L.W. and R.D. Cramer, "Shading Devices to Limit Solar Heat Gain But Increase Cold Sky Radiation," *Transactions of the American Society of Agricultural Engineers*, Vol. 8, No. 4 (1956), pp. 470, 471, 472, & 475.

Neubauer, L.W., R.D. Cramer, and Melvin Laraway, "Temperature Control of Solar Radiation on Roof Surfaces," *Transactions of the American Society of Agricultural Engineers*, Saint Joseph, Michigan, Vol. 7, No. 9 (1964), pp. 432, 433, 434, & 438.

University of California Agriculture Extension Service, *The Climate of Yolo County* (1971).

Ordinance No. 787
Ordinance Amending Section 6 of
Ordinance No. 784 (Ordinance Establishing
Energy Conservation Performance Standards
for Residential Construction within the City
of Davis) Relating to Energy Conservation
Performance Standards for Residential
Construction on Lots Created Prior to
September 1, 1974

The City Council of the City of Davis does hereby ordain as follows:

Section 1. Section 6 of Ordinance No. 784 is hereby amended to provide as follows:

Section 6. Partial Exemption.
"Structures designated U.B.C. Group I to be built on lots which are unimproved with structures and for which a tentative subdivision map has been approved prior to September 1, 1974, shall be exempt from requirements adopted by resolution pursuant to Section 4 of this ordinance. To the extent that the exemption from requirements causes a structure to exceed the performance standards established by Section 3 of this ordinance, such incremental excess shall be permitted."

Section 2. This ordinance shall become effective concurrently with Ordinance No. 784.
Passed and Adopted by the City Council of the City of Davis on this 5th day of November, 1975.

Resolution No. 1833, Series 1975
Resolution Adopting Procedures for
Compliance with the Energy Conservation
Performance Standards for Residential
Construction within the City of Davis

Whereas, the City of Davis has, by ordinance, established certain energy conservation performance standards for new residential construction within the City of Davis; and
Whereas, the ordinance which establishes energy conservation performance standards provides that standard methods for

determining compliance of proposed buildings shall be established by resolution:

Now, therefore, be it resolved by the City Council of the City of Davis as follows:

Section 1. Application.

Compliance with the energy conservation performance standards established by the City of Davis shall be determined by reference to the provisions of this resolution and any amendments thereto.

Section 2. Definitions.

For purposes of this resolution and the energy conservation performance standards ordinance of the City, the following words and phrases shall have the meanings respectively ascribed to them by this section.

A. *R Values.* $(1/U = R)$ Thermal Resistance (R) is the measure of the resistance of a material or building component to the passage of heat. The units of measurement are: (Hours) (Degrees Fahrenheit) (Square Feet)/BTU. The resistance value (R) of mass-type insulations shall not include any value for reflective facing. (**Note:** For reflective foil insulation, use ASHRAE procedures only. Calculate both the winter and summer composite resistance value and use whichever is less.)

B. Composite Thermal Resistance (Rt) is the sum of each of the resistance values of the parts of an assembly of materials which together form an external skin element of the structure. For example, a commonly used wall is one which has an interior air film, one-half (1/2) inch thick plaster board, three and one-half (3-1/2) inches batt insulation, stucco, and finally, an exterior air film, all of which have R values which are added together to derive the Rt value for the wall element.

C. *Orientation.* The compass directions are designated as follows when the attached tables are used.

North	337.5°–022.5°	South	157.5°–202.5°
Northeast	022.5°–067.5°	Southwest	202.5°–247.5°
East	067.5°–112.5°	West	247.5°–292.5°
Southeast	112.5°–157.5°	Northwest	292.5°–337.5°

D. *Exterior Surface Area.* The area for each dwelling unit of walls, ceilings, suspended floors, glazing, doors, etc. enclosing conditioned spaces and exposed to ambient climatic conditions.

E. *Heavy Exterior Building Elements.* The walls, suspended floors and/or ceilings which contain a heat storage capacity of 30

BTUs/Day for each square foot of surface area are considered to be heavy (see definition K). Only those materials located on the interior side of insulation materials may be counted. (An eight [8] inch thick lightweight concrete block wall with exterior insulation slightly exceeds these requirements.)

F. *Color.* Surfaces with a Munsell lightness value of 6.0 to 10.0 are to be considered *light in color.* Surfaces with a Munsell lightness value of 9.0 to 10.0 are to be considered *very light in color.* Unpainted wood surfaces are to be considered *light in color.* The Building Inspector shall prepare two (2) representative collections of materials and surface covering materials, one with Munsell lightness values greater than 6 and one of materials with Munsell lightness values greater than 9. These collections shall be available for inspection by the public.

G. *Glazing.* All vertical, horizontal, and tilted translucent or transparent exterior building elements shall be considered glazing with a thermal resistance and daylight transmittance as specified by the manufacturer or as calculated by ASHRAE methods or other reliable references or procedures.

H. *Shading Coefficient.* The ratio of the solar heat gain through a shading-glazing system to that of an unshaded single-pane or double strength window glass under the same set conditions.

I. *Hour's Solar Heat Gain.* The amount of energy transmitted through an area of glazing oriented to a particular direction in one (1) hour. The following formula is used for calculation:

$$HSHG = (SC)(SHGF)(A)$$

Where:

HSHG = Solar Heat Gain through the glazing for one (1) hour (BTUs/hour)

    SC = Shading Coefficient

SHGF = Solar Heat Gain Factor for the hour from attached Table 1 [omitted] (BTUs/square foot of glazing) using December 21 for winter and August 21 for summer.

     A = Area in square feet of glazing exposed to the sun (square feet).

J. *Solar Heat Gain Factor.* The number of BTUs of solar energy transmitted through one (1) square foot of clear 1/8-inch glass in one (1) hour. This is determined by using the attached Table 1 [omitted] which applies to 40°. North latitude and the eight (8) compass orientations (see definition C).

K. *Heat Storage Capacity.* The mass located inside the insulated shell of the structure that fluxes through a temperature cycle each day in summer and winter, absorbing heat during overheated periods and storing it for release during underheated periods. Heat storage capacity shall be estimated by the following procedure:

$$HS = (WM)(SH)(\Delta T)$$

Where:

HS = Heat Storage Capacity (BTUs/Day)

WM = The weight of the materials (lbs.) inside the insulated shell of the building to a depth yielding a resistance of R-1, except in the case of slab floors where only the slab itself is credited.

SH = Specific Heat of those materials (BTUs/[lb.] [degree F])

ΔT = Temperature flux; 5°F will be the maximum allowable for calculation purposes, except that light weight frame construction will be allowed to flux 10°F. (In order to determine the heat or cold available for storage, see Path II, Section 5.)

This total stored heat may be subtracted from the day's heat loss or gain to yield the adjusted Total Day's Heat Loss or Total Day's Heat Gain. Mass located in exterior elements to which the Equivalent Temperature Differential Method (E.T.D.) is applied to calculate summer heat gain shall not be included in the summer heat storage capacity credit.

L. *Floor Area.* Total habitable area of a dwelling unit (expressed in square feet) which is within the exterior face of the insulated shell of the structure and which is heated or cooled.

M. *Accepted References.* The following are useful and acceptable references:

Handbook of Fundamentals 1972, American Society of Heating, Refrigerating and Air Conditioning Engineers, Inc. (ASHRAE), N.Y., N.Y., 1972.
Architectural Graphic Standards, Charles G. Ramsey and Harold R. Sleeper, John Wiley & Sons, Inc., N.Y., N.Y., Sixth Edition, 1970.
Design with Climate, Victor Olgyay, Princeton University Press, Princeton, New Jersey, 1963.

Concepts in Thermal Comfort, David Egan, Tulane University, School of Architecture, New Orleans, Louisiana, 1972.

Thermal Design of Buildings, Tyler Stuart Rogers, John Wiley & Sons, Inc., N.Y., N.Y., 1964.

Sun Angle Calculator, Libbey-Owens-Ford Company, Toledo, Ohio, 1975.

Energy Design Manual for Residential Buildings, State of California, Department of Housing and Community Development, Division of Codes and Standards, Sacramento, California, 1975.

Section 3. Standard Methods of Building Performance Calculation.

A. There are hereby adopted two (2) alternative standard methods of determining compliance with the City of Davis energy conservation performance standards. The two (2) alternative standard methods shall be referred to as Path I and Path II approaches.

B. Structures utilizing either Path I or Path II shall comply with the following:

1. *Infiltration.* All swinging doors and windows opening to the exterior or to unconditioned areas such as garages shall be fully weatherstripped, gasketed or otherwise treated to limit infiltration. All manufactured windows and sliding glass doors shall meet the air infiltration standards of the 1972 American National Standards Institute (A134.2, A134.3, and A134.4), when tested in accordance with ASTM E 283-73 with a pressure differential of 1.57 lbs./ft.² and shall be certified and labeled.

2. *Loose Fill Insulation.* When blown or poured type loose fill insulation is used in attic spaces, the slope of the roof shall be not less than 2-1/2 feet in 12 feet and there shall be at least 30 inches of clear headroom at the roof ridge. ("Clear headroom" is defined as the distance from the top of the bottom chord of the truss or ceiling joists to the underside of the roof sheathing.) When eave vents are installed, adequate baffling of the vent opening shall be provided to deflect the incoming air above the surface of the material and shall be installed at the soffit on a 45-degree angle. Baffles shall be in place at the time of framing inspection. When loose fill insulation is proposed, the R value of the material required to meet these regulations shall be shown on the building plans or calculation sheet.

3. *Pipe Insulation.* All steam and steam condensate return piping and all continuously circulating domestic or heating hot water piping which is located in attics, garages, crawl spaces, underground or unheated spaces other than between floor or in interior walls shall be insulated to provide a maximum heat loss

of 50 BTU/hr. per linear foot for piping up to and including 2-inch and 100 BTU/hr. per linear foot for larger sizes. Piping installed at depth of 30 inches or more complies with these standards.

Section 4. Path I (Prescriptive Method).

Buildings meeting all of the following criteria will fulfill the required energy conservation aspects of this code with no overall performance calculations required.

Calculations using the applicable methods outlined in Path II may be employed to demonstrate compliance of alternatives to any particular section of Path I. Thermal trade-offs between sections of Path I must be done by using Path II or by referring to approved thermal trade-offs table developed by the Building Inspector.

A. *Walls.* All exterior walls (excluding windows and doors) shall use R-11 batt insulation between studs. Group H structures must have light colored walls or shaded walls. Fifteen percent (15%) of the wall area may be dark colored to allow for trim and color accents. (Group I structures have no wall color requirement.)

Exceptions:

1. All exterior walls shall achieve a composite resistance value (Rt) of 10.52 if the insulation is not penetrated by framing, and Rt of 12.50 if the insulation is penetrated by the framing or furring. (California Administrative Code, Title 25, Chapter 1, Subchapter 1, Article 5, Section 1094[a].)
2. Heavy walls with exterior insulation not penetrated by furring or framing shall have an Rt of 7.36, and Rt of 8.75 if the insulation is penetrated by furring or framing.
3. Group H structures with dark colored walls shall increase their applicable Rt requirements by twenty percent (20%).

B. *Roof/Ceilings; Ceiling/Attics.* All roof/ceilings and ceiling/attics must use insulation achieving a minimum resistance of R-19 for the insulation itself. Group H occupancies having roof surfaces unshaded on August 21, at 8:00 a.m., 12:00 noon, or 4:00 p.m., shall be no darker than No. 6 on the Munsell color chart. Unshaded roof areas on Group I occupancies shall be no darker than No. 4 on the Munsell color chart. Roofs having unshaded areas and color darker then No. 6 or No. 4 respectively must increase the total insulation to yield R25 for the insulation itself.

Exceptions:

1. All roof/ceilings and/or ceiling/attics sections shall achieve a composite resistance value (Rt) of 16.67 if the insulation is not penetrated by framing or furring and Rt of 20.0 if the insulation is penetrated by the framing or furring. (California Administrative Code, Title 25, Chapter 1, Subchapter 1, Article 5, Section 1094[c].) Blown insulation (loose fill type) shall be considered to be penetrated by the framing.

2. The roof/ceiling and/or ceiling/attic sections of the dwelling unit as a whole may be insulated to values greater and/or less than required in (1) above if the resulting heat loss equals or is less than that which would occur if the values required in (1) above were met, or if the thermal resistance values of the ceiling areas satisfy the following equation:

$$1/\text{Rt required} = (\text{Area A}/\text{Total Area})(1/\text{RT achieved})$$

$$+ (\text{Area B}/\text{Total Area})(1/\text{Rt achieved})$$

$$+ \ldots + (\text{Area N}/\text{Total Area})(1/\text{Rt achieved})$$

3. In Group H occupancies, roof/ceilings or ceiling/attics located beneath dark colored roofs shall achieve composite resistance values (Rt) 30% greater than the values in (1) and (2) above, i.e., Rt = 21.67 and Rt = 26.00 respectively. In Group I occupancies, roof/ceilings or ceiling/attics located beneath roofs that are darker than Munsell Color No. 4 shall achieve composite resistance values (Rt) 30% greater than the values in (1) and (2) above, i.e., Rt = 21.67 and Rt = 26.00 respectively.

C. *Floors.* Suspended floors over a ventilated crawl space or other unheated space shall have insulation with a minimum resistance of R-11. Concrete slabs on grade require no insulation.

Exceptions:

1. Suspended floors over an unheated space shall achieve a composite resistance value (Rt) of 10.52 if the insulation is not penetrated by framing, and Rt of 12.50 if the insulation is penetrated by framing.

2. Heavy suspended floors with exterior insulation shall achieve a composite resistance value (Rt) of 7.36 for insulation not

penetrated by framing members, and Rt of 8.75 for insulation penetrated by framing members

D. *Glazing Area.* In Group H occupancies, exterior singlepane glazing (windows, skylights, etc.) may not exceed 12-1/2% of the floor area. Exterior double-pane glazing may not exceed 17-1/2% of the dwelling unit's floor area. In Group I occupancies, a glazing constant of 20 square feet in single-glazing and 28 square feet in double-pane glazing may be added to the percentage figures allowed above.

Exceptions:

1. A combination of single and double-pane glazing may be used so long as the area of the single plus the area of the double glazing divided by 1.4 is not greater than 12-1/2% (plus 20 square feet for Group I occupancies) of the dwelling unit's floor area.
2. A combination of single and/or double-pane glazing with interior shutters may be used to increase the allowed glazing provided that:

   i. The interior shutters are of a permanent construction and installed so that they are operable, and tight fitting or weatherstripped so that a seal is created.
   ii. The areas in each treatment do not exceed those allowed by the following procedure.

$$GC + (FA)(.125) = Area_s + (Area_D)(.64) + (Area_{shut})/Rt$$

Where:

GC = Glazing constant (square feet) taken at 20 square feet in Group I and zero in Group H occupancies.

FA = Floor Area (square feet).

$Area_s$ = Area in single-pane glazing (square feet).

$Area_D$ = Area in double-pane glazing (square feet).

$Area_{shut}$ = Area in interior shuttered glazing (square feet)

Rt = The composite resistance of the shutter-glazing systems.

3. When the area of glazing allowed by application of (1) or (2) is exceeded, the excess area will be considered justified if all the following conditions are met:

   i. Glazing must be south facing. If it is mounted other than vertically, it must be tilted at least 30° up from the horizontal to face south.
   ii. It must be clear. (Shading coefficient numerically greater than or equal to .80 for the glazing itself.)
   iii. It must receive full direct sun from 10:00 a.m. to 2:00 p.m. (P.S.T.) on December 21.
   iv. For each square foot of glazing being justified, the building must contain a heat storage capacity (HS) equivalent to 750 BTUs/Day, located inside the insulated shell of the structure, and not covered with insulation materials such as carpet yielding an Rt of 1.0 or greater. The following will allow a quick method for calculation of mass needed for each square foot of exempted glazing:

59	Square feet of interior stud partition wall (2" X 4"s–16" o.c. with 1/2" gypsum two sides).
117	Square feet of interior stud wall or ceiling (2" X 4"s–16" o.c. with 1/2" gypsum inside, insulation, and with various external treatments).
21	Square feet of 8-inch lightweight concrete block masonry exterior wall insulated externally, cores filled for structural support only.
15	Square feet of concrete slab floor provided with a steel trowel finish, exposed aggregate, tile (vinyl, asbestos, or ceramic), terrazo, or hardwood parquet not greater than 1/2-inch thick.

Note: Lightweight stud frame walls are assumed to flux 10°F; heavy walls are assumed to flux 5°F. See Definitions E and K.)

E. *Glazing Shading.*

1. All glazing which is not oriented to the north must be shaded to protect it from direct solar radiation for the hours of 8:00 a.m., 12:00 noon, and 4:00 p.m. (P.S.T.), August 21. Glazing facing SE or SW must also be checked for shading at 10:00 a.m. for SE and 2:00 p.m. for SW in addition to the standard

three hours. For each check hour the area of glazing not shaded is calculated and accumulated. In Group H occupancies the total accumulated amount of unshaded glazing may not exceed 1.5% of the dwelling unit's floor area. In Group I occupancies the total accumulated amount of unshaded glass may not exceed 3% of the dwelling unit's floor area. Shading shall be demonstrated to the satisfaction of the Building Inspection Division of the Community Development Department. Drawings showing shadows cast by shading systems, or scale models suitable for use in the solar-ranger setup by the Building Inspection Division, or the use of approved shade screen systems may be employed to demonstrate compliance. Tinted, metalized, or frosted glass shall not be considered self-shading.

2. Interior mounted shutters meeting the following specifications may be utilized to meet the shading requirements:

   i. The exterior oriented side must be very light in color (Munsell of 9.0 or greater) and flat.
   ii. The shutters must be tight fitting or all cracks or edges in the system must be weather stripped to create a seal.
   iii. The shutters must be opaque.
   iv. A composite resistance value of Rt = 1.0 for the shutters must be achieved.

3. Exterior mounted shading systems meeting the following specifications may be utilized to meet the shading requirements:

   i. They shall be of permanent materials and construction. A permanent frame with sheathing having a life expectancy of five years minimum must be provided and guaranteed by the builder.
   ii. For the required design hour, the shading device must be capable of intercepting 100% of the direct beam solar radiation, or provide a minimum shading coefficient of 0.2 or less. If the shading system at a design hour does not perform to these standards, then the portion of the glazing which is left exposed is to be calculated and added to the accumulated unshaded glazing total.

4. Other types of shading systems are allowed if they comply with either of the following:

i. All on-site and off-site obstructions to the sun, providing 80% attenuation of the direct solar beam, may be considered as external shading devices and may be accounted for in the summer shading calculations.

(**Note:** If during the life of the structure the off-site obstructions to the sun used to achieve shading standards compliance are modified or removed, then the structure may be found to be in violation of the Code if other compensating obstructions to the sun or shading devices have not been deployed.)

ii. A shading system may be temporary, provided that it is designed and constructed to function to the standards above and built to last until its function is replaced by plantings. Plan and elevation drawings must show expected plant configuration and accurately state the number of years required for the projected plant growth. Final occupancy permits shall not be issued until the specified plants are in place.

F. *Ventilation for Summer Night Time Cooling.* Where design of the dwelling unit is such that openable windows may only be provided along one elevation, mechanical cross ventilation must be installed to provide 15 air changes per hour ducted to the exterior.

Section 5. Path II (Performance Method).

Buildings regulated by the Residential Energy Conservation Code that do not meet the criteria of Path I must be calculated by a registered architect, engineer, building designer, or other qualified person to show that the proposed building will not exceed the standards set forth in Section 3 of Ordinance No. [blank in original]. The required calculation schedule is outlined below.

(**Note:** More precise calculations may be submitted using ASHRAE or other comprehensive methods provided that the same design days are used.)

Commonwall U.B.C. Group I dwelling units may increase the permissible thermal standards for Heat Loss or Heat Gain using the following equation:

$$TS = TS_H + (TS_I - TS_H)(1 - SAC/[1.5][FA])$$

Where:

TS = The Thermal Standard which is applicable to the dwelling unit (BTUs/[sq. ft.] [Day])

TS_H = The Thermal Standard for Group H structure (BTU's/ [sq. ft.] [Day]

TS_I = The Thermal Standard for a detached Group I dwelling unit of the same floor area (BTUs/[sq. ft.] [Day])

SAC = The Surface Area in Common with other dwelling units such as ceilings, walls, and floor (square feet)

FA = The dwelling unit's Floor Area (square feet)

A. *Winter Calculations.*

1. The Total Day's Heat Loss shall not exceed the standards set in the Residential Energy Conservation Ordinance, Section 3.
2. Winter heat loss calculations shall be based on the following formula:

$$TDHL = (DHL - SHGC)/(FA)$$

Where:

TDHL = Total Day's Heat Loss (BTUs/sq. ft] [Day])

DHL = Day's Heat Loss (BTUs/Day)

SHGC = Solar Heat Gain Credit (BTUs/Day)

FA = Floor Area of dwelling unit (sq. ft)

3. The Design Day for sun angle considerations is December 21 at latitude 40°N or 38° 32' N. The outside daily temperature average for December and January is 45°F, yielding a 23°F difference between the inside (68°F) and the outside (45°F) average daily temperatures. The number of degree hours in the design day is the temperature difference times 24 hours or 552 for Davis. This figure is used as described in Paragraph (4)(i) below.

(Note: This design, outdoor condition, is not intended to be for equipment sizing, but rather is meant to serve the purpose of performance design for energy conservation by more closely predicting the long term average conditions and energy use of the structure. Equipment sizing will require additional standard peak load calculations.)

4. Calculation of Day's Heat Loss (DHL): Winter heat loss is determined by the composite resistance (Rt) of the exterior building surface to heat transfer to the outside air from the heated interior spaces.

DHL = HL + SHL

Where:

DHL = Day's Heat Loss (BTUs/Day)

HL = Heat Loss from outside surface elements (except slab) (BTUs/Day)

SHL = Slab on grade Heat Loss (BTUs/Day)

i. The heat loss for all surfaces (except slabs on grade) facing the outside air or unheated spaces may be determined by the following formula:

$$HL = (A_1/Rt_1) (552)$$
$$+ \ldots + (A_n/Rt_n) (552)$$

Where:

HL = Heat Loss from exterior surface element except a slab on grade (BTUs/Day)

A = Area of the exterior surface element (sq. ft.)

Rt = The element's composite thermal resistance ([hours] [Deg. F] [sq. ft.] /BTU)

552 = Davis Design Day Degree Hours ([Deg. F] [hours] /Day)

All exterior elements (walls, ceilings, doors and suspended floors) which are exposed to unheated enclosed or partially enclosed spaces shall be calculated as if they are exposed to outside conditions, or the temperature difference may be altered according to accepted ASHRAE procedures for surfaces adjacent to unheated spaces.

    ii. Concrete slab floors on grade lose heat in direct relation to the perimeter dimension in linear feet. The following formula applies:

$$SHL = (F)(P)(552)$$

Where:

. SHL = Heat Loss from Slab (BTUs/Day)

    F = The thermal conductivity of the edge of the slab with $F = 0.81$ (BTU/[foot][hour][Deg. F]) where no insulation is used and $F = 0.55$ where slab is insulated with edge insulation of $R = 4.5$ minimum. The insulation shall come within one inch of the top of the slab and extend sixteen inches below grade.

    P = Perimeter dimension (feet)

  552 = Davis Design Day Degree Hours ([Deg. F][hours]/[Day])

5. *Calculation of Solar Heat Gain Credit (SHGC).* Direct use of solar energy is dependent on the Day's Solar Heat Gain (DSHG) through the glazing, the Heat Storage (HS) characteristics of the building, and the Solar Climatic Variable (SCV). The following steps are to be followed to calculate the SHGC:

    i. Calculate the Day's Solar Heat Gain (DSHG), by adding up the Solar Heat Gain for each daylight hour of December 21 design day for each square foot of glazing receiving sun.

$$DSHG = (HSHG_1 + HSHG_2 + \ldots + HSHG_n)(SCV)$$

Where:

  DSHG = Day's Solar Heat Gain (BTUs/Day)

  HSHG = Hour's Solar Heat Gain. HSHG is found according to the procedure described in Definition I. The number of hours added depends on the hours of sunlight on the glazing surface in question (BTUs/hour)

    SCV = Solar Climatic Variable (no units). SCV = 0.56 for Davis. This was determined by averaging the mean fraction of possible sunshine available for each month of the winter heating season (November, December, January, February, March)

  ii. Calculate the Heat Storage capacity of the building (HS). (See Definition K for calculation procedure.)

 iii. Then the Solar Heat Gain Credit (SHGC) (BTUs/Day) equals:

SHGC = DSHG or HS, whichever is less.

B. *Summer Calculations.*

1. The Total Day's Heat Gain (TDHG) shall not exceed the standard set in the Residential Energy Conservation Ordinance, Section 3.
2. Summer heat gain calculations shall be based on the following formula:

TDHG = (DHG − HS)/FA

Where:

TDHG = Total Day's Heat Gain (BTUs/[sq. ft.] [Day])

  DHG = Day's Heat Gain (BTUs/Day)

    HS = Heat Storage (BTUs/Day)

    FA = Floor Area of the dwelling unit (sq. ft.)

3. The calculations below are based on the design day cited in the Residential Energy Conservation Ordinance taken at the five hours of 8:00 a.m., 10:00 a.m., 12:00 noon, 2:00 p.m., and 4:00 p.m.
4. The Day's Heat Gain (DHG) is based on the weighted sum of calculations done at each of the five heat gain calculation hours (see equation [a] below). Structures without elevations oriented to the intercardinal directions may delete calculations for 10:00 a.m. and 2:00 p.m. and equally weigh the remaining three calculation hours by multiplying them by four (see equation [b] below). The following two weighted sum equations hold respectively.

(a) DHG $=$ ($[HG_{8:00 \text{ a.m.}}][3] + [HG_{10:00 \text{ a.m.}}][2]$

$+ [HG_{12:00 \text{ noon}}][2] + [HG_{2:00 \text{ p.m.}}][2]$

$+ [HG_{4:00 \text{ p.m.}}][3]$)

or

(b) DHG $=$ ($[HG_{8:00 \text{ a.m.}} + HG_{12:00 \text{ noon}} +$

$HG_{4:00 \text{ p.m.}}][4]$)

Where:

DHG $=$ Day's Heat Gain (BTUs/[Day])

HG $=$ Heat Gain at the hour calculated (BTUs/hour)

(Note: More detailed analysis of Heat Gain may be done by calculating each hour's heat gain for the daylight hours. The digits "2", "3", and "4" in equations (a) and (b) above have the units of hours.)

5. The Heat Gain (HG) may be calculated by using the following formula:

HG $=$ WHG + OHG

Where:

HG $=$ Heat Gain (BTUs/hour) at one of the design hours

WHG $=$ Heat Gain through Windows (BTUs/hour)

OHG $=$ Heat Gain through Opaque surfaces (BTUs/hour)

i. *Heat Gain through Opaque surfaces.* Calculations will be based on the Total Equivalent Temperature Differential Method (TETD) as described in ASHRAE Handbook of Fundamentals 1972, Chapter 22, pages 411–417. The TETD appropriate for the wall or roof section is found in attached Tables 2 and 3. Since the average Davis design day temperature is 5°F less than that used by ASHRAE, 5°F should be subtracted from the TETD values given in attached Tables 2 and 3 in accordance with ASHRAE procedures, as shown in the calculation below. (The interior temperature is assumed to be 75° F in accordance with ASHRAE.) The Heat Gain through Opaque surfaces is calculated as follows:

$$\text{OHG} = A_1(\text{TETD} - 5)/Rt_1 + A_2(\text{TETD} - 5)/Rt2$$
$$+ \ldots + A_n(\text{TETD} - 5)/Rt_n$$

Where:

OHG = Heat Gain through opaque surfaces at the calculation hour (BTUs/hour)

A = Area of the outside surface element (sq. ft.)

Rt = The element's composite thermal Resistance ([hours] [Deg. F] [sq. ft.] /BTU)

TETD = The element's Total Equivalent Temperature Difference from attached tables 2 and 3

ii. *Glazing* Summer Heat Gain through windows (WHG) shall be calculated using the following formula:

$$\text{WHG} = ([A][SC][SHGF] + [\Delta T][A]/Rt_1 + (A \ldots)_2$$
$$+ \ldots + (A \ldots)_n$$

Where:

WHG = Direct solar heat gain plus conducted heat gain through windows at the calculation hour (must be done for each wall or roof section with glazing). (BTUs/hour)

A = Area of glazing surface being calculated (sq. ft.)

SC = Shading Coefficient (see Definition H). (Unitless)

SHGF = Solar Heat Gain Factor at the hour being calculated. (BTUs/[hours] [sq. ft. of glazing])

Rt = Thermal Resistance of the glass (0.9 for single weight glass and 1.7 for double-pane). ([hours] [Deg. F] [sq. ft.] /BTUs)

ΔT = Difference between the outside and the inside temperatures, with 75° F being taken as the inside temperature. (Deg. F)

6. *Heat Storage Capacity (HS)*. Where the building design provides for ventilation in minimum conformance with section 4F, credit can be taken for the Heat Storage capacity of the structure.

(Note: When calculating the heat storage capacity for the summer, no credit may be taken for exterior elements.)

Section 6. Fees.

The following schedule of fees shall be applicable for the checking of plans for conformity with the performance standards of the Residential Energy Conservation Code:

Path I (No Exceptions)	No Charge
Path I (Exercising Exceptions)	$20.00
Path II	$25.00

Passed and Adopted by the City Council of the City of Davis on this 15th day of October, 1975.

NOTES

1. See Research Bibliography.
2. R.D. Cramer and L.W. Neubauer, "Solar Radiant Gains Through Directional Glass Exposure," American Society of Heating, Refrigeration and Air Conditioning Engineers, 1958; presented at Lake Placid, New York, June 22–29, 1959; *ASHRAE Transactions* (1959), Vol. 65, No. 59, p. 499.
3. L.W. Neubauer, "Shapes and Orientations of Houses for Natural Cooling," *Transactions of the American Society of Agricultural Engineers*, Vol. 15, No. 1, pp. 126, 127, 128 (1972).
4. R.D. Cramer and Loren W. Neubauer, "Thermal Effects of Floor Construction," *ASHRAE Journal* (January, 1961), six pages.
5. Jonathan Hammond, Marshall Hunt, Richard Cramer and Loren Neubauer, *A Strategy for Energy Conservation* (1974).
6. University of California Agriculture Extension Service, *The Climate of Yolo County (1971)*.
7. Ibid.
8. Infiltration and internal heat production are not considered under the requirements of these standards. These are very important considerations in the real performance of a building and must be estimated when sizing heating and cooling devices whether conventional or solar. However, for the present purpose they are too variable to be standardized.

Index

About the Author

Grant P. Thompson is a senior associate at The Conservation Foundation, Washington, D.C., where he directs the energy program. He is a graduate of Pomona College, Oxford University (England), and Yale Law School. Prior to joining The Conservation Foundation, he was an Institute Fellow at the Environmental Law Institute, where he headed the institute's energy research program. He has been actively involved for many years in energy public policy research and has written books and papers in the field of energy conservation, energy pricing, and solar energy law. He has been consultant to, among others, the Pacific Northwest Regional Commission, the Office of Technology Assessment, the Federal Energy Administration, the Department of Energy, Brookhaven National Laboratory, and Resources for the Future.